LDAP Directories Explained

Independent Technology Guides

David Chappell, Series Editor

The **Independent Technology Guides** offer serious technical descriptions of important new software technologies of interest to enterprise developers and technical managers. These books focus on how that technology works and what it can be used for, taking an independent perspective rather than reflecting the position of any particular vendor. These are ideal first books for developers with a wide range of backgrounds, the perfect place to begin mastering a new area and laying a solid foundation for further study. They also go into enough depth to enable technical managers to make good decisions without delving too deeply into implementation details. The books in this series cover a broad range of topics, from networking protocols to development platforms, and are written by experts in the field. They have a fresh design created to make learning a new technology easier. All titles in the series are guided by the principle that, in order to use a technology well, you must first understand how and why that technology works.

Titles in the Series

Brian Arkills, *LDAP Directories Explained: An Introduction and Analysis*, 0-201-78792-X

David Chappell, *Understanding .NET: A Tutorial and Analysis*, 0-201-74162-8

Eric Newcomer, *Understanding Web Services: XML, WSDL, SOAP, and UDDI*, 0-201-75081-3

For more information check out http://www.awprofessional.com/

LDAP Directories Explained

An Introduction and Analysis

Brian Arkills

✦✦ Addison-Wesley

Boston ■ San Francisco ■ New York ■ Toronto ■ Montreal
London ■ Munich ■ Paris ■ Madrid
Capetown ■ Sydney ■ Tokyo ■ Singapore ■ Mexico City

The publisher offers discounts on this book when ordered in quantity for bulk purchases and special sales. For more information, please contact:

U.S. Corporate and Government Sales
(800) 382-3419
corpsales@pearsontechgroup.com

For sales outside of the U.S., please contact:

International Sales
(317) 581-3793
international@pearsontechgroup.com

Visit Addison-Wesley on the Web: www.awprofessional.com

Library of Congress Cataloging-in-Publication Data

Arkills, Brian.
     LDAP directories explained : an introduction and analysis / Brian Arkills.
          p. cm.
     Includes index.
     ISBN 0-201-78792-X (alk. paper)
     1. LDAP (Computer network protocol)   I. Title.

  TK5105.5725 .A75 2003
  004.6'2—dc21
                                                    2002038354

ISBN: 0-201-78792-X
Text printed on recycled paper
1 2 3 4 5 6 7 8 9 10—MA—0706050403
First printing, March 2003

*To my wife, Janet, who gave me support when
I didn't believe in myself. I look forward to returning
the favor on your book. Hopefully, it won't be
a saga of the lark and the owl.*

*And to Zooba Dooba—I won't know who
won the race for another couple months, but you
already have my heart in chains.*

Contents

Foreword

LDAP recently celebrated its tenth birthday. For comparison, that's about the same age as the World Wide Web, half as old as the domain naming system, and around a third as old as the Internet itself. In its relatively short life, LDAP has grown from its obscure roots as an easier way to access the X.500 directory into the Internet standard for directories, used by virtually every e-mail client, browser, and a host of other applications, with more being developed every day. Like any successful technology, LDAP has taken on a life of its own, being used in ways its designers never imagined. I, for one, never thought when helping to design LDAP ten years ago that it would be used in the diversity of applications that it is today.

When I started work on LDAP, my ambitions were much smaller. I was simply trying to solve a problem on my own campus at the University of Michigan. I wanted to give desktops across the campus access to the central university-wide directory, which was based on X.500. This desire led to the creation of a protocol similar to LDAP called DIXIE. The popularity of DIXIE among a small community of similarly minded directory developers led to my joining forces with Steve Kille and Weng Yeong and to the creation of a standard version in LDAP.

LDAP's breakthrough to the mainstream, so to speak, came in 1996 when Netscape galvanized the industry around adopting LDAP as the Internet's commercially accepted directory protocol. Soon, all major vendors were on board, announcing plans to develop their own LDAP implementation, and LDAP was on its way to being a part of most users' everyday computing lives.

Often people that use LDAP are not even aware they are using it. It is the protocol used to access your corporate e-mail directory; LDAP may be consulted every time you access a private Web page; LDAP often stores configuration for the services you access. In these applications and others, LDAP provides the behind-the-scenes support needed to control access to resources and look up information. LDAP has also been used for applications ranging from storing and retrieving images to calculating chess moves.

In this book Brian Arkills has put together a broad treatment of LDAP for readers of varying technical backgrounds. It should prove useful to those seeking a more accessible introduction to the topic than has been previously available. As for me, I look forward to seeing what the next ten years will bring for LDAP.

Timothy A. Howes, Ph.D.
Opsware Inc.
Co-creator of LDAP

Preface

Lightweight Directory Access Protocol (LDAP) is the predominant protocol used to communicate with directories. These days, directories are everywhere. Many enterprise software packages require a directory, for example, and companies seeking to reduce costs and streamline their business also implement a directory.

Not so long ago, I knew nothing about LDAP. Because Stanford University, my employer, was implementing and integrating Active Directory with its existing directory, I needed to understand LDAP and how directories worked. However, I found that the resources for a novice were sparse and hard to find, and that none of the books on the subject took me from novice to competency. During the course of the Stanford project, I met David Chappell and worked closely with him. This led to an invitation from Addison-Wesley, and I embarked on writing this book. I hope it fills the gap I found.

Audience

This book is part of the Independent Technology Guide series, which focuses on providing an independent look at a technology combined with a no-nonsense approach. David Chappell, the series editor, likes to say that the series should be called "Big Pictures 'R' Us." Each of the books in the series explains how the technology fits into the larger world. Technical managers turn to this series for explanations of all the acronyms and buzzwords they hear.

This book is also appropriate for someone who is more technically savvy, but looking to break into LDAP and directories. Almost every LDAP book on the market is written for developers, and those who don't write code are left in the dark. This book takes a different approach by providing a thorough introduction for newcomers regardless of their orientation or technical background. Once you've finished this book, you might turn to *Understanding and Deploying LDAP Directory Services* by Tim Howes, Mark Smith, and Gordon Good to continue learning about LDAP, especially in the context of developing LDAP code.

About the Book

The book is divided into two parts. Part I explores how LDAP and directories work in general. This book is unique in its approach to the topic from a standards-based, non-product-centric perspective. Part II explores three products to highlight how LDAP is used. If you don't have a lot of time to do research, this overview of the most popular LDAP products will help you compare existing products.

Appendixes

There are also several appendixes to augment the material presented in the chapters. When additional material is available, I have included references in the relevant chapter. I'd like to call your attention to two of the appendixes in particular. Appendix C is a case study of Stanford University's directory architecture. It is intended to give you a real-world sense of how integral an LDAP directory can become to your business. Appendix G contains URLs for all the online reference material that I used while writing this book. Many people have indicated to me how invaluable this compilation of online resources was to their research.

Brian Arkills, October 2002

Acknowledgments

I'd like to thank David Chappell, whose friendship and guidance made this book possible. David's openness about his own technical writing and interest in my writing led to this book. He also provided feedback on the organization of this book that was priceless.

My editor Stephane Thomas was unfailingly supportive, as were all the production staff at Addison-Wesley. Special thanks go to Elizabeth Collins for the detailed copyediting. Thank you all!

There are many reviewers whose contributions significantly improved the quality of writing and technical accuracy. Many thanks to Rob Weltman for reviewing the entire book from start to finish. Other reviewers include: Megan Conklin, Gabor Liptack, Jim Sermersheim, Ian Redfern, Jeff A. Dunkelberger, and Howard Lee Harkness.

Ross Wilper made several significant contributions to the Active Directory chapter through his technical expertise.

I'd like to thank two good friends, Brad Judy and Michael Snook, who both gave invaluable feedback throughout the book. Your honest comments and friendship mean a lot.

I'd also like to thank my father and mother. The discipline and positive attitude you instilled in me were invaluable in helping me finish this book.

Finally, to my high school English teacher Mrs. Perri, who endured my inane comments about how studying English lacked importance. You were ultimately right; I use English skills far more now than the math skills I so highly valued then. Thank you for your persistence, and all the difficult writing assignments.

Part I
How LDAP Works

1

Overview of LDAP

Introducing Directories

Directories are designed to help people find their way. We've all entered an unfamiliar building and used the building's directory. Without the directory, we'd have to wander the building in search of our destination. We rely on that directory without thinking much about it, unless the information leads us to the wrong place.

With the advent of computers, there is no end of information that needs organizing so people can easily find it. Computers have always relied on directories. Even early operating systems such as DOS had a file directory so a user could keep track of data files. Directories seem to be everywhere online today, with directories that list contact information for high school graduating classes, directories that list all the movies showing, and so on. All directories have the same goal of helping us eliminate aimless searching for the information we seek.

Directories help people by organizing information

Directories allow data to be managed

However, a directory should be more than just an efficient way to find information; it should also provide an efficient means of managing that information. If there are many sources for the information we seek, we may get contradictory or out-of-date information, and sifting through can be just as frustrating as aimless browsing. The directory should be a centrally managed repository. It's important to have a single, authoritative source for a particular type of information. That way, we don't have to search in several places for the information we want, and then painstakingly decide which information is correct.

Many applications and services can take advantage of data that is central-ized in a directory

There are many uses for a directory, beyond the direct interac-tion a person has when manually looking up information. Application software can leverage the information in a directory to provide a more informed and better experience. Backroom services that work without our being aware of them can also make use of centralized information. These services provide the foundation that lets us interact in the digital world, identifying us to others, establishing our authority, allowing us to commu-nicate with each other, even protecting us. Each of these foun-dational services, sometimes called *infrastructure*, must either have its own source of information about identities or rely on a common set of information. Clearly there is a benefit to having only a single set of information to manage, along with a clearly defined method of accessing this data. And there are many uses for the same piece of data, as the example that follows shows.

The directory can streamline your business processes

A directory should enable an organization to manage its busi-ness processes better. Imagine the following scenario as an ex-ample of why directories are making such an impact.

An important new executive joins your place of business. On her first day, the security officer stops her at the front door to request a long list of information for her security badge. Once she has passed by the security officer, her first visit is to the HR department, where she is asked to fill out a form with her name, social security number, birth date, home address, department, supervisor, and so forth so she can be added to the payroll system. Then she is shown to her office. There a young technician gives her a user account and password for accessing network resources. The technician needs her name and department to give her access to the appropriate network resources.

Throughout the day, administrative assistants stop by for information. One needs to take down the asset information for her new computer and assign it to her by name. Another is from the HR department again with a form for benefits. Another is from the budget department, to give her the proper budget codes for requisitions and spending accounts. The forms don't seem to stop . . . and much of the information is requested on multiple forms. Naturally the executive wonders why all these people can't share her information. Ideally, she would enter the information into the directory and then other people who needed the information could query the directory without wasting her valuable time. The people performing these business tasks could manually query the directory for the appropriate information, or better yet software could be used to interact directly with the directory and automate the entire process after the executive entered the personal data.

There are as many uses for a directory as there are types of information to organize. The amount of information being stored on computers is increasing at an exponential rate, so finding a good directory solution has become more important than ever. Fortunately for the computer industry, a common standard for directories has emerged in LDAP. This chapter introduces LDAP, highlights its capabilities, and explains why it has garnered widespread support as the best directory solution.

The LDAP standard has been widely accepted as the ideal solution

To this point, I have discussed directories through common examples in everyday experience. Now it is time to look at what a

My Company Won't Buy a Directory

Maybe it should. The potential savings over the long run are more substantial than you think. For example, think of all the business processes that are keyed to correct and up-to-date contact information. When my contact information changed recently, I notified all the companies with which I did business. But I still had a difficult time because many businesses didn't use a single, unified repository for tracking that information. In some cases, I stopped doing business with them because I didn't appreciate spending my time troubleshooting their poor business process.

On another track, your company may just as easily end up with a directory because it is a required component for implementing some other essential product. Directories are becoming a common prerequisite. For example, almost all network operating systems require a directory to get the most out of product features. A lot of server software requires a directory to store its configuration information. So even if your company wouldn't buy a directory to actively solve a business need, you will probably end up with one.

directory is, and what is unique about the directory structure that makes it useful. This examination focuses on two properties:

- **Structure**—How does a directory store information?

- **Content and usefulness**—What can be put in a directory, and why would someone choose a directory over something else?

This general examination of directories sets the stage for the following introduction to LDAP.

Structure

The entry is the unit of the directory

A directory is composed of entries. The *entry* is the basic unit of the directory. These entries usually contain a similar kind of information. For example, my directory could have entries about people (commonly called person entries) that include a person's name along with a phone number, and perhaps other relevant personal information. There would be an entry for each person, and each entry would consist of all the personal information known by the directory about that person. The term "entry" is synonymous with the term *record* or *directory object*; these terms are used interchangeably in the literature on the subject.

The information associated with an entry is called the *attributes* or *properties* of the entry. Again, the literature is not uniform; "attribute" and "property" are used interchangeably. An entry is essentially a collection of attributes. For a person entry, the person's name is one of the attributes, as is the phone number. Depending on how the directory is defined, entries can have a set of mandatory attributes as well as a set of optional attributes. For example, my directory might have entries with mandatory common name (full name) and surname (last name) attributes along with optional phone number, fax number, and e-mail address attributes. The entry is incomplete, and therefore not allowed, without the presence of every mandatory attribute. Figure 1-1 shows an example entry for myself.

The entry is composed of a set of attributes

Each attribute is composed of a pair of elements. The *attribute type* is a label for the kind of information being stored. The

The attribute is composed of a type and value pair

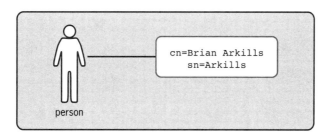

Figure 1-1   A person entry with two attributes

attribute value is the actual data being stored. For example, cn=Brian Arkills is an attribute pair, where cn (or common name) is the attribute type, and Brian Arkills is the attribute value. Incidentally, some attributes can have multiple values, which is an important feature for maximizing the flexibility of the data structure. The ability to have multiple values is a key advantage that LDAP possesses over common database solutions. Figure 1-2 shows an entry with a multivalued cn attribute.

The objectclass *attribute defines what rules the entry follows*

There is a special attribute that is mandatory to all entries, called the objectclass attribute. This attribute determines what rules the entry follows. These rules govern the content of the entry by specifying the set of attributes that are mandatory and another set that is optional. The objectclass attribute is multivalued, so the set of mandatory and optional attributes for an entry is the union of all the values of the objectclass attribute. The rules may also include the possibility of restrictions on where entries of that object class can be created. At the most basic level, the object class defines what attributes can be used in the entry. The schema of the directory determines which object classes are available in the directory. The *schema* essentially defines the set of rules the directory data must follow.

Many types of entries are possible

A directory can have many different types of entries. A directory can have person entries with name attributes, phone attributes, and others. But it can also have entries that represent products

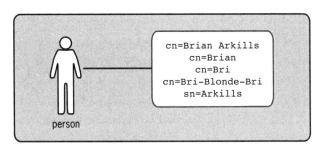

Figure 1-2   A person entry with a multivalued attribute

What's the Difference Between Object Class and Objectclass?

The terms are closely connected and very similar. `Objectclass` is an attribute of an entry; you use the term only when you refer to a specific entry. Every entry in a directory has the `objectclass` attribute with one or more values that denote the object classes to which the entry belongs. An object class is a definition of rules that an entry of that object class will follow. The term "object class" is used to abstractly discuss a set of entries that follow the same rules. All of these entries have the same `objectclass` attribute value. It isn't the entries themselves that are being referenced; it is the set of rules that define that class of entries.

with a name, UPN serial number, and manufacturer attributes. You could delineate these different types of entries by using different object classes, or you could set up the entries to share the same object class, depending on the class's flexibility. The example shown in Figure 1-3 uses different object classes. Despite what is shown in Figure 1-3, different types of entries can exist side by side as long as structural rules don't prohibit such juxtaposition.

There is a special type of entry known as a container. A *container* helps to organize other entries by establishing a parent/child relationship. A commonly used container object class is *ou,* organizational unit. In my directory, we might want to place all of the person entries in a container named People while placing all the product entries in a container named Products. In general, this choice might make it easier to find or manage entries; however, in our example, you could just as easily find all the product entries by searching the directory for entries with the `objectclass` attribute equal to "part". But separating all the product and person entries into different containers makes it easy to delegate management of the entries to different people. For example, I might delegate management of the People OU to the HR department and of the Products OU to the product manager.

Container entries provide a structure for organization and management

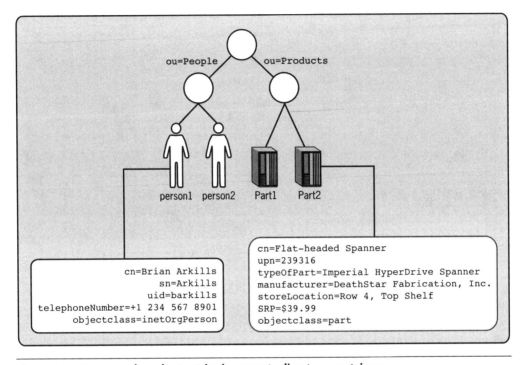

ou=People   ou=Products

person1   person2   Part1   Part2

cn=Brian Arkills
sn=Arkills
uid=barkills
telephoneNumber=+1 234 567 8901
objectclass=inetOrgPerson

cn=Flat-headed Spanner
upn=239316
typeOfPart=Imperial HyperDrive Spanner
manufacturer=DeathStar Fabrication, Inc.
storeLocation=Row 4, Top Shelf
SRP=$39.99
objectclass=part

Figure 1-3   Person and product entries in separate directory containers

Containers have rules, but you decide how to use them to organize

Containers can have other containers as children, but child entries can have only a single container as a parent. So a pyramid (or upside-down tree) organizational structure is possible, but web or hub structures are not possible. To what extent containers are used is left to the details of implementation. You could choose to have an extensive structure of containers to provide critical organization, an arbitrary structure of containers, or no containers at all.

Content and Usefulness

The leading alternative to a directory is a database, and comparing the two helps illustrate both the nature of a directory and its usefulness. After this comparison, this section provides some examples to highlight typical directory content. Note that the comparison considers only relational databases. Object databases are similar to directories, but the technology is not widely adopted.

Directories Versus Databases

A directory usually contains entries that are static or change infrequently, because it is designed to provide very fast response to searches and lookups. A database often contains entries that can change frequently. Databases are designed to provide data that can be easily manipulated and sustain intense processing, with both reading and writing of that data. So if you want to keep track of your company's sales, you'd pick a database, not a directory, because (one hopes that) your company would be constantly writing new sales quotes. In contrast, your company's sales contacts would be best suited for a directory, because this information doesn't change often. In general, if the entries you'd like to store change less than once a day, a directory is probably the best solution.

Directory=read; database=read and write

Relational databases and directories also differ in terms of internal structure, and looking at this difference provides another measure of both what a directory is as well as how it is useful. Entries in databases have certain attributes that are called keys. *Keys* provide critical functionality for database technology by allowing you to sort entries. Additionally, you can use the keys to cross-reference information about an entry in one table to information about an entry in another table. The entries in a database have no inherent structural relationship to one another, and they don't really have names, aside from the keys (special attributes) that must be unique among all records in that table. In contrast, a directory is extremely structured. Each directory entry has a name that also defines that entry's location in a hierarchy. This relationship is discussed in more detail shortly. Another structural difference is that the attributes of a directory entry regularly have multiple values, whereas only denormalized relational databases have multiple values per attribute.

Relational databases and directories have key structural differences

The structural dif-ferences highlight special uses of databases and directories

These key structural differences mean that each technology has strengths and weaknesses that predispose it toward specific uses. Databases excel at storing objects that can be sorted in different ways. Databases usually implement a locking mecha-nism to prevent two parties from writing the same information, whereas directories don't. Complex queries that cross-reference multiple entries are typically quicker in a database than in a directory. Databases manage large data objects pretty well, whereas a directory is not designed for this purpose. The struc-ture of a database lends itself to tables, whereas a directory is not well suited to store tables. Databases let you store proce-dures for efficient processing of complex requests.

Directories are suited for several commonly required purposes

Directories are really specialized data storage systems. Directories are much more suited for objects that need a hierar-chy. Directories can be replicated across servers to allow access from multiple locations. They are more than a name service, because they allow both searching and retrieval, whereas name services just perform retrieval. Text-based information is particu-larly well suited for a directory because it can be easily searched; however, any type of data can be stored in a direc-tory. Directories manage user attributes and policies well, be-cause most services simply need to search and retrieve these

Do I Need to Choose Between a Database and a Directory?

No. They simply have different strengths and weaknesses. Each has a valid place, and it is likely that you will have both databases and directories. In fact, directo-ries usually have a specially configured database running behind them. It might help you to think of a directory as a layer on top of a database, except that you can't access the database directly through normal means. In some cases, your company may want to synchronize some of the data elements stored in a direc-tory and a database. For an example, see Appendix C.

attributes. Directories also manage information for machines and applications well, especially when the information is configuration-centered or is management information. Directories usually support a very fine level of access control, allowing information to be restricted as desired.

Typical Directory Use

You can use a directory to organize or manage just about any kind of information so people can easily find that information. Directories are most commonly used for personal information, but they can be used just as readily for information about any real-world object. For example, you could have a directory with products from your place of business. People could search the directory, based on the part number or type of product, to find information about the product they need and its physical location in a store. The directory could include pictures of the products and have a nice application interface (maybe Web-based) integrated with other functionality, such as an online ordering system, so products could be ordered.

You can use directories for information about people or real-world objects

The directory excels at storing personal information because information about people is fairly constant. Again, the directory is optimized to respond to queries about information that remains constant over time. Person-related information is of high value to the clients of a directory, whether they are people or applications. Person-related information also has a great need to be centrally managed so it is consistent, up-to-date, and secure. Think about personal contact information. The list is lengthy: a postal address, home address, office address, multiple phone numbers, e-mail addresses, a URL to a homepage, and so on. Obviously, there is more personal information than just contact information. However, personal contact information illustrates one inherent problem that a directory helps solve, in that I must first be in contact with you in order to get your contact information. A directory can let you store your personal contact information for easy retrieval by others—subject, of

Important personal information abounds, and a directory excels at storing it

course, to the access controls applied to protect that contact information from untrustworthy folks who might use it to spam or harass you.

Applications use the directory on our behalf

However, the directory isn't just useful for others to find out about us. Often there are computer applications that need to check information associated with us. These applications do work for us behind the scenes. For example, it's fairly common for an e-mail service to query a directory with your e-mail address to find out which server your mailbox resides on, so it can deliver your e-mail to you. Additionally, some e-mail services automatically create an address book (which is stored in a central directory) so the user can simply pick a name instead of remembering an e-mail address. Many other applications and services are capable of looking up information in a directory, and some even provide an interface so people can modify directory information.

Authentication credentials can be placed in a directory

As another example, almost every time you log in, you are *authenticating* to some form of a directory. The directory validates the *credentials* you provide (a password or a ticket encrypted with your password) so everyone else on the network knows for certain that you are who you say you are. This authentication is critically important because it prevents someone else from impersonating you. Many network operating systems (NOSs) use LDAP as the basis of their internal directory functionality. This close integration can be an incredible benefit but also can have some drawbacks. I'll look a bit more at how a NOS might use LDAP shortly.

People are more productive with a directory to support them

Without the directory behind the example situations I've explored, people would be much less productive. Managing e-mail addresses and authenticating to every network resource (instead of authenticating just once) are tasks that people don't want to be bothered with, and the directory helps people manage this information. Directories have many of these behind-the-scenes uses, which ultimately benefit all of us. In fact, the major benefits of a directory are behind-the-scenes types of services, with a computer application or a computer running more smoothly because the directory is there.

Another perfect use for a directory is in managing machines. Networked machines inevitably have configurations that need to be managed. These configurations are largely static, but keeping the information centrally lets changes be easily implemented. Networked computers have even more specialized uses for a directory. Computers that are members of a NOS service usually need to authenticate themselves. This information needs to be centrally maintained. Computers also have many characteristics such as software, environment configuration, and access privileges. Network administrators appreciate any tool that will help them manage this information, which generally changes infrequently. Microsoft's Active Directory (an extension of Windows 2000 Server) provides a good example of a specific implementation of this type of use. For example, Active Directory allows a directory administrator to define *group policy* directory entries that are a set of configuration information, and apply these policy entries to computer entries. This process facilitates computer management and demonstrates one way in which LDAP can be used.

Machine and computer management information belong in a directory

Users also experience the benefit of machine management via a directory. The previous examples may appear to benefit only computers and computer support personnel, but they also benefit other employees and customers of the company. Users don't want to memorize obscure naming conventions in order to find a network resource. Directories can help address this issue by helping users locate network resources via the directory. Imagine, if you will, the harried user who desperately needs to print a document for an important presentation in a remote location at your place of business. How does she find a printer? There are no support personnel at hand. The directory comes to the rescue, because it knows where all the printers are and the user can easily ask the directory for a printer at that

Directory management of computers helps people

location. The directory might interface with the user's laptop to configure the needed printer settings. The directory might further address the issue of multiple obscure naming conventions by providing a unified and user-friendly naming convention that hides the real naming conventions being used.

Benefits of a Directory

Many IT personnel know that implementing a directory is important for their business but don't quite know how to justify the cost and effort required to their managers. Benefits 1-1 consolidates the relevant points into a useful form that you can use in such a situation. Benefits 1-2 later in the chapter is a similar summary that focuses on the benefits unique to LDAP. Use Benefits 1-1, Benefits 1-2, and Figure 1-4 to begin to build a case to your manager for implementing an LDAP directory.

Benefits 1-1   Benefits of a directory

- Make network administration easier

    - Central management of people information
    - Central management of computer and machine configuration
    - Central management of user accounts
    - Reduced support costs from centralized management

- Unify access to network resources

    - Uniform naming convention
    - Potential for single login to network resources

- Provide single destination for users to search for information

    - Contact information
    - Central location of network resources
    - Potential as a catalog for any data, for example, product documentation

- Improve data management

  - Improve the consistency of data that is widely used
  - Provide centrally managed security for business-critical data
  - Organize data in a logical structure

- Help streamline business processes

- Provide repository and lookup for application and service data

Introducing LDAP

How does LDAP work? Why has LDAP been adopted as the directory standard by so many large companies, as well as by all the major software vendors? This section provides an overview of how LDAP technology functions and why LDAP is considered so highly by the industry. Later chapters in the book expound on this overview in more detail.

LDAP (Lightweight Directory Access Protocol) originated out of the X.500 series of International Telecommunication Union (ITU) recommendations. ITU is an international standards body, and X.500 is a set of recommendations about directories. Because of this relationship, the structure of X.500 and LDAP directories is similar. LDAP directory implementations are often also X.500 compliant, and gateways between the two directories are also plentiful. LDAP was pioneered at the University of Michigan, and there is still a free implementation available from their Web site, along with documentation, source code, and other resources.

LDAP came from X.500

LDAP is defined by a set of published Internet standards, commonly referenced by their Request For Comment (RFC) number as published at the IETF Web site: http://www.ietf.org. The Internet Engineering Task Force (IETF) helps manage a rigorous

A set of nine RFC documents defines LDAP

What Happened to X.500?

There were a host of problems with X.500. It was too tied to the OSI (Open Systems Interconnection) protocols, and so wasn't well suited for the TCP-dominated world that emerged. It used a complicated encoding mechanism (although to be fair, LDAP uses pretty much the same one). Its creators were very ambitious, and so X.500 was probably too complicated for the kinds of problems that people really wanted to solve. And finally, X.500 was meant to be a global directory service, even though it wasn't clear that everyone thought this was a good problem to solve. In short, LDAP and the Domain Naming System (DNS) solved in a simpler fashion the real problems that people faced.

proposal process in which ideas such as LDAP are reviewed in drafts until they are ready to be published as an Internet standard. Don't be confused about the number of RFC documents associated with LDAP. LDAP version 3 (v3) is defined by nine RFC documents. RFC's 2251 through 2256 give the core details, and were later followed by RFC 2829 and 2830. RFC 3377 followed shortly prior to the time this book went to press. It tied all of these RFCs together as the official LDAP v3 standard. In addition to these nine documents, you will find many other documents that address technology based on the core LDAP standard. LDAP comprises a wide set of technology and continues to be developed, so several documents are needed to help define its many facets. This book includes coverage of the material in the core RFCs as well as most of the other LDAP RFCs. Although the RFC documents define the standards, they don't tell the whole story, and they are certainly not enjoyable reading. But for further reference, when the RFC documents provide more detail than is appropriate for this book, they will be cited.

To summarize LDAP, we'll be looking at four areas:

- Namespace
- Client operations

- Schema
- Management

These four areas coincide with the next four chapters of the book, which expand the summary information found here in greater detail. In the second section of the book, each of the chapters looks at specific vendor implementations. These chapters also use these four primary areas to organize the information.

Mycompany.com

Prior to looking at the four LDAP areas, I need to introduce the example company that is used throughout the book to provide a concrete context for abstract concepts. Mycompany.com is a typical company, with sophisticated technical requirements for carrying out its business. I've intentionally left the profile of Mycompany generic, to maximize the relevance of the example. Figure 1-4 shows a representative sample of the types of business applications and IT infrastructure services that Mycompany has deployed and would like to integrate with an LDAP directory.

Trying to Read the RFCs?

If you try to read the RFCs on the IETF Web site, you may encounter several problems. You may come across references to X.500 documents that you can't find online. This is because X.500 is maintained by the ITU international standards body. ITU asks that you pay to receive a copy of its standards, and you can order a copy online from its Web site. Alternatively, I've listed a few online X.500 references at the back of the book, including an entire online book on X.500. Second, you may not understand the special coding system used in some of the definitions. It is called Backus-Naur Form (BNF), and you can read more about it in RFC 822. The RFC is oriented toward simplifying the encoding of e-mail; but if you skip several of the messaging-specific parts, you can get an idea of how to use the BNF format.

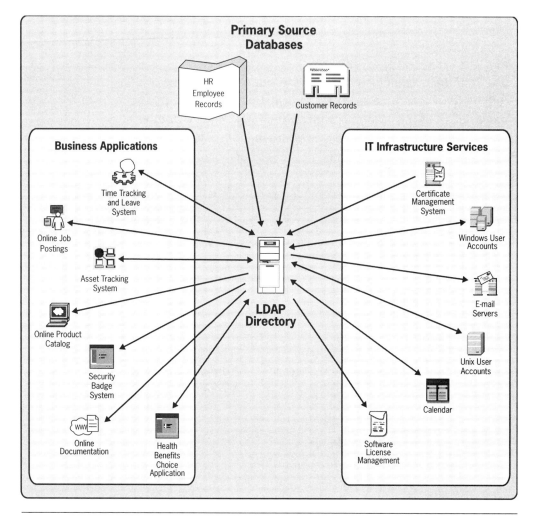

Figure 1-4   Integration of Mycompany.com's applications and infrastructure with LDAP

Mycompany would like to use an LDAP directory to tie these applications and services together to simplify data management, cut development and support costs, and provide a single point of IT infrastructure management. Figure 1-4 further shows how each of these applications, databases, and services might inter-act with data in the LDAP directory. Arrows out of the directory represent a search operation (also called a query) that is the source of information for the service or application. Arrows into the directory represent a source of directory data or potential modification of existing directory data.

Namespace

Every directory needs a namespace. What, you might ask, is a namespace? As you might expect, *namespace* refers primarily to how entries are named. However, it can also imply other things, such as an organizational structure for the entries. Incidentally, the term "namespace" can also be used in a general sense to refer to all the objects in a specific container.

To find information in a directory, a common set of naming rules is needed; these rules are called a namespace

In general, the LDAP namespace is the system used to reference objects in an LDAP directory. Each object must have a name, and the name of each object serves two purposes. First, it allows the object to be referenced. Second, it allows the object to be organized into a logical structure. Understanding the namespace is the key to understanding the structure of the directory.

The namespace serves two functions: to identify objects and to define the hierarchical structure

Each entry in the directory needs a name for the purposes of referencing that entry. These names must be unique in an LDAP directory so you can designate a specific entry. But instead of simply naming each entry with a unique name, the namespace goes a step further and designates where in the directory's organizational structure each entry belongs. So if you know the name of an entry, you also know where that entry resides in the directory structure.

Because each entry indicates a location in the directory, its name must be unique

Because the namespace is organized in a hierarchical fashion, management control can be delegated at multiple points in the hierarchical structure. The hierarchy that is inherent in the namespace conveniently provides an effective means for cooperative delegation of management. This is a significant advantage of LDAP over databases, and it is usually one of the primary factors in deciding how to organize data in the directory.

Namespace hierarchy allows management control

DNS is one common namespace

Many of the directories you may have used share a common namespace, which happens to be an Internet standard: DNS. For example, when you send an e-mail to another person's mailbox across the Internet, you address it in a way (person@domain.com) that conforms to the DNS namespace. The e-mail is delivered to only one person because the mail service using the DNS namespace also enforces uniqueness of names. DNS provides a namespace for many computer services.

The LDAP namespace is very similar to DNS, and DNS can be employed

DNS is by definition hierarchical in nature. The LDAP namespace is hierarchical too. Because the namespaces are so similar, many LDAP directories leverage the DNS namespace, so the LDAP namespace works seamlessly with DNS. This reliance helps make LDAP more attractive and provides for future development of globally integrated LDAP directories. LDAP vendors that adopt DNS compatibility allow for the possibility of seemingly independent directories being more easily connected in a global hierarchy at a later time, just as an intranet-based DNS zone might be connected to the global DNS namespace. Chapter 5 examines the integration of independent directories, and Chapter 2 introduces some of the primary concepts. Formalizing the relationship of LDAP to DNS is one of the tasks of an IETF working group; Chapter 2 also examines this relationship.

DNS is not required but usually is preferred

With some directory servers, clients or users can automatically locate directory servers for their local DNS zone without any prior knowledge or configuration (for more detail, see Chapter 2). But to be clear, LDAP does not require that DNS be used in forming a directory namespace. With the help of a name resolution service like DNS, a client locates a directory server on the network. Other name resolution services can be used to locate the LDAP server; however, the trend is definitely to implement LDAP with a reliance on the DNS namespace. The benefits of doing so are greater than the alternative, but there are reasons not to do so as well. These reasons are usually limited to LDAP directories with an isolated use.

Figure 1-5 shows a simple version of Mycompany's directory. The name of the root of the directory is known as the directory's *base DN*. The directory root is not necessarily a directory entry. The server's base DN typically matches the DNS name of the directory server and uses the *domain components (dc)* attribute to represent the DNS zones. However, the server's base DN does not necessarily have to coincide with the server's DNS name. The directory server's base DN might be different to allow greater flexibility in designing a distributed directory architecture across multiple directory servers. The flexibility to create a distributed directory via the namespace is a key advantage of LDAP over databases. Chapter 2 covers some of the foundational concepts behind a distributed directory architecture, like referrals, replication, and the full details of namespace. Chapter 5 addresses distributed directory architecture models, as well as the issues and solutions to integrating directories.

The root of the directory has a name

But how do you reference an entry within my LDAP directory? Each entry in the directory has a unique name known as the *distinguished name (DN)*. Each entry also has a name local to its immediate container known as the *relative distinguished name (RDN)*. The RDN is unique among all entries in that container. For now, think of a container as being similar to a directory or folder in a file system; Chapter 2 covers containers in more detail. The DN of each entry is formed by concatenating the RDN of the entry with the RDN of the containers between the entry and the directory root. There is a comma between the RDNs in the DN. Neither the DN nor the RDN is an attribute of the entry, but the RDN consists of one of the attributes of the entry.

The DN is the name of an entry

The RDN is an attribute type and value pair. More precisely, it can be any attribute pair (or combination of attributes) that is unique in the entry's immediate directory container. The RDN does not have to be unique across the entire directory. You can compare the RDN to the hostname, like myserver, which is

The RDN is the local name of an entry

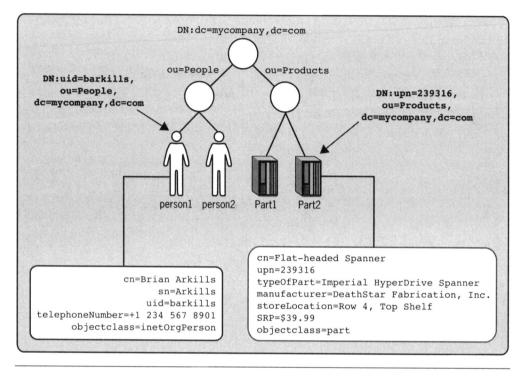

Figure 1-5   Person and part records with DNs in an LDAP directory that integrates with the DNS namespace

unique within the mycompany.com DNS zone, but is not necessarily unique among all DNS zones in the world.

Example to illustrate DN usage

The DN of the person entry shown in Figure 1-5 could have been cn=Brian Arkills,ou=People,dc=mycompany,dc=com instead of uid=barkills,ou=People,dc=mycompany,dc=com. Notice that each RDN component includes both the attribute type and value. For example, the single component cn=Brian Arkills has both the attribute type cn and the attribute value Brian Arkills. The attribute value without the attribute type would not be sufficient to distinguish the entry, because the value might refer to different attribute types on many entries. The *common name (cn)* of the entry in Figure1-5 is Brian Arkills. Note that cn=Brian Arkills must be unique among all entries in the container `ou=People` to qualify as an RDN. As you might realize, uniqueness of a person's name isn't guaranteed, so another attribute is often used instead as the RDN. Mycompany might choose the user identity `uid=barkills` instead as the entry's RDN, because login IDs are unique within Mycompany. The DN `uid=barkills,ou=People,dc=mycompany,dc=com` refers to exactly the same record in the directory namespace as the DN above. This second DN simply uses a different RDN to identify the entry desired, where the *uid* is my user identity or account name.

Based on the desired integration noted in Figure 1-4, Mycompany's directory namespace might look something like Figure 1-6. For simplicity, almost no directory entries have been shown, but each of the containers shown (open circles) would have entries (closed circles) and possibly additional containers for further organization or delegation. For example, the People namespace might be divided with containers by department, with the entire Sales department in a container and the entire Engineering department in another. The layout shown in Figure 1-6 could be implemented differently and still meet the desired integration requirements.

The namespace that LDAP employs has substantial benefits. First, it provides a naming model that uniquely identifies entries but is flexible in that more than one name may be valid. Second, it is inherently hierarchical. This allows entries with the same naming attribute to exist in the directory in different containers. It provides a vehicle for delegation of management, application of access controls, and organization of data. Third, it usually leverages DNS, which gives an LDAP directory an advantage in integrating with other technologies, and service location resolution from anywhere. Fourth, the namespace allows LDAP to distribute a directory across multiple servers. For more detail on this topic, see Chapter 5. This benefit is significant because greater reliability, distributed load, and localized

LDAP's namespace provides many advantages

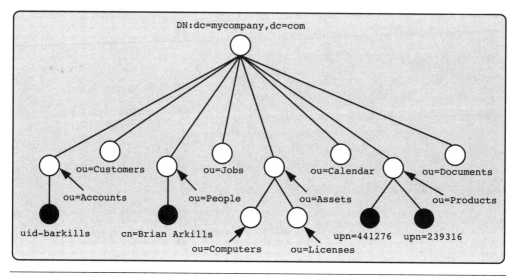

DN:dc=mycompany,dc=com

ou=Customers
ou=Accounts
uid-barkills

ou=Jobs
ou=People
cn=Brian Arkills
ou=Computers

ou=Calendar
ou=Assets
ou=Licenses

ou=Documents
ou=Products
upn=441276   upn=239316

Figure 1-6   Mycompany directory namespace

directory data are additional benefits that can be realized from this distribution.

Protocol

LDAP is primarily a set of server operations

At its heart, LDAP defines a set of server operations (the directory access protocols) used to manipulate the data stored by the directory. But there are many other aspects to LDAP, and people are hard at work developing draft standards that might be added to the accepted Internet standards that comprise LDAP. Some of these extensions may comprise the rules that govern the method in which data is stored in an LDAP directory, extensions of the protocol and server operations, standards for secure client authorization, architecture for ensuring directory reliability, and so forth.

Client-Server Model

TCP/IP is required for LDAP

As an Internet protocol, LDAP uses TCP/IP for its communications. For a client to be able to connect to an LDAP directory, it must open a TCP/IP session with the LDAP server. LDAP minimizes the overhead to establish a session allowing multiple operations from the same client session. It also gains traffic efficiencies from compression because the majority of data stored in the directory is discrete text-based information. LDAP employs *BER encoding* to encode the attribute value data passed between the server and client. This overly complicated encoding method is retained from LDAP's X.500 roots.

Interestingly enough, the set of LDAP operations correspond one to one to a set of standard application programming interfaces (APIs) in different languages. An *API* is a set of functions that programmers can use in writing software. These functions provide a higher-level deliverable by hiding the messy guts of the code from those that use it. Some APIs are *closed source*, meaning that the guts are intentionally hidden from everyone. Others are *open source*, meaning that anyone can view the details and even contribute improvements. The LDAP APIs are all open source. For an example of a function from an LDAP API, take the server operation used to add entries. There is a standard LDAP function `ldap_add()` in the C language API that an application would use to ask the server to perform the add operation. Similarly, the standard APIs define functions for each of the server operations defined by the LDAP specifications. Any application that used an LDAP API to interact with an LDAP server is called *LDAP-enabled*. The standard C language version of the API is documented in RFC 1823.

Any LDAP client can speak with any LDAP server

Clients

The LDAP client can be either standalone software that a person interacts with by typing in the syntax as required, or it can be an integrated piece of software with much of the operation automated and the syntax requirements hidden from the user. For example, the Windows 2000 operating system has integrated the LDAP client functionality into several of its core applications. In Windows 2000, you can choose the Search option from the Start menu, and look up person or printer entries in the Microsoft Active Directory (in other words, the

The LDAP client can be standalone or integrated software

LDAP server) to which the computer is connected. There are many LDAP-enabled Web sites that provide a single interface (sometimes called portals) for people to use in searching and modifying entries in their company's LDAP server. In addition to these Web sites, most modern browsers support the LDAP protocol and are completely functional clients for retrieving information from LDAP. The flexibility of integration is one of the primary reasons why many software companies have embraced the LDAP protocol.

The open standards model means LDAP is very easy to integrate

The beauty of the LDAP open standard becomes evident when you realize that any LDAP client or LDAP-enabled application can successfully communicate with any LDAP server, regardless of the client's or server's particular operating system. The open standard, multiple-platform model makes integration easy, in a marketplace that makes integration difficult. This means that implementing LDAP in a complex, nonhomogeneous operating system environment is significantly easier than implementing other technology.

LDAP has only ten operations, and this is good

Operations
There are ten LDAP operations. The limited number of operations is quite important, in that client programs that interact with the directory are much simpler than client programs that interact with other similar technologies. These operations can be grouped into three basic categories with one outlier, as shown in Table 1-1.

Table 1-1 LDAP operations

Category	LDAP Operations
Client Session Operations	Bind, unbind, and abandon
Query and Retrieval Operations	Search and compare
Modification Operations	Add, modify, modifyRDN, and delete
Extended	Extended

The extended operation is unique among the operations. The extended operation is a placeholder for specific directory implementations to extend the functionality of the protocol but still have a predefined syntax for doing so. The LDAP designers showed a lot of forethought by including the extended operation. By standardizing a way to expand the operational functionality, they eliminated any perceived liability in the limited number of operations.

The client session operations help to control the client-server session context for all subsequent LDAP operation requests from that client. The bind and unbind operations allow the client to establish an identity with the directory. This identity can be used by the directory to determine authorization to perform the other operations, and can be used to control access to directory information. The abandon operation allows the client to cancel an outstanding operation request.

Session operations affect how the client interacts with the directory

The query operations allow the client to look up information in the directory. Most readers new to LDAP need to know how to intelligently search an LDAP directory. The search operation is the most frequently used, and skill in using it will be repeatedly valuable. The search operation has many parameters, in fact, more parameters than any other operation. This greater complexity is worthwhile, however, because it allows the user to designate sophisticated queries in a search for data within the directory. Because of the importance of the search operation, be sure to closely peruse the details and examples provided in Chapter 3. The compare operation allows a client to request a verification of the information associated with an entry. The client sends the purported value(s) of the entry, and the server responds with success if it matches or failure if it doesn't.

Query operations allow data to be found and retrieved

The modification operations allow the client to change information in the directory. These operations might be restricted in some instances, for example, in the case of a public read-only directory. Of these operations, the modifyRDN operation is the

Modification operations allow a variety of changes to be made

only one in need of any summary explanation. The modifyRDN operation allows the client to change the name of an entry and possibly move the entry to a different container.

Referrals and Unicode support extend the functionality of LDAP

Two other notable protocol features of LDAP are referrals and Unicode UTF-8 support. *Referrals* allow an LDAP server to redirect a client to a different LDAP server to locate the data the client requests. This functionality enables integration or cooperation between directory servers and even independent directories. *Unicode* is a specific method of representing data in character sets that are specific to a language or locale. This means that any written language can be represented if Unicode is used to encode the data. Not all data is represented in Unicode; for example, you may have heard of ASCII encoding. Data encoded in ASCII would not allow most of the languages in the world to be represented. Unicode support extends the usefulness of LDAP to virtually any language, making LDAP a global solution. For details of the LDAP protocol, see Chapter 3.

Schema

The schema defines the rules

A game without rules is chaotic and subject to the players' whims. The popular comic strip *Calvin and Hobbes's* "Calvinball" game zealously demonstrates how out of control life can be without rules. In this game, Calvin and Hobbes make up the rules as they play, which inevitably leads to disaster. The set of rules that defines what types of entries can be in the

Is LDAP the Final Word for Directories?

Probably not. In fact, there is evidence that the Web services movement with the XML standards may add something significant to the future of directories. A new standard called DSML is emerging. This standard, however, assumes the presence of an LDAP directory. Perhaps in the future it will evolve beyond this. For more information on DSML, see Chapter 5.

directory is known as the *schema*. If a particular object class isn't in the schema, you can't create an entry with that object class. You extend the schema to include a new object class or to allow new optional attributes on an existing object class. The schema further defines pertinent rules like what type of value can be placed in an attribute, and what operators are valid for those attributes. The *operators* are what the directory uses to compare one attribute's data value to another value. Greater than, less than, and equality are examples of common data operators.

Schema Checking

The addition of any new entry in your directory is subject to a schema-checking process. Should any of the data not meet the applicable definitions, the addition of the entire entry fails. The schema is not something one can ignore—it has teeth that bite! Some LDAP implementations allow you to turn off this schema checking, but doing so is not wise. The data would lose its uniformity.

All new entries must pass the schema-checking process

Default Schema

The minimum set of schema objects required by the LDAP standard, as listed in RFC 2252 and 2256, will give Mycompany a functional directory. The minimum LDAP schema is largely formed from the set of X.500-defined schema objects and follows the basic rules for the X.500 schema. This is the key reason why so many LDAP products can also be X.500 compliant. Directory vendors take care of implementing this minimum set of schema objects, so you only need to be familiar with what these schema objects are and how you might use them. Most software vendors that leverage a directory find this minimum set insufficient for their purposes and further extend the schema with their own definitions.

The LDAP schema comes from X.500

Extending the Schema

Although the schema is arcane because of its syntax format, it is also the source of most of the flexibility of LDAP. Mycompany's directory can implement schema extensions to include whatever

Schema syntax is hard to read, but it is very flexible

types of data the company deems necessary. The schema also lets you define new ways to interact with the directory and new ways to work with the data. Chapter 4 considers schema extensions that others have found significant.

The schema is published so clients know what is supported

LDAP publishes the directory schema so any client can determine what definitions and rules the server employs. The location where the schema is published is stored on every entry, and this information tells you where to look for the schema. The location is called the *root DSE* (Directory Systems Agent Specific Entry) container. Most LDAP directories have a single schema that applies to the whole directory, so the location is the same for all entries. Some LDAP servers may allow the definition of unique schemas for different parts of the directory.

Here is a sample schema definition for the `person` object class:

```
person OBJECT-CLASS ::= {
    SUBCLASS OF { top }
    KIND abstract
    MUST CONTAIN { sn, | cn}
    MAY CONTAIN { userPassword | telephoneNumber |
        seeAlso | description }
    ID 2.5.6.6}
```

If your curiosity is piqued, see Chapter 4, which addresses the schema in more detail.

Management

Information that is centrally organized in an LDAP directory lends itself to management. In fact, an LDAP directory can become the hub of IT management. Figure 1-4 shows how centrally important the LDAP directory is to Mycompany.com, and you can easily imagine how this architecture would make management tasks easier. The support for LDAP directory management functionality is therefore very important. Management functionality that is easy to use or provides ways to simplify integration is highly desirable. Some directory management

Does the Schema Look Complex and Tedious?

For the most part, it is both complex and tedious. Don't underestimate the importance of the schema. You may feel like the schema is boring, and the syntax not worth learning. However, the schema employed by LDAP is one of the greatest features of LDAP, because it lets you design how data is represented, what data is allowed, where it is allowed, and what additional operations can be performed on that data. The other areas of LDAP may be flashy, but they all derive their functionality from definitions in the schema. Without the flexible model LDAP uses with the schema, a lot of the flashiness and all of the extensibility would be gone.

functionality is not addressed by the LDAP standards. For example, LDAP leaves the implementation of storing and retrieving the data on the server up to the vendor. Usually, a specialized database is used. This functionality can introduce a variety of management tasks and functionality, depending on what software component is chosen. In most cases, management tools are best left to vendors and market-driven competition.

Distributed Directory

Possessing a fault-tolerant directory is of high importance to Mycompany because the company wants to make the directory a central focus of critical business data and processes. Most vendors have implemented some form of *replication* to allow portions of the directory to be copied to multiple servers. Employing replication copies a directory or portions of a directory across multiple LDAP servers. Distribution via replication provides several advantages, including load distribution and protection against data loss. For more details on replication, see Chapter 5.

The LDAP standard leaves the implementation of replication to vendors

However, replication is not the only way to have a distributed directory. Different LDAP servers can host different portions of the directory namespace with references to the other LDAP

A distributed directory has many advantages

servers. The namespace can be divided in any way desired.
This type of distribution provides advantages, such as storing
information about your European office on LDAP servers located in that office. This would decrease the dependency on
long-distance connectivity between geographical locations.
Another advantage might allow politically divergent departments to run their own server. This would enable separate management of information that each department feels that it owns.
The flexibility that LDAP provides in terms of namespace provides benefits in simplified management.

Integration and Data Manipulation

Integrating independent LDAP directories and servers from
rogue departments or mergers will further empower the value of
Mycompany's directory. As discussed previously, LDAP supports referrals that allow one LDAP server to reference another.
These referrals can be used to connect servers. Integration via
other methods can also be critical to keeping data consistent
and authoritatively controlled across your organization. For
some other methods, see Chapter 5.

*LDIF and other
features allow
duplication of data
between servers*

There is also an LDAP standard that allows directory data to be
copied between servers. The *LDAP Data Interchange Format
(LDIF)* standard provides a means for a directory administrator
to move directory data between servers in a file format. The
LDIF standard also gives the administrator a way to make batch
modifications to many entries using search-and-replace text-
manipulation tools. For more detail on the solutions LDAP provides in this area, see Chapter 5.

Security

*Authentication,
authorization, and
encryption are
needed to secure
information*

The term "security" is used in a broad sense in the computer
industry. In discussions of computer security, typically two areas
are of concern: authentication and authorization.
Authentication is the means of proving we are who we say we
are. *Authorization* is the means of designating access permissions to users. When we add the complexity of operating on a

network, there is a third area of concern: privacy. *Privacy* is the means of ensuring that data is kept safe so that it is available only to those for whom it is intended. Some form of encryption is usually used to keep data private.

LDAP supports many authentication methods. LDAP v2 and v3 both support *simple authentication* (cleartext), Kerberos, and *digital certificates.* LDAP v2 supports Kerberos v4, whereas LDAP v3 adds support for Kerberos v5 via *Simple Authentication and Security Layer* (SASL). You can find the standard designation for Kerberos under RFC 1510 and 1964. LDAP v3 also supports the SASL. SASL offers a way to add authentication mechanisms to any protocol. Examples of such mechanisms are Kerberos 5 and DIGEST-MD5. The SASL standard designation is specified in RFC 2222. LDAP v3 identifies Transport Layer Security (TLS), the successor to Secure Sockets Layer (SSL), as the way to authenticate with digital certificates. TLS is documented in RFC 2246. Given that LDAP is an Internet standard, you are probably not surprised to learn that Kerberos, SASL, and TLS are also Internet standards.

LDAP supports cleartext, Kerberos, and SASL for authentication

Currently, LDAP has no specifications for authorization. With authorization or access control, you can control access to entries and even attributes. You can allow or deny specific users or groups of users access to entries. The access levels vary between permission levels such as being able to read or write to the entry. Because there is no agreement on authorization in the LDAP standard, vendors are left to implement their own authorization model. Discussion and work is under way in the IETF on this subject, so in the future this may be part of the LDAP standard. This lack of standardization means that this is one of the areas Mycompany will want to scrutinize closely with respect to its choice of a vendor.

Implementation of authorization is left to the vendor

LDAP also supports session encryption for privacy. All information that is communicated during the client-server session can be encrypted so eavesdroppers are foiled. Both SSL and TLS are

LDAP supports SSL and TLS for data encryption privacy

supported. TLS is the successor to SSL, and can be thought of as SSL v3.1. Both SSL and TLS are based on *public key certificate* technology, which depends on the server having a certificate from a trusted certificate authority server. Additionally, clients can obtain certificates and in some cases use them as a valid form of identification (authentication). Although this requirement may pose some hurdles, including management of certificates, the resulting security can be deemed well worth the trouble. Encrypting the session can provide privacy to the directory information passed over the wire. The information in your organization's directory may be some of the most sensitive data you have, possibly personal and proprietary, and your organization won't want this information passed "in the clear" for the advantage of outsiders. Session encryption is critically important if simple authentication (cleartext) is the only available authentication method for a specific client.

Does LDAP Provide Security?

I often talk to people who confuse LDAP as a generalized solution to security concerns. There is a perception that "LDAP" is a security buzzword. LDAP is a directory technology, not a security technology. LDAP directories commonly use security technology, like Kerberos, to provide secure access to the directory, and they may also be used to store security-related information such as X.509 certificates or authorization information. But LDAP itself doesn't provide any security services. LDAP as a standard or a protocol still has room to grow before I'd associate security with it. Don't get me wrong, in most products it is implemented relatively securely. However, the IETF should standardize many of the security features that vendors have implemented. Additionally, the protocol should require some input stream validation mechanism so a client can't pass commands to the directory server via a buffer overflow or other nastiness.

Vendor LDAP Products

Part II covers several of the most popular LDAP products. A few notes about the trends and diversity of offerings are worth mentioning here.

One strong trend has vendors using LDAP to support their network operating system (NOS). This is innovative and provides nice opportunities to integrate many infrastructure services with all the benefits of LDAP. However, the offerings from these companies usually limit the integration with products outside that vendor's software suite. This is made worse when you must employ the vendor's NOS to use the LDAP directory. Integration is nice, but not integration without freedom to choose the best components.

Vendors often use a directory to enable their network operating system

Another trend that has continued throughout LDAP's history is the open source movement. This movement is important in light of the previous trend. The open source movement has helped ensure that some minimum level of integration is kept standard and, in turn, has put pressure on vendors to work with others. Open source LDAP software offers the ability to choose components and eliminate dependence on a single vendor.

LDAP has a strong open source movement

A final trend to note is that almost every large software company has an LDAP directory offering. In addition, several small company offerings also offer LDAP directory products. This diversity of products is great for the consumer, because it provides greater choice and means that vendors have to provide real competitive advantages to capture our attention. Table 1-2 lists most of the LDAP server offerings.

There are a lot of LDAP product offerings available

Why Choose LDAP?

The reasons to use LDAP are overwhelming. Simply put, LDAP is the best show in town if you want to use a directory.

Table 1-2   LDAP servers

Vendor	Product Name
Computer Associates	eTrust Directory
Critical Path	CP Directory Server
IBM	SecureWay
Sun AND Netscape	Directory Server (used to be iPlanet and Netscape Directory Server)
Microsoft	Exchange 5.5 AND Active Directory
Netscape	Directory Server (no longer offered)
Novell	eDirectory (formerly NDS)
OpenLDAP	OpenLDAP
Oracle	Internet Directory
Syntegra	Global Directory AND Aphelion Directory
University of Michigan	Slapd

Consider the many companies and organizations that have already adopted the technology. Benefits 1-2 summarizes a list of advantages of LDAP, but you probably are already familiar with them. This list, together with Benefits 1-1 and Figure 1-4, would make a good start on justification for deploying a directory.

Benefits 1-2   Summary of LDAP Advantages

- Entries are organized in a distinct hierarchy. This provides the means to delegate administration, apply access controls, and enjoy other information management benefits. Even the name of an entry reveals information about the entry.

- Attributes of an entry can have more than one value. The structure of an entry doesn't need to be extended to permit additional data. An entry can also have multiple names, each of which is unique across the directory.

- An LDAP directory can be distributed across multiple servers. This design distributes the load and provides other management benefits.

- LDAP is an open standard, with multiple-platform support. An LDAP client on any platform can communicate with any LDAP server. So there is less reliance on a single vendor.

- The LDAP client requires very few resources to run, and it can easily be integrated into other software. The LDAP operations are few in number, which makes it easy to interact with the directory. Session traffic is encoded and uses TCP, so network communications are economical.

- LDAP has a standardized API for multiple platforms. As a result, your developers can leverage the information in the directory when developing new applications instead of having to rebuild this information. This saves money and time, while opening up the possibility for new cross-functional applications based on access to data that was not previously available.

- LDAP provides easy integration with existing standards because LDAP uses other accepted standards, including TCP/IP and DNS. Standardization of integration methods with other standards is an ongoing process. Later chapters note the results of this process.

- LDAP supports strong authentication and encryption methods.

- LDAP uses Unicode UTF-8 so almost any language character set can be represented. This makes an LDAP directory capable of supporting international organizations in the native language.

- LDAP employs an extensible schema, which allows further operability to be added. Operations and data must conform to the schema, which improves the quality of data.

- The usefulness of LDAP is being extended constantly, because of the widespread adoption of the view that it is the future of directory services.

Cross-technology integration has become a strength of LDAP

Most organizations are now taking the next step and looking for further ways to integrate LDAP with existing technologies. This step extends the usefulness and value of the investment made in LDAP. There are many examples of leveraging other technologies to extend the usefulness of LDAP. This is because LDAP is based on a clear standard that easily integrates with other existing standards.

2

LDAP Namespace

"Namespace" implies that a name is not simply a name, but holds meaning in terms of structure as well. The term takes two different aspects of the directory and seeks to tie them together: how to name things and how to organize them. The definition of a service's namespace is critical. It may be obvious, but a namespace lets you find things. Namespace is the set of conventions used to identify all the objects in a given environment; in other words, it is the naming system. Without a namespace that we agree on, you and I might be referring to the same thing, but using different languages. A good namespace also ensures that one object's name doesn't conflict with that of another object. Namespace is probably the hardest concept presented in this book, so take solace if it seems confusing. To help introduce the concept of namespaces, the next section examines some examples and the properties of namespaces. The rest of the chapter focuses on the namespace that LDAP employs.

The namespace includes more information than just the immediate identifier

A good analogy that illustrates the use of a namespace in the real world is the postal address system used worldwide. In the postal namespace, a letter is addressed (or named if you will) as follows:

> Person's name
>
> Street number Street
>
> City, State/Province/Region Zip code
>
> Country

This name (address) tells us many things by the way it is constructed and the value of each component, while also uniquely designating the recipient. We know that the person lives in the country listed, in the state listed, in the city listed, on the street listed, and so on. We further know the letter is intended for the person who lives at this address, not a person by the same name who lives elsewhere.

By using a hierarchical namespace, you can delegate information management

But consider another point that is well illustrated by this postal example. Because this namespace is organized in a hierarchical fashion with locales of diminishing scope clearly designated, management involving the object (in other words, the recipient) can be delegated. In other words, when the reader drops a letter in the mailbox to this person, it can first be sent to the postal service responsible for the country listed. After that, it can be sent to the state postal service, and so on, until it reaches the local post office and can be delivered. The hierarchy that is inherent in this namespace conveniently provides an effective means for cooperative delegation of management.

You can use the namespace for other management purposes

The postal example illustrates a namespace that is used to uniquely identify objects and establish structured relationships between those objects. Besides identification and structure, the namespace can be involved in accomplishing several other directory management operations. As examples of such functionality, most vendors implement data partitioning and replication. Chapter 5 covers these and other special structural concepts.

When the term "namespace" is used in the context of a specific directory namespace, a slightly different meaning is intended. In this context, it isn't the naming system being referenced. In this context, the term refers to all the objects in that directory and the specific structure that was chosen. With LDAP, there are seemingly two names for every directory term, so be prepared for a multitude of new vocabulary words with duplicate meanings. You may hear the term *directory information tree (DIT)* being used to refer to a specific directory namespace.

Namespace can also refer to a specific directory implementation

DNS

The domain naming system forms a portion of the foundation for the LDAP namespace, and it is also a good example of a namespace. Exploring how DNS works will help underline key points about LDAP. As noted in Chapter 1, the DNS name of the LDAP directory server can be particularly important in determining the name of the root of the directory, which is the directory's base DN. Whether DNS is used in naming affects the implementation of an LDAP namespace. A directory's base DN doesn't have to match the DNS name of the directory server, and usually the two don't match when a directory distributed across multiple servers is desired. Aside from this connection to the namespace, DNS can also play a critical role in the process of the LDAP client locating the LDAP directory server. DNS does not have to be used in the location of the server, but frequently it is.

The server's DNS name is the basis for the name of the root of the LDAP directory

DNS is a distributed directory service that is maintained by thousands of servers across the globe. There are billions of records in this directory, which map an IP address to a computer name and vice versa. IP addresses are numbers that are the "name" that

DNS maps a human-readable name to a computer-readable name

one computer uses to refer to another computer. People know computers by alphanumeric names. A sample record could be *host.mycompany.com. IN A 127.42.12.6*. This record denotes that host.mycompany.com is the human-readable name of the computer at the IP address 127.42.12.6.

DNS Hierarchy

A hierarchy is employed to provide a clear basis for authoritative name resolution

These records are distributed across millions of files called *zones*. Each zone holds a copy of records for the DNS namespace for which it is authoritative. In other words, each zone allows changes to only a small portion of the entire DNS namespace. The host.mycompany.com computer record belongs to the mycompany zone. The mycompany zone belongs to the com zone. The com zone belongs to the root zone. The root zone is the topmost zone in all of DNS. Figure 2-1 shows a diagram of the hierarchy of DNS zones. The zone file is kept on the authoritative DNS server for that zone. Each parent zone is the authority for distinguishing which DNS server is authoritative

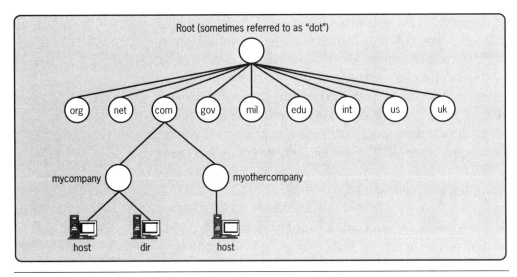

Figure 2-1   Hierarchy of DNS zones (the DNS namespace)

for any child zone. A single root zone holds the authoritative records for each of the first-level DNS zones. This forms a hierarchy, which client computers can query with a reasonable assurance of getting authoritative name resolution.

DNS Resolution

The DNS namespace provides a system both for organizing computer name records and for resolving the location of the computer name. The client computer is typically directed to query the authoritative DNS server of the local zone for name resolution. For example, the computer host.mycompany.com would be configured to query the DNS server for mycompany.com. Should host.mycompany.com want to know the IP address for unknown.whitehouse.gov, it would first ask the DNS server at mycompany.com. mycompany.com would refer it to the com DNS server. The com DNS server would refer it to the root DNS server. The root DNS server would refer it to the gov DNS server. The gov DNS server would refer it to the whitehouse.gov DNS server. The whitehouse.gov DNS server would then reply to the client with the IP address of unknown.whitehouse.gov. Usually DNS servers cache information about important zones like the root and first-level DNS servers, so in reality the process described would follow a much shorter path.

The hierarchy provides an efficient way for a client computer to perform name resolution

Basic DNS Record Types

There are several basic types of DNS records. Table 2-1 lists these records along with a short explanation.

How LDAP Uses DNS

Chapter 1 describes an informal connection between LDAP and DNS. This connection primarily provides a mechanism for an LDAP client to locate the directory server for a particular directory. The RFCs that define LDAP don't refer to DNS, but they allude to it. For example, RFC 2255 defines the LDAP

Table 2-1   Basic types of DNS records

Record Type	Class	Explanation
Address	A	Address records simply map a computer name to an IP address. More than one IP address can be assigned to a computer name by using a second A record. More than one computer name can be assigned to a single IP address, but you should use a canonical name record for this purpose.
Canonical Name	CNAME	The canonical name record is sometimes known as the alias record. It is used to allow a computer to be referred to by more than one name; the secondary name is entered in a record with the IP address of the primary name. Multiple canonical name records are allowed.
Mail Exchange	MX	The mail exchange record is used to indicate the IP address e-mail for a given name. You can designate that all mail for a zone should be delivered to a single IP address.
Pointer	PTR	The pointer record has the opposite function of an address record. It maps an IP address to a computer name. This allows computer services to verify that a request coming from a client is not being hijacked by a nonauthorized computer.
Name Server	NS	The name server record is used to denote the authoritative name servers for the zone.
Start of Authority	SOA	The start of authority record is used to communicate with other authoritative name servers in the DNS hierarchy. Information on how often to check for updates is stored in this record.
Service	SRV	The service record is used to indicate a network service. Several LDAP vendors use this record to provide client location of a server.

URL syntax, which I return to later in this chapter. On close examination, you would find that the hostname component of this syntax clearly relies on DNS, although DNS isn't mentioned. So the reliance on DNS is informal, but in practice every LDAP product expects LDAP clients to use DNS to locate their LDAP directory server. There are good reasons for this dependency. One reason is that DNS is the dominant name resolution standard, and another is that the transmission protocol that LDAP uses is TCP, which relies on DNS.

One important implication of LDAP using the DNS namespace is that by registering a DNS domain name to connect a host or zone of hosts to the Internet, you may inadvertently also register for a directory service namespace. There is a parallel in the e-mail delivery namespace with the MX record and many other network-based services. When I register an A record for mycompany.com with an authoritative DNS server, mycompany.com may become a valid directory service namespace. Most vendors currently expect that your LDAP directory has an A record for each directory server. Some vendors further expect that if you deploy a directory that is distributed across multiple directory servers, you will make each of the directory servers subordinate in the DNS namespace. So for example, if I distributed the mycompany.com directory, the directory servers might have A records of dir1.mycompany.com, dir2.mycompany.com, and so on.

DNS is used to register a directory service

In addition to the informal expectations that have become practice, there has been some formal work with regard to the relationship between DNS and LDAP. RFC 2247 provides a clear standard for DNS to easily be incorporated into the namespace that LDAP uses within the directory. The domain component (*dc*) attribute is defined, and it can be used as a naming attribute in the directory for container objects. Within the IETF, there is other extensive work on using DNS to extend the LDAP namespace functionality. Draft documents include a proposal to use DNS SRV records for clients to locate an LDAP directory for a given namespace. This proposal has gained significant support, as Microsoft's directory implementation of it demonstrates. It will probably supplant the existing informal practice within a few years. Another proposal suggests using DNS SRV records with referrals. Chapter 5 discusses referrals.

LDAP is making increasing use of DNS for its namespace functionality

LDAP Object Structure

The internal structure of an LDAP directory primarily provides organization of entries via a hierarchy. The structure is critical to the usability and manageability of the directory. The structure can also allow the benefits listed in Benefits 2-1 to be easily provided.

Benefits 2-1   LDAP namespace benefits

- The structure can make it easier to distribute information across multiple servers. A directory distributed across multiple servers in turn provides greater reliability and the possibility of locating directory information close to remote locations.

- The structure can make management of access control simpler.

- The structure can enable applications with specific directory requirements to be integrated into your directory.

- The structure can simplify directory maintenance by grouping similar entries together.

The structure itself does not provide these benefits. For Mycompany to realize these benefits depends on its directory implementation and design of the namespace. How each of these benefits is provided is a topic in itself (see Chapter 5).

A namespace with a hierarchy of structure has other benefits

As noted in the postal example, organizing directory objects hierarchically provides an effective means for delegating management of the entries. To add entries, you would need some type of delegated authority in the appropriate place in the directory. The layer of management that is created by the existence of a structure helps to enforce consistent data in entries.

Containers enable structure

A hierarchy is possible in the LDAP directory because of container entries. *Container entries* are special entries that allow other entries to be placed hierarchically beneath them. An entry beneath a container is sometimes called a *child* of the container, or a *subordinate entry* to the container. The container is sometimes called the *parent* of the entries beneath it. You can also refer to the relationship between the container and entries beneath it by saying the entries are *contained* by the parent.

Allowed Structures

The namespace in an LDAP directory allows no arbitrary connections within the structure. Structures similar to the linked relationship between Web pages (in other words, a Web structure) are not allowed. More specifically, a container can have only a single parent directly above it. A container can have multiple child containers, but only a single parent. This type of structure is commonly called a *tree structure.* This term may remind you of the alternate term for namespace: directory information tree (DIT). Figures 2-2 and 2-3 show examples of valid and invalid namespace structures. The regulated approach to the structure leads to little service disruption when new entries are added, because only the new entry is written, and no existing entries must be modified.

Only a specific kind of structure is allowed in LDAP

LDAP Containers

You may assume that containers in an LDAP directory have an attribute that identifies the entry as a container. But this isn't the case. An entry becomes a container when entries are placed under it, but the LDAP directory makes no modification of the container entry when this happens. With LDAP, every entry holds the possibility of becoming a container, and this design supports many hierarchical opportunities.

With LDAP, any entry can become a container

You might also assume that container entries have an attribute that lists all the entries that are contained within that container. This also isn't the case. The hierarchical structure is not stored by any special mechanisms aside from the name of each entry. You create a container by creating an entry beneath another entry! This concept takes some getting used to, as logic suggests

You create a container by creating an entry below another entry

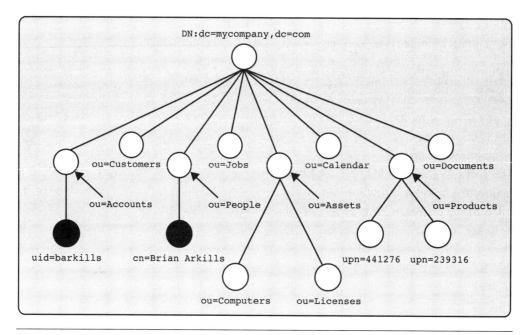

Figure 2-2   Example of valid hierarchical namespaces in an LDAP directory

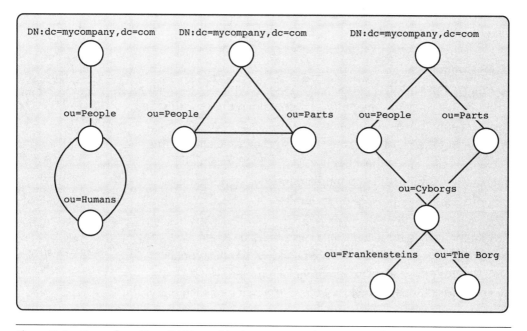

Figure 2-3   Examples of invalid hierarchical namespaces in an LDAP directory

that the container entry would need to be modified. However, specific LDAP implementations may go beyond the LDAP specification and have special attributes for child information in order to offer additional management functionality.

In some LDAP server implementations, there may be restrictions on which object classes an entry must have to become a container. These restrictions are called *structure rules* (for more details, see Chapter 4). In general, there are several object classes that are regularly used as containers for historical reasons. These object classes are favorites because they are the only allowed containers in X.500. Table 2-2 lists these object classes with a short description of each object class along with why they might be useful as a container.

Although every entry can be a container, some object classes may make more sense

Among these object classes, the organizational unit is used most widely. It is frequently employed for a wider variety of purposes than simply political structure. You don't have to use these object classes as the containers in your directory, but you may find that there are good reasons why these classes are favored.

Structure Rules

LDAP also supports structure rules specific to an object class (for detail beyond what's here, see Chapter 4). This functionality

Structure rules restrict where an entry of an object class can be created

Table 2-2   Common object classes used for containers

Object Class Type	Attribute Name	Explanation of Use
Country	c	The country entry can provide geographical structure. As such, you typically use them when you want to split directory information across servers based on geography.
Locale	l	The locality entry also provides geographical structure to subdivide the country container.
Organization	o	The organization entry provides a political structure.
Organizational Unit	ou	The organizational unit entry also provides a political structure.

is not necessarily part of the LDAP standard, but it is implemented by several vendors. Object class structure rules impose restrictions on where an entry of a particular object class may be created. For example, I might associate a structure rule with the organizational unit object class. This structure rule might require that all entries of `objectclass=organizationalUnit` be immediate children of entries of `objectclass=organiza-tion`. This rule imposes an additional restriction in the namespace, and it also limits functionality. Structure rules are enforced by the schema-checking process. Mycompany will want to review any structure rules specific to its chosen vendor.

Naming Contexts

Naming contexts are used to refer to portions of a directory

The name of each top-level container has the distinction of also being called a naming context. The naming context is greater than just the container, though. A *naming context* is a contiguous subtree beginning at a top-level container. For example, if you referred to the Accounts naming context in Mycompany, you would mean the Accounts container, all its child entries, and all containers and entries beneath the Accounts container, as shown in Figure 2-4. In this way, you can conveniently refer to portions of the directory. The naming context is the same terminology as a directory suffix (or a context prefix in X.500). The Accounts naming context is the Accounts suffix.

The directory has no single root entry; instead, all the naming contexts are peers connected by the root DSE

There is really no directory object at the root of an LDAP directory. Instead, there is a special entry that is like a root object, called the *root DSE entry*, that lists all the naming contexts on the directory server. The directory uses the naming contexts to quickly differentiate whether a request for an entry is within the known naming contexts.

A flat namespace allows quick growth

In a directory with a flat structure, organization and management are typically disregarded, while adding new entries is increasingly easy. As you can see in Figure 2-5, the lack of structure

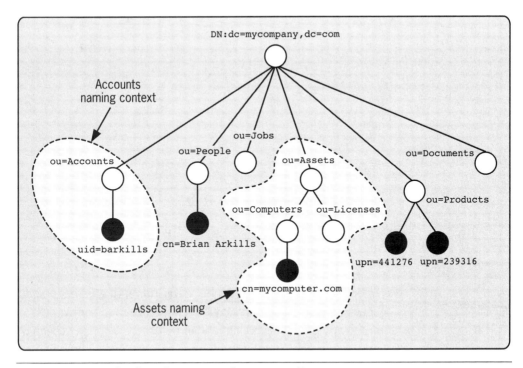

Figure 2-4   Example of naming contexts in an LDAP directory

encourages easy growth because there is only a single organizational container in use, with little to no restriction placed on additions. But in this model, consistency and scalability can
become a nightmare. Scalability becomes an issue when generic
queries regularly return large numbers of entries. Scalability can

Don't Be Fooled by the Figures

Note that the figures throughout the book include a root entry, when in actuality
there is no such entry. This is purely to allow you to know the context of the namespace being pictured. It is a common practice in diagramming directory namespaces, but it fooled me for a long time into thinking there really was a root entry.

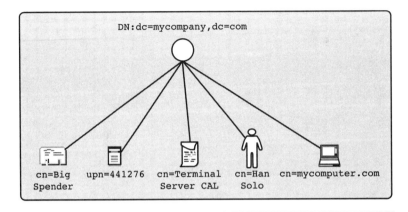

Figure 2-5   A flat namespace in an LDAP directory

also be an issue when the number of useful unique names reaches its limit. This limit may be reached because only one entry in any particular container can be named with any specific name. A hierarchical model sidesteps these problems by organizing entries at multiple levels in the hierarchy.

There are four basic divisions of a directory namespace that are useful:

1. **Political/functional**—Dividing information based on an organization, or difference in functional needs. For example, you might separate the HR directory information from the Marketing directory information.

2. **Geographic**—Dividing information based on the location of the clients who will be accessing the information or based on the location of the real objects that the information in the directory represents. For example, you might separate the personal information for individuals in Europe from the same information for U.S. citizens.

3. **Resource-based**—Dividing information based on the type of resource. For example, you might separate the

printer information from the server information, or separate public resources from private resources.

4. **User classification**—Dividing information based on users' needs. For example, you might separate information for managers from information for staff.

How Do I Decide How to Structure My Directory?

The decision on how to structure a directory can be a difficult one. Equally hard can be the decision as to when to divide up a flat structure or a single container. Hybrid combinations of the four basic divisions of a namespace can frequently fit a situation very well. Usually a geographical division is accompanied by distributing the directory namespace across multiple servers. Chapter 5 covers distributed directory servers in more detail. Another factor in the decision is a requirement to provide certain kinds of directory data in a more fault-tolerant manner by replicating it across multiple servers. LDAP vendors have differing requirements on what the smallest unit of replication can be, and this will affect design decisions.

Keep in mind that the single biggest reason to implement structure is to simplify management of the information. If you implement a structure with no clear management goal, you will come to regret your choices. While looking at each of the models for implementing a hierarchy, you should consider the following questions:

- Will users of the directory need different levels of access to the information? If so, what structure can be implemented to simplify the access management?

- Does the directory help to provide management of computers or other devices? If so, are there compelling reasons to manage specific computers differently from others?

- Are the political or organizational divisions under consideration? If so, make sure that you make it easier to manage resources, users, or directory information. The most frequent mistake is to blindly implement the structure based on internal organizational boundaries that require no different level of management.

- For every new container, ask, "What administrative management purpose does this container serve?"

Try to keep your directory as flat as possible, while having enough structure to delegate management and accomplish other goals like those in Benefits 2-1. Too much structure can be restrictive in future situations. For example, if an extensive political structure is used as the basis of division of the namespace, a later reorganization or company merger may pose serious issues. Interestingly, the LDAP standard has a requirement that also may influence the design you implement. LDAP clients are only required to support a hierarchy with ten levels between the root and any entry. If you implement something more complex, it may not work! These guidelines may not create your structure for you, but they should help.

LDAP Object Naming

With a firm grasp on DNS and the acceptable structures allowed in an LDAP directory, you are ready to consider the internal details of the LDAP namespace. The namespace that LDAP employs is highly flexible, allowing for multiple names for each entry and the possibility that different attributes can be used in forming the name. The naming flexibility LDAP provides doesn't come at the cost of ensuring that each entry has a name that is unique across the directory.

Relative Distinguished Name (RDN)

The RDN is an entry's naming attribute; it has a unique value in the container of the entry

The relative distinguished name attribute provides a unique name identifier for each entry within a container. For example, Figure 2-6 shows a person entry with an RDN of `cn=Brian Arkills`. There cannot be two entries with the same RDN

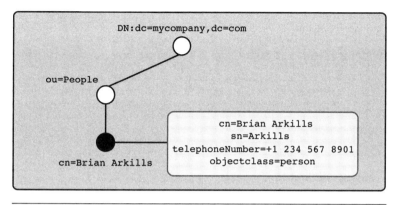

Figure 2-6   An example of an RDN

value within the same container. So there can be no other person entry in the People container with `cn=Brian Arkills`, and within any specific container the `cn` attribute value must be unique for subordinate person entries to that container. The RDN attribute is one of the entry's attributes, known as the *naming attribute* for that type of entry. But generally speaking, the naming attribute for any particular object class is not forced to be a specific attribute. In the object class definition, some LDAP vendors do force a specific attribute to be the naming attribute, but this is not part of the LDAP standard. In the example in Figure 2-6, the `cn` (common name) attribute is the naming attribute of the person object class.

You can use a special string of numbers called an *object identifier (OID)* in place of the attribute type. Every attribute type has a unique OID assigned to it. For example, the `cn` attribute's OID is `2.5.4.3`. The OID is used to uniquely identify an attribute type. For example, you might define an attribute type called `myattribute`. I might also define an attribute type called `myattribute`. How can we know if they are the same attribute? By comparing the OIDs of the two attributes. For more detail on OIDs, turn to Chapter 4; for now, you need to know that an OID can be substituted for the name of an attribute type. The

You can substitute a unique string of numbers called an object identifier for the attribute type in an RDN

OID is relevant to namespace when an OID is used as the naming attribute. For example, a valid RDN of the entry in Figure 2-6 is `2.5.4.3=Brian Arkills`.

cn is frequently used in RDNs, but other types are possible

The `cn` attribute is the most commonly used naming attribute; however, there are several other attribute types that are commonly used (see Table 2-3).

Naming Attributes

You can use any attribute with a unique value in the RDN

You can form the RDN using any attribute type on the entry that has a unique value among the entries in that container. Although this rule may seem confusing, it allows the client more flexibility to identify an entry in an unexpected form. Generally speaking, the schema checker must ensure that each new entry or modification to an existing entry leaves the entry with at least one unique RDN, so the entry has a unique name. Some LDAP implementations do standardize the naming attribute for any given object class; and in this case, attributes that are designated as naming attributes must meet the uniqueness rule that

Table 2-3   Common attributes used as naming attributes

Attribute Type	Attribute Used For:
cn	common name
l	locality name
st	state or province name
o	organization name
ou	organizational unit name
c	country name
street	street address
dc	domain component
uid	user identity

the schema checker enforces. Either way, there is a guarantee that every entry has a name that is unique across the directory.

You can also use more than one attribute in the RDN. This is called a *multivalued RDN*. This functionality lets you specify a unique entry with an intersection of two attribute values when one or both of the attribute values doesn't meet the uniqueness requirement. For example, consider the situation shown in Figure 2-7. There are two people with the same phone number, and two people with the same surname. You can't use either the phone number or the surname attribute to uniquely indicate Luke Skywalker's entry, but a combination of both attribute types will create a unique combination. The RDN would be `sn=Skywalker+telephoneNumber=+1 222 222 2222`. Of course, in this case you could more easily use `cn=Luke`

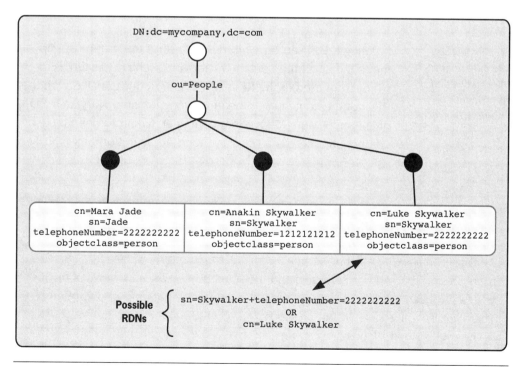

Figure 2-7   An example of a multivalued RDN

`Skywalker` as the RDN; but there might be instances in which you do not know the `cn` value, so it would be more efficient to use the multivalued RDN. Not all vendor implementations fully support this functionality. Use it only with careful planning.

Distinguished Name (DN)

A DN provides a name for users to uniquely refer to each directory entry

The DN provides a fully qualified name to each entry, so it is clear exactly which entry is referenced, and also where in the hierarchical structure that entry is located. Under the LDAP specification, each entry does not store its DN, nor does the directory index the DNs of directory entries. Instead, a DN is primarily for the users of the directory to be able to indicate to the directory which entry is desired. A DN is presented by a client operation request, and the directory dynamically looks to see whether an entry matches this purported DN. Specific vendors may store the DN as an attribute of the entry or index all the DNs, but this is neither required nor expected.

The DN is a concatenation of the entry's RDN and the RDN of every container between the entry and the directory root

Forming a DN can be a bit tricky because the user must know the RDNs of all the containers above the entry. The DN is a string composed of the RDN of the entry concatenated with the RDN of the container of the entry concatenated with each RDN of every container above that container. Commas delimit each component. Here is a simpler, recursive definition of a DN: The

What's This Phone Number?

Attributes that express a phone number have a commonly accepted syntax so users around the world will understand the number. The accepted syntax begins with a plus sign and the country code, followed by the national phone number. There are two plus signs in the previous multivalued RDN example. One is part of the multivalued RDN syntax to link the two RDNs into a single DN, and the other plus sign is expected in a phone attribute.

DN is the string composed of the RDN of the entry concatenated with the DN of its container. As shown in Figure 2-7, the
entry on the right has two possible DNs:

```
cn=Luke Skywalker,ou=People,dc=mycompany,dc=com
```

or:

```
sn=Skywalker+telephoneNumber=+1 222 222
   2222,ou=People,dc=mycompany,dc=com
```

Using Naming Attributes Appropriately

Naming attributes are critically important to your directory. The users of your directory will constantly be referencing the values of these attributes to find and
modify entries. This design has several implications.

The value of these attributes should not contain information that is considered
private. Otherwise, you will need to place access controls on the attribute, and
this will prevent the attribute from being used as an RDN. Using access controls
can also lead to some entries being left out of critical business processes. Both
vendors and deployment teams alike can make the mistake of using an attribute
with information that may be considered private as the naming attribute of a critically important object class.

The value of the naming attribute should be static. Changes to a name can cause
undesirable behavior in programs that have been "hardcoded" to use a specific
name. Just as a program is hardcoded, so are people. They won't always know
when a name change has been made, and they can have difficulty finding this renamed entry or knowing that the renamed entry is the same as the original.

One way to sidestep both of these problems is to use an arbitrary, public, but
unique value in the naming attribute. This approach may feel wrong from a design perspective because the name is less personal, but it is effective. It guarantees that everyone can query all the entries, and that the entry's name won't
change.

Naming Special Characters

You should treat some special characters differently when they are used in a DN

You must treat several characters specially when they are used in a DN. You can store these special characters as naming attribute values without the escape character; but when referring to these characters in a DN, you must escape them. You specially notate these characters by preceding them with a backslash character (\) to avoid mistakes in meaning. This is sometimes called *commenting* or *escaping*. For example, designating a DN with an RDN that has a comma in its value would cause confusion because the directory uses commas in the DN to separate the DN components. Treat the characters listed in Table 2-4 specially by escaping them in DNs.

RFC 2253 makes it clear that vendors can make other characters special, so take care to examine vendor implementations for special cases.

Table 2-4   Special characters in distinguished names

Character	Escaped Character
Comma (,)	\,
Plus (+)	\+
Double quotation marks (")	\"
Backslash (\)	\\
Less than (<)	\<
Greater than (>)	\>
Semicolon (;)	\;
Space at beginning or end of an RDN	\<space>
Octothorp (#) at beginning of an RDN	\#

LDAP Hacking: Possible Code Injection?

Code injection and format string attacks are common security exploits in other technologies these days. SQL, printf, Web servers, and homegrown Web applications have all exhibited this vulnerability in recent years. These types of vulnerabilities are based on poor coding of exceptions or parsing of user input, and they allow a malicious attacker to insert commands or code on a server. These types of vulnerabilities usually surround special characters and ambiguous behavior on what to do with these special characters when a user presents them as input. Although there are no known LDAP vulnerabilities in this area, I have to believe that there will be exploits discovered in the near future. With more organizations centralizing data into LDAP directories, more scrutiny will produce the trial and error needed to discover the coding mistakes behind these vulnerabilities.

URL Naming

Most Web browsers today support LDAP client functionality. As a result, you can perform searches conveniently via a browser. The naming format of the LDAP URL is fully specified in RFC 2255. This format is slightly different from that used by standard LDAP clients. URLs have a large set of special characters that must be treated in a special way as designated in RFC 1738, and the different format accommodates this. The LDAP URL-naming format is not exclusively used by Web browsers; standard LDAP clients must also be able to use it to support referrals.

When using a Web browser as an LDAP client, you should use a special naming format

An LDAP URL begins with the protocol designation `ldap://`, followed by the hostname and port of the directory server, then the base DN and other designations, such as the scope, filter, and attributes desired. The syntax is

How to use LDAP URL syntax

```
ldap://[hostname][/dn[?[attributes][?[scope]
    [?[filter][?[extensions]]]]]
```

The components of the syntax are

- **hostname**—The hostname specifies the LDAP server and the TCP/IP port used by the LDAP server. As indicated by the brackets, both the hostname and port are optional. A default of port 389 is used if the port isn't specified. If the hostname isn't specified, the client must have prior knowledge of which server to contact. Separate the hostname and port with a colon, mycompany.com:389, as specified in RFC 1738.

- **DN**—The DN component specifies the base distinguished name for the search.

- **attributes**—The attribute component specifies the attribute types to return from the entries that match the search parameters. If left unspecified, all attributes are returned.

- **scope**—The scope component specifies the scope of directory entries to return. As with typical LDAP searches, base, one, and sub are possible values. If the value is left unspecified, sub is assumed.

- **filter**—The filter component specifies a limiting filter on which entries should be returned. It follows the same syntax as typical LDAP searches. If left unspecified, (objectclass=*) is assumed, so that all entries are returned.

- **extensions**—The extensions component specifies optional LDAP URL extensions. These extensions can be defined as needed, and they don't necessarily correspond to LDAP extended operations. Only one such extension has been standardized, called the bindname extension. The *bindname extension* allows the client to specify the DN of a directory entry to use in authenticating to the directory. A subsequent authentication challenge would then be initiated. You can find more details in Section 4 of RFC 2255.

Here is an example of an LDAP URL:

```
ldap://mycompany.com:389/cn=Brian
    Arkills,ou=People,dc=Mycompany,dc=com?sn
```

Given the sample directory shown in Figure 2-6, this search would return the `sn` attribute of the entry `cn=Brian Arkills,ou=People,dc=mycompany,dc=com`. The search has the subtree scope, but the entry at the specified base DN has no children, so only one entry is returned.

There are several illegal and special URL characters. These characters include the special characters noted earlier in this chapter as well as almost all nonalphanumeric characters (the notable exceptions include $-_.!*'()). You must escape these characters when you use them in an LDAP URL component. The escape method is fully described in RFC 1738, but it amounts to substituting the % character and the two-digit hexadecimal ASCII code for the character in question. Most browsers automatically translate illegal URL characters into the escaped version.

Special URL characters must be treated in a unique way

LDAP v2 Naming Conventions

In addition to the special naming syntax restrictions defined by the LDAP v3 standard, LDAP v3-compliant implementations must also support LDAP v2-compliant naming. LDAP v3 implementations can't generate LDAP v2-compliant names, but they must accept and process those names by translating the names to the LDAP v3-compliant standard. RFC 2253 Section 4 spells out this compatibility. There are distinct differences between the

LDAP v3 must support all LDAP v2 naming conventions

two versions. LDAP v2 differs from LDAP v3 on the following points of syntax:

- LDAP v2 uses semicolons as RDN separators.

- LDAP v2 allows spaces before and after each of the following:

  – RDN separators (either comma or semicolon)
  – Equal signs between the attribute type and value
  – Plus signs in a multivalued RDN

- LDAP v2 allows quotation marks at the beginning and end of an RDN value, which are not part of the RDN attribute value. If you use quotation marks in this way, all the special DN characters that usually require escaping do not need to be escaped.

- LDAP v2 allows the text `OID.` or `oid.` to prefix an OID attribute type string.

Again, an LDAP v3-compliant directory accepts all these differences in syntax, but it automatically translates them to the correct LDAP v3-compliant syntax for processing.

Designing Your Directory to Be People Friendly

Although you can store the special characters listed in Table 2-4 as naming attribute values, carefully consider the alternatives. For example, imagine that you are planning to store the cn of a person object in the format *lastname, firstname*. Because of the comma in the CN, searches for those person entries would have to escape the comma to successfully find the entry. Users would have to be familiar with the characters that are considered special so they could successfully use the directory. Avoiding special characters in naming attribute values isn't required, but by doing so you will create a more friendly experience for your users.

Special LDAP Structural Concepts

As LDAP has matured, extensions to the structural functionality have rapidly developed to reflect the distributed computing model. Certain structural features are needed to support a directory housed on multiple servers, greater directory reliability, integration with other directories, and localizing directory data on a geographical basis. Replication, referrals, and aliases are the advanced features used to enable this functionality. Some of these special features are part of the LDAP standard, while others are available only in certain vendor implementations. To explore further how to extend the LDAP namespace, see Chapter 5, which focuses on directory management.

Summary

In summary, the namespace employed by LDAP directories follows an ordered hierarchical model. The preexisting DNS namespace at an organization is usually used to augment this model. The hierarchical model provides many advantages, but perhaps the most critical is that knowing the name of an entry tells you where the entry is located within the directory structure.

The namespace provides the structure to store and find directory information

3

Client LDAP Operations

While crafting the namespace structure is critical to the directory administrator, the LDAP operations are at the heart of the client-to-server interaction. The LDAP operations are therefore what the typical user of your directory needs to know about, although good client software abstracts even this interaction from view. Users probably need only the search operation, which happens to be the most detailed operation. There are ten primary operations defined by the LDAP standard. Administrators and programmers use this full set as they manage directory information and create special business processes that interact with the directory information. This chapter describes the purpose of each of the ten operations, and along the way I discuss issues that relate to the client-server interaction.

One of the most obvious topics involved in the client-server interaction is the LDAP client itself. The client software is the key to people finding the LDAP directory useful and easy to use. If the client software requires people to understand this

The LDAP client is what a user sees of a directory

book, or even a fraction of this chapter, they won't use the directory. Therefore, well-designed applications that hide LDAP from users are important. Because the search operation is the most prominent operation, it is addressed early in the chapter. You can explore how to create complex searches, how to use comparison operators, and what client options affect the search operation. By understanding how the client should work and what the common client configuration options are, you can educate users even if the client software isn't friendly.

LDAP operations, extensions, client services, and APIs are examined

After addressing the topics of immediate concern to users, I turn next to other standard operations and technical topics connected with the LDAP operations. In addition, I examine some extended operations and controls that can make an LDAP directory more valuable. The chapter ends with a look at the details of using an LDAP API. An organization that is developing a directory-enabled application or service needs to look at these details. Directory users will employ LDAP client software that was written using these underlying APIs, but typical users won't need to know about the API. For example, a programmer might design a program that automatically fills out all the paper forms needed when a new employee joins the organization. The new

Client Software

The typical user cannot be expected to remember LDAP syntax. Good client software is necessary to help users interact with the directory. You need to review a vendor's client software just as carefully as you review the server features. The client software should focus on making the search operation, especially the creation of a search filter, easy to perform. If a good client isn't available, your organization may have to create a client interface that fits its needs. A programmer can design a client with search filter options that include a user-friendly version of the filter and match operators desired.

executive at Mycompany that was introduced in Chapter 1 would have a less painful first day with such a program in place. These standard APIs are the primary reason why LDAP is such a popular choice, because they work regardless of the client's operating system, making a multiplatform implementation possible. Appendix A summarizes the standard C version of the API, as defined in RFC 1823. In addition, this chapter takes a brief look at some of the functions in the C version of the API.

Directory-Enabled Services and Applications

Many applications benefit from being able to interact with the directory to find information. An application or service that is capable of being an LDAP client is called *directory-enabled*.

Applications that can interact with a directory are called directory-enabled

Among the most common directory-enabled applications are e-mail services. When an e-mail server receives an e-mail, it can query the directory to find out whether the e-mail address recipient resides at the local site and what e-mail server that person's mailbox resides on. Centralizing this information in the directory simplifies the administration of the e-mail servers by eliminating the need for a synchronized copy of this information on each e-mail server. For example, sendmail is a common UNIX mail server that can be directory-enabled (for more details, see Appendix C). Microsoft recognized the importance of directory-enabling their mail server, Microsoft Exchange 2000, and has integrated it with Active Directory (see Chapter 7).

Many e-mail services are directory-enabled

Similarly, e-mail clients can be directory-enabled, and they provide a valuable service by looking up a destination e-mail address given a person's name. Several e-mail clients allow the user to browse a directory via an interface within the e-mail application and pick out recipients for an e-mail.

E-mail clients can also be directory-enabled

A Web-Based Client Interface

Many organizations implement a Web-based client interface for their directory. This approach removes the cost of distributing client software and locating an adequate client for every platform. It can even help provide some limited integration of multiple directories. However, if you want to maximize the potential benefits of a directory, implementing more than a Web-based client interface would be wise. A Web-based client integrates poorly with other software. Restricting the client interface to a browser limits the usefulness of the data obtained by searching the directory.

Extending the functionality of existing user applications is a good way to help users take advantage of the directory. For example, if you configured the users' mail application to search the directory for an e-mail address through a simple command, users would see how the directory benefits them.

The limits of directory-enabled services haven't been reached yet

Directory-enabled services have few boundaries. For example, you could use an LDAP directory

- As a certificate authority store associated with public-private certificate technology. This also allows you to provide a service to verify the validity of those certificates.

- To catalog the location of HTML and other types of electronic documents. You could then query and return a list of appropriate documents, just as a library catalog would do.

Microsoft's Active Directory LDAP implementation is a good example of how a variety of directory-enabled services can be integrated. Via Microsoft's Active Directory, software can be distributed to computers, user and computer configurations can be set, printers can be advertised to clients, and so on. Clearly, there are significant benefits to centralizing information in a directory, especially information that helps manage resources.

Mycompany simply needs creativity and integrated services that take advantage of the directory to realize this potential.

Search

All the LDAP operations consist of the client sending the operation request along with parameters to the server. The server then performs the operation and sends a result code back to the client. The result code indicates the success or failure of the operation. When the operation is a search operation, the server sends all the entries that match the search parameters prior to sending the result code. There is no read operation, so if a directory user wants to read a specific entry, she must perform a search operation specifying the entry.

An LDAP operation consists of a client request, server work, and the results

The search operation has many parameters that modify how the server performs the operation. There are mandatory parameters that are required or the search will fail, and there are optional parameters that have default values if not set otherwise. The search parameters affect only the single search operation for which they are set. Should you want to modify all LDAP operations for a session, you must use an *LDAP option*, if there is an appropriate one. LDAP options are discussed a little later in this chapter. Do not confuse LDAP options with optional search parameters or the attribute options introduced in Chapter 4.

Search parameters define what entries the server returns to the client and how it finds those entries

Mandatory Search Parameters
The mandatory search parameters are

- **A base DN to begin your search**—An idea of how the directory is structured is helpful here. In other words, if you want to look up person entries, are they all in a common container? The base DN is sometimes also called the *baseObject*. If I didn't know where to begin, I could start at the root of the directory. In Mycompany's directory, this

Where does the server begin looking?

would be `dc=mycompany,dc=com`. So at a minimum, I must know the naming contexts of the directory.

How far does the server look?

- **The scope of the search**—There are three options for the scope. A *base* scope means to search only the single entry at the base DN. A *one* scope means to search all entries at the same level in the hierarchy within the container of the base DN. A *subtree* scope means to search the base DN and all entries beneath the base DN, regardless of their level in the hierarchy.

What special characteristics do the entries have?

- **A search filter**—Search filters are composed of an attribute type, a *comparison operator*, and an attribute value. These three components are surrounded by parentheses and form a *search filter item*. The simple syntax of the search filter item is "`("attributetype operator attributevalue")`" with no spaces between any of these mandatory elements. The quotation marks enclose text that is constant in the syntax. For example, `(objectclass=person)` would be a valid search filter item. One or more search filter items can be combined with filter operators to form the *search filter*, so the example is also a valid search filter. Filter operators are introduced shortly.

To illustrate the use of a search filter, if I wanted to find my entry as shown in Figure 3-1, I might use the following search parameters:

Base DN: `dc=mycompany, dc=com`

Scope: `Subtree`

Search Filter: `(cn=Brian Arkills)`

You can use filter operators to combine filters

You can combine filter items within the search filter parameter by using filter operators. *Filter operators* can modify a filter item specified within the search filter parameter, and they can be used to combine multiple filters to designate intricate sets of entries.

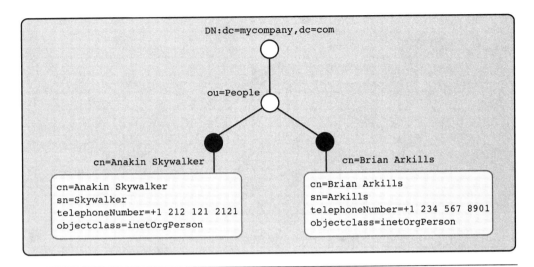

Figure 3-1   Mycompany with my person entry

The filter operators available are

- &   AND

- | OR

- !   NOT

These operators should precede the filter they modify. This pre-
cession is very similar to how functions in the LISP language or
operations in reverse polish calculators are represented. The
following filters illustrate the use of the filter operators with
the directory shown in Figure 3-2. All the examples provided
assume a base DN at the root of the directory, along with a
subtree scope.

The filter

```
(|(cn=Brian Arkills)(cn=Chewbacca))
```

returns the entries of Chewbacca and me.

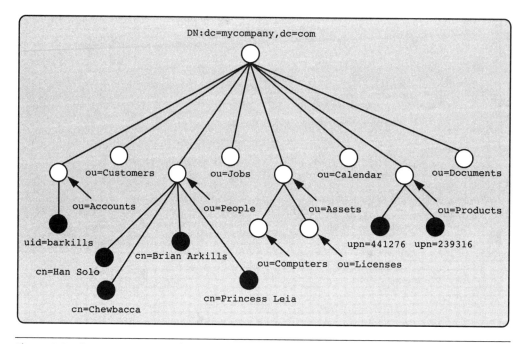

Figure 3-2   Mycompany example for search filter operators

The filter

`(!(|(cn=Brian Arkills)(cn= Chewbacca)))`

returns all entries in the entire directory except Chewbacca or
my entry, so it would return the entries of cn=Princess Leia,
cn=Han Solo, uid=barkills, upn=441276, upn=239316, as
well as the ten ou entries pictured. Containers are still entries.

The filter

`(&(!(|(cn=Brian Arkills)(cn=`
`    Chewbacca)))(objectclass=inetOrgPerson))`

finds all the inetOrgPerson entries except Chewbacca's or
my entry, so it would return the entries of Princess Leia and
Han Solo.

The Search Operation Is Too Complicated for My Users

Explaining how the search operation works and the valid values for the mandatory parameters (and the optional parameters that haven't been introduced yet) is a daunting task. Most users won't understand (or worse, will be intimidated and won't try) even with good documentation for reference. This is where client software comes into play. Good client software might have the most common search types already defined. For example, a user could simply enter a name to search for a person. The software would recognize the type of search and would supply the correct parameters to the directory.

For example, the Pine e-mail program (UNIX, Windows, or Web-based) can be preconfigured to search your directory with a given base DN and scope. A user enters a name on the To: field of a new e-mail, and the program looks up the address in the directory and enters it in the e-mail message.

Search filters are the most dynamic and interesting parameter in the LDAP search operation. For more details on search filters, see the following section, Search Filters.

Optional Search Parameters

The optional search parameters are

- **What attribute information to return**—If you don't specify what you want, all the attributes of the entries the server finds will be returned. You can list the attribute types you want in a list separated by commas. The *operational attributes*, which are the attributes that the directory uses for its own purposes, are never returned unless explicitly specified. You can also specify that no attributes should be returned by denoting the attribute *1.1*. This designation holds significance as a special OID number that is not associated with any attribute type. See Chapter 4 for more information on both operational attributes and OID numbers.

Should the server return the entire entry or just some of the attributes?

How should the server treat alias entries?

■ **derefAliases**—Denotes how to deal with alias entries. An *alias entry* is a dummy entry that references or points to another entry. *Dereferencing* an alias simply instructs the server to go to the object that the alias references, and for the purposes of the search, treat the referenced object as if it were the alias object. The following options are available (for more information on alias entries, see Chapter 5):

– neverDerefAliases	Don't look up any alias reference.
– derefInSearching	Look up all alias references except on the baseObject.
– derefFindingBaseObj	Look up alias references only on the baseObject.
– derefAlways	Look up all alias references.

How many entries should the server return?

■ **sizeLimit**—Limits the number of entries to return on the search. The default value of 0 denotes no limit. If a search finds more entries than what is specified as the limit, only the first set number is returned. In this case, a result code of LDAP_SIZELIMIT_EXCEEDED is returned to indicate that more results were available.

Settings in other places can modify the effects of this parameter

Many LDAP server implementations allow the directory administrator to set a mandatory upper sizeLimit for all client operations. In this case, the client can set a limit with a lower value, but limits greater than the server limit are disregarded. Some LDAP servers have a special user that can override the size limit. Another modifier called an LDAP control can be used to tell the server to send the results back to the client in pages. For example, the directory might have a sizeLimit of 50, and a search that yields 100 entries normally only returns the first 50. But if I ask for a page size of 50, the server would send the first 50 entries to my client, then the second 50, and I'd see all the entries. LDAP controls are modifiers that apply to a single LDAP operation. LDAP controls, including this one, are discussed later in this chapter.

- **timeLimit**—Limits the time in seconds allowed to complete the search. The default value of 0 denotes no limit. If a search operation takes longer to complete than the specified limit, the operation will finish at the time limit. Only the entries found in this time period are returned. In this case, a result code of `LDAP_TIMELIMIT_EXCEEDED` is returned to indicate that more results were available. Some LDAP server implementations allow the directory administrator to set a mandatory upper `timeLimit` for all client operations. Some LDAP servers have a special user that can override the server time limit. The client can set a limit with a lower value, but limits greater than the server limit are disregarded.

  How long should the server work on this request?

- **typesOnly**—If set to `true`, the results will list only the attribute types, not the values. The default value of `false` denotes that both the attribute types and values should be returned.

  Does the client want the attribute pair or just the type?

Search Filters

In addition to the filter operators, other operators, called *match operators* or *comparison operators*, can modify the search filter. Most documentation on the subject confuses match operators with filter operators. But match operators do not operate on the entire filter expression, only on the attribute value. The match operators are usually common mathematical operators, such as equality or greater than or

You use match operators to limit the attribute values specified in the search filter

Does the Search Operation Really Need These Parameters?

If you omit the optional parameters in a client request, the default values will be assumed. However, in the larger design sense, yes, all of these parameters are useful. The optional parameters provide a greater level of control over what information is returned, and how much work the directory performs for any client request. This level of control makes the interaction more efficient.

equal. You use match operators to help designate the entries that match the attribute value parameters desired. The operations used to match vary depending on the specific type of data stored in the attribute. Most attributes store some type of string value, in other words, text. Therefore, the most common match operators you will use are string match operators. Here are the string match operators:

- **= Equality**—We have already looked at a few examples together.

- **<= Less than or equal to**—(sn<=Arkills) would return entries alphabetically prior to Arkills in addition to Arkills, for example sn=Adams. Note that in combination with the not filter operator, you can create a greater-than operation that doesn't include the entry that is equal.

- **>= Greater than or equal to**—(sn>=Arkills) would return entries after Arkills in addition to Arkills, for example sn=Chewbacca. Note that in combination with the not filter operator, you can create a less than operation.

- **~= Approximate**—(sn~=Cat) would return entries like sn=Scat, sn=Cast, sn=Hat, and sn=Mat. The algorithm employed for the approximate match filter varies depending on the implementation, so these examples may not work in your environment. Usually a single character wildcard is permitted in any position, but this is not standardized, and the approximate match operator isn't always implemented.

You can use a wildcard to match substring values

Finally, you use the asterisk (*) as a *wildcard* for zero or more characters in the values of strings. You can use the wildcard by itself to detect the presence of an attribute or in combination with other characters to find *substrings*. In the example directory shown in Figure 3-3, a search filter of (cn=*Skywalker) would return the entries of both Luke and Anakin Skywalker.

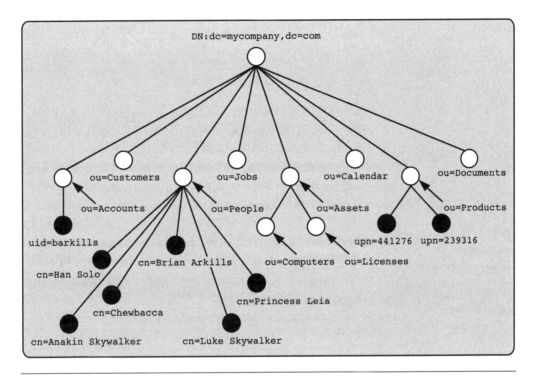

Figure 3-3   Example directory for wildcard match

Both the presence and substring capabilities that the wildcard
provides are very useful.

As noted already, the list contains only the match operators for
the string type. There are other match operators for other types
of data. However, most of these operators work with other data
types because these operators are fairly common across all the
syntaxes.

*The available
match operators are
linked to the type
of the attribute*

Extended Match Filters

LDAP v3 lets you define additional match operators and rules
in the schema for specific data types. How you define these
match operators for data and attribute types is covered in
Chapter 4, in the section on attribute-matching rules. You can

*New match opera-
tors can be defined
with LDAP v3*

specify these extended match operators in the search filter by using an extended match filter syntax, which is slightly different from the simple search filter syntax already described. The extended syntax of the search filter is

```
"(" attributetype [":dn"] [":" extendedoperator]
    ":=" attributevalue ")"
```

The optional elements are in [brackets]. The extended operator is usually an OID, but a descriptive name can also be assigned in the schema and used here in the filter.

The filter (cn:1.2.3.4.987:=Brian Arkills) would match any entry by comparing "Brian Arkills" with the values in their cn attributes, using the matching logic defined by the matching rule denoted by OID 1.2.3.4.987. Should this OID not denote a matching rule that the directory supports (and in this case the OID is a fabrication of the author), the directory will return an error code.

The DN of entries can be searched with an extended match filter

Extended match filters also let you search the DN of an entry for value matches. This may be a bit confusing at first. An entry's DN contains all the RDNs of the object above it in the directory structure. These RDNs may or may not be attributes of the entry. So if you wanted to find all the entries with ou=People in the DN, you would need to use an extended match filter. Now you may be thinking, "Why wouldn't you use a search with a base DN at the People OU, and a one-level scope?" This seems to accomplish the same thing. But consider the possibility that a referral might reside in the People OU. The more simple search would return records via this referral that technically do not have ou=People in their DN. Also consider the possibility that there might be more than one container with an RDN of ou=People in the directory. In this case, a single search without extended match filters would fail to capture all the entries. Multiple searches would work, but that approach might be inconvenient. Not all LDAP servers support extended match filter searching for DNs.

Special Characters in Search Filters

There are several special characters that must be treated differently when used in the attribute value portion of a search filter. You must escape these characters just as you had to escape the special characters in the DN or LDAP URL format. Table 3-1 lists the special search filter characters along with the escaped character sequence.

You must treat special characters differently when they are used in the attribute value portion of an LDAP search filter

You must use the hexadecimal value of the character, which is different from quoting the special characters in DNs.

LDAP Protocol

The LDAP client-server session minimizes client processing overhead. The server is responsible for performing the operations requested and bears the processing load, while satisfying the client request. In the client-server model, the server is designed to handle large computing loads, with larger processing and memory capacity, while the client may have little to no computing power. After the server performs the requested operation, the client receives a response or error from the server.

The server does most of the work

Table 3-1   Special search filter characters

Character Desired in Attribute Value	Escaped Character
*	\2A
(	\28
)	\29
\	\5C
NUL	\00

The client does little work other than sending the request and receiving the answer.

The client can make multiple requests to multiple servers

LDAP is message based, so the client can make multiple requests with a single session. These multiple operations from the same session each receive server attention at the same time, and therefore a great deal of work can be performed in parallel. Multiple sessions from the same client are also possible at the same time, so a single client can interact with more than a single LDAP server.

The result code indicates the end of the client operation

If the client submits a search request that returns several entries, several messages are returned to the client. Each returned entry is enclosed in a separate message to the client; and when all the entries are returned, a final result code message is sent to the client. Should a referral be returned, then, depending on the applicable settings, additional client or server traffic may result prior to the final result code indicating completion of the operation. Asynchronous LDAP APIs change this behavior; for more details, see the following section, APIs.

LDAP uses TCP/IP and is a very efficient communicator

The LDAP transport makes very efficient use of network traffic. LDAP uses TCP/IP for network communication. TCP/IP is processor and memory intensive, with error checking built into the protocol, and it is most efficient for sessions of more than trivial length. Startup and shutdown of TCP sessions can be a costly use of computer and network resources. The ability to perform multiple operations makes LDAP capable of making good use of communication resources.

The client-server interaction usually follows this pattern:

1. Client connects to server and requests a bind operation.

2. Server returns bind operation result code (success or the process ends here).

3. Client requests a search operation (or some other operation).

4. Server returns message with located entry or entries from search operation. If no entries are found, no entry messages will be sent.

5. Server sends search operation result code to client.

6. Client requests an unbind operation.

7. Server sends unbind result code and closes connection.

Note that result codes are important, in that they signal the completion of an operation as far as the server is concerned.

There is a form of interaction with an LDAP directory that uses even less communication overhead than the traditional LDAP protocol based on TCP interaction. This form is called *connectionless LDAP,* sometimes abbreviated as *CLDAP.* RFC 1798 defines CLDAP, which uses UDP instead of TCP. A CLDAP transaction can use up to a third fewer network packets than LDAP. CLDAP further simplifies the directory model by restricting the number of operations available. CLDAP is primarily intended for use by very simple clients that need to quickly look up information in a directory. The low overhead and even more simplified operations available may be appropriate for some uses at your organization. Very few LDAP servers or client APIs support CLDAP yet. Messaging Direct is an example of one product that supports CLDAP to enable a high volume of messaging service queries.

CLDAP uses UDP instead of TCP and uses considerably fewer resources than LDAP

LDAP Operations

The ten operations that LDAP defines cover the necessary interaction with a directory. The limited number of operations means that both the client and server are simple to implement and require limited resources.

Problems with CLDAP

The primary problem with CLDAP is acceptance and deployment in existing LDAP products. There are many uses for an even simpler interaction, but only a limited number of products have implemented CLDAP. I'd like to see the IETF include CLDAP in the LDAP core standard in order to more strongly promote its acceptance.

A secondary problem arises from the fact that CLDAP is UDP-based. UDP transactions are vulnerable to attacks, and provide very little in the way of error checking and handling. This might cause problems for directories on the Internet that support CLDAP. But as long as CLDAP is configurable with an on/off toggle, I'd rather see it included in all products.

Bind

Bind establishes the identity of the client

The bind operation is the first request a client sends to the server. Binding is the same task as authenticating to the directory. The client is verifying its identity to the directory, so all future operations can be performed in the context of that identity. A client that doesn't bind, or that binds with an empty string as the identity, is said to be anonymous. One identity may be allowed to view directory information that another identity can't. Binding to the directory provides an authorization context for allowing or denying the subsequent operations. The bind operation has two parameters: a DN and a set of credentials. Some LDAP directories are configured to support anonymous binding, and others are designed to allow no requests from anonymous clients. This design choice is typically linked to the sensitivity of the data in the directory.

Search

The search operation is discussed in detail earlier in this chapter.

Compare

Compare verifies that an attribute value is known

The compare operation simply verifies whether the information passed by the client matches the information stored in the directory. The compare operation is less useful than the search operation, except for one key situation in which it works differently from the search operation. If you ask to compare an attribute of an entry, but the attribute isn't present on the entry, a special result code is returned. A search operation for an attribute that isn't there returns no entries but a success result code. The compare operation has three parameters: a DN, an attribute type, and an attribute value.

For example, a compare operation request with the following parameters, against the directory pictured in Figure 3-1, would return a TRUE response.

DN: `cn=Anakin Skywalker,ou=People,`
          `dc=mycompany,dc=com`

Attribute: `telephoneNumber`

Value: `+1 212 121 2121`

Add

The add operation allows the client to create a new entry. For it to be successful, the add operation requires that the client specify what object class(es) the new entry will contain, and that all mandatory attributes of that object class be supplied with values. The schema-checking process on the server enforces these requirements. Additionally, the container object of the new entry must already exist, and no existing entry can have the same DN. If there are structure rules for the entry's object class, they also must be met. Finally, the DN (and any RDNs) must be in the proper form with any illegal, special characters escaped. The add operation has primarily two parameters: a DN (of the new entry) and the attribute pairs (type and value) that you want to include on the entry. You can specify as many attribute pairs as you want (or as many as are required by the object class).

Add creates new entries

As an example, an add operation request to the Mycompany directory with the following parameters would be successful.

I've denoted the list of attributes with semicolons delimiting the attribute pairs and with an equal sign connecting each pair. The actual syntax would depend on the API used.

DN: `cn=Boba Fett,ou=People,dc=mycompany,dc=com`

Attributes: `cn=Boba Fett;sn=Fett;objectclass=person;`

Delete

Delete removes entries

The delete operation removes an entry from the directory. All information associated with that entry (the values of the entry's attributes) is removed. Of course, for the operation to succeed, the entry specified must exist. Additionally, that entry cannot be a container with child entries. A delete operation has a single parameter: the DN of the entry.

A delete operation request with the following parameter would delete the entry we just created in the previous Add section.

DN: `cn=Boba Fett,ou=People,dc=mycompany,dc=com`

Modify

Modify changes the attribute values of an entry

The modify operation allows the client to modify existing attributes of an entry, delete attribute values, or add a value to one or more attributes. The entry designated must exist for the operation to succeed. All the attribute modifications must succeed or the entire operation will fail. This condition avoids an inconsistent entry state in which the operation only partially succeeds. It also avoids the need for the client to order the attribute modifications in a least-to-highest risk order. The modify operation has two parameters: a DN and the set of attribute modifications desired.

Anakin's phone number has changed, and he is anxious to make sure the directory reflects his new number so he doesn't miss any calls from any ladies. He would also like to update his `homePostalAddress` so the Jedi Academy knows about his new home. A modify request with the following parameters will get the job done:

DN: `cn=Anakin Skywalker,ou=People,`
           `dc=mycompany,dc=com`

Attributes: `telephoneNumber=+1 212 121 2121;`
           `homePostalAddress=31580749 Sith Way $ Jedi`
           `Academy $ Coruscant;`

ModifyRDN or Rename

The modifyRDN operation allows the client to rename the directory entry. The existing DN is specified, and the new RDN is supplied. The rename operation has four parameters: the DN to be renamed, the new RDN for the entry, a flag to tell the server whether to keep or delete the old RDN as an attribute of the entry, and an optional parameter for specifying a new parent container DN. This last optional parameter is important; it doesn't exist in the LDAP v2 standard. It lets you move an entry anywhere in the directory. The entry being moved can be a container with child entries beneath it. If the entry (or entries) being moved is being relocated to a DN on another server, the operation may fail depending on the vendor implementation. In this case, the client should be prepared to receive an `affectsMultipleDSAs` error in the result code. Even though the ability to specify a new parent DN is an essential requirement of meeting the LDAP v3 standard, some LDAP servers that advertise themselves as LDAP v3 compliant do not support this functionality.

ModifyRDN renames the entry or moves the entry within the directory

The modifyRDN operation's ability to move an entry or even an entire portion of the directory tree can be confusing. The following examples should help to illustrate how this operation can be used. Each example is accompanied with a figure that shows how the directory looks before and after the operation.

Leia's name must be updated to reflect her marriage to Han Solo. The following modifyRDN operation parameters are used.

Original DN: `cn=Princess Leia,ou=People,`
                    `dc=mycompany,dc=com`

New RDN: `cn=Leia Organa-Solo`

Delete-Old-RDN: `TRUE`

New Parent DN:

Figure 3-4 shows how the directory looks before and after the operation.

Mycompany's Sales department manages the Customers container in which all customer contact information is kept. The Sales department is now a division of the HR department. Because the HR department manages the People container, the HR department wants the Customers container moved under

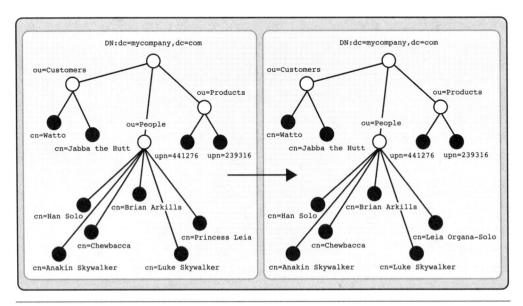

Figure 3-4   ModifyRDN used to modify only the RDN

the People container to reflect the organizational change. The HR department also wants to rename the Customers container to Customer Contacts. The following modifyRDN operation parameters are used.

Original DN: `ou=Customers,dc=mycompany,dc=com`

New RDN: `ou=Customer Contacts`

Delete-Old-RDN: TRUE

New Parent DN: `ou=People,dc=mycompany,dc=com`

Figure 3-5 shows how the directory looks before and after the operation.

Many people know Chewbacca by his nickname Chewie. His name must be updated to include both his formal name and

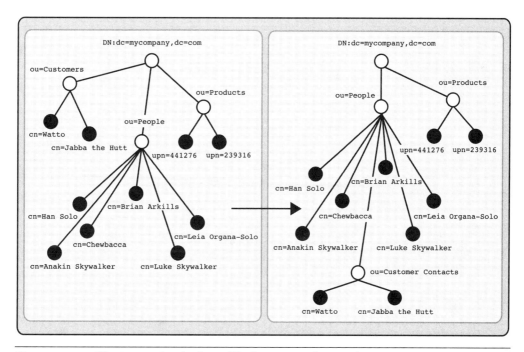

Figure 3-5 ModifyRDN used to both modify the RDN and move the entry

nickname. The following modifyRDN operation parameters are used. After this operation, the original RDN will no longer be a valid DN, but it will remain as an attribute of the entry.

Original DN: `cn=Chewbacca,ou=People,dc=mycompany,`
                    `dc=com`
New RDN: `cn=Chewie`
Delete-Old-RDN: `FALSE`
New Parent DN:

Figure 3-6 shows how the directory looks before and after the operation.

You may have expected to see both "Chewie" and "Chewbacca" in the second tree. But because of space restrictions, I can't list all the attributes of each entry . . . so pretend you can see the additional attributes associated with all these entries.

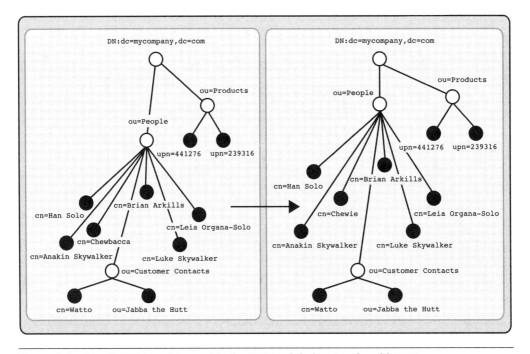

Figure 3-6   ModifyRDN used to modify the RDN, while leaving the old RDN

Why Can't the ModifyRDN Operation Have Just Three Parameters?

It seems more efficient to use just these three parameters: the DN to be renamed, the new DN, and the flag on whether to delete the old RDN. But keeping backward compatibility with LDAP v2 servers is more critical than simplifying the operation by making a major change between versions. Both LDAP v2 and X.500 support this operation with less functionality, so the LDAP v3 operation has simply added an additional parameter.

Unbind

The unbind operation allows the client to close its existing session with the directory. The directory obliges by discarding any client credentials it is holding, and it ceases any work on behalf of the client session, effectively terminating the session. Note that the connection, in other words, the TCP session between the client and server, isn't necessarily terminated. After an unbind operation, if the client requests a new operation without binding, the new operation will be evaluated in the context of an anonymous client. The unbind operation has no parameters. If the client terminates the session without issuing an unbind operation, most LDAP implementations use a session timeout parameter to accomplish the same end. The directory administrator can set this directory-wide timeout parameter.

Unbind cleanly ends the client session

Abandon

The abandon operation allows the client to tell the directory to cancel a specific previous operation it requested. This eliminates the need to unbind and rebind, should the client not want to wait for the results of a lengthy operation. This operation improves the potential efficiency of the client and server. The abandon operation has a single parameter: the message ID of the operation the client wishes to cancel. Note that a timing issue is possible with this operation. The client could send an

Abandon cancels a specific client operation request

abandon request that arrives at the server after the server has sent the complete result code (and entries) from the operation the client is canceling.

Extended

Extended operations allow new operations to be defined and used

The extended operation is a placeholder for specific directory implementations to extend the functionality of the directory but still have a predefined syntax for doing so. Additional security functionality such as session encryption is a good example of an extended operation. An extended operation can have parameters just as any other LDAP operation does. An LDAP directory must advertise what extended operations are available in the root DSE object in the `supportedExtension` attribute. The *root DSE object* is a special directory entry with an empty DN: *""*.

RFC 3062 defines an extended operation to modify passwords

An example of an extended operation that has reached RFC status is the *password modify extended operation* as defined in RFC 3062. This operation addresses a common need of organizations. Traditionally, LDAP directories stored authentication information internal to the directory so each authentication identity had its own DN. In other words, the username and password were integrated with the LDAP namespace. Now, however, many LDAP directories use primarily SASL as the means of authentication. This allows for an external store of authentication information, using a non-LDAP namespace. Therefore, the traditional method of changing a password using the modify operation won't work in this instance. This extended operation provides a way to modify a password external to the directory.

LDAP Controls

LDAP controls allow a client to ask the server to perform a standard operation in a slightly different way

LDAP controls constitute an extra parameter that alters the behavior of one of the standard LDAP operations. A control allows an LDAP client to take advantage of a special feature that an LDAP server supports. An LDAP directory must advertise what controls are available in the root DSE object in the `supportedControl` attribute. The special feature provided by the control can affect how results are returned, allow the client to access entries that are usually ignored, perform a task that is normally impossible with a single operation, or other added functionality that could accompany one of the standard LDAP operations. LDAP controls are designated with an OID and are used in the extended versions of the client API functions.

A common example of an LDAP control is the *paged search control.* This control supports a way to retrieve search results from the server a few at a time, instead of all at the same time. This capability is helpful when there is low bandwidth between the client and server, or when the expected number of entries is large. The client specifies a desired page size (in other words, the number of entries per LDAPMessage), and the server returns the smaller set along with a message that the results are paged and the expected number of entries so the client can request the rest by asking for the next paged set. This control provides the only way to circumvent a mandatory upper `sizeLimit` that is set at the server and affects all sessions. For example, if a directory administrator set a server mandatory `sizeLimit` of 500 entries, a normal client search would return only the first 500 entries and not reveal any other matching entries. But a search using the paged search control would allow the client to see all the matching entries in pages of 500 at a time. The limit of 500 due to the `sizeLimit` is still enforced, but the client can still accomplish its task.

The paged search control modifies the search operation by asking the server to return entries in pages

Another well-known LDAP control is the *server-side sort control* defined in RFC 2891. This control works in conjunction with the search operation and asks the LDAP server to sort the entries it returns based on the parameters the client requests. The parameters can include one or more attribute types, matching rules, and ascending or descending order. This control is intended to save the client processing time and resources.

The server-side sort control returns sorted search results

Persistent search control continues to return results indefinitely

Another extended search control is the *persistent search control*. This control allows a client to receive constant updates on entries that fit the search profile submitted, in other words, the base DN, scope, and filter. When the specified entries change, the client is notified. This type of functionality is extremely useful, especially in a context in which you'd like the directory to feed information to a program or other directory. Unfortunately, this control is not documented in an RFC, but several vendors, including Netscape and Microsoft, have implemented it. Three different designs of this control have been submitted to the IETF for comment: PSEARCH, TSEARCH, and DIRSYNC. These nicknames represent so-called Internet-drafts, which are proposals that were submitted but didn't make it to Internet standard. To make matters worse, vendors have begun implementing slight variations of these three. For example, Microsoft's Active Directory implements a version of PSEARCH with a different OID than that specified in the Internet-draft: 1.2.840.113556.1.4.528. Fortunately, an effort known as LDAP Client Update Protocol (LCUP) is seeking to bring these three different implementations together in an RFC. For your reference, you can find information about these draft controls and LCUP in Appendix A.

LDAP controls are constantly in development to extend the functionality of LDAP

There are many other controls under development. For example, one draft control allows the client to direct the directory server how to handle referrals when chaining is supported. Another draft control called *virtual list view* lets the client specify that the server return search results in a special order and number designated by the client. This draft control is designed to replace the existing paged search control and will help e-mail clients more fully integrate with LDAP, so long lists of e-mail addresses can be browsed in a list by a specified number of entries. Clearly LDAP controls are an area in which considerable development is under way, and the functionality of LDAP is being extended to meet many needs. You'll see more examples of LDAP controls in Part II, when we look at several LDAP server products.

Controls Are More Important Than the Extended Operation

The extended operation provides a mechanism for an additional operation to be defined and used. But controls allow an existing operation or many existing operations to be modified. This turns out to be far more important, because the existing operations are comprehensive. As a point of reference, far more new controls have been defined than extended operations.

LDAP Client Options

LDAP client options allow the LDAP client to specify standard settings for the duration of an LDAP client session, as opposed to a single operation. LDAP client options apply to a server session; so if a client has a session open to two different servers, the options set on one session do not apply to the other server session. LDAP client options are different from LDAP attribute options (for more detail on these, see Chapter 4). The LDAP C API designates several standard client options, and any LDAP implementation can define new ones. The following list comprises some of the options listed in the API RFC:

LDAP client options set parameters for an entire session

■ **LDAP_OPT_DEREF**

This option allows the client to control how aliases are handled. The valid values are

- **LDAP_DEREF_NEVER**: Never dereference aliases.

- **LDAP_DEREF_SEARCHING**: Don't dereference an alias at the base DN, but dereference otherwise.

- **LDAP_DEREF_FINDING**: Dereference an alias at the base DN, but don't dereference otherwise.

- **LDAP_DEREF_ALWAYS**: Always dereference.

- **`LDAP_OPT_SIZELIMIT`**

  This option controls the maximum number of entries that can be returned.

- **`LDAP_OPT_TIMELIMIT`**

  This option controls the maximum amount of time the server spends completing an operation.

- **`LDAP_OPT_REFERRALS`**

  This option controls whether the client chases referrals. The valid values are

  - **`LDAP_OPT_ON`**: Chase all referrals.
  - **`LDAP_OPT_SUBORDINATE_REFERRALS`**: Chase only subordinate referrals.
  - **`LDAP_OPT_EXTERNAL_REFERRALS`**: Chase only external referrals.

  Significant options not defined in the API RFC that Mycompany may want its vendor to support include:

- **`LDAP_OPT_SSL`**

  This option directs the client to use SSL on client connections.

- **`LDAP_OPT_REFERRAL_HOP_LIMIT`**

  This option sets the maximum number of referrals a client will chase on a single operation.

APIs

The LDAP API is an important component of the LDAP framework

The C language LDAP application program interface (API) specified in RFC 1823 is not part of the LDAP standard. However, it is critically important because it helps to define a base framework for programmatically interacting with an LDAP server. Even though this RFC is not part of the standard, almost all vendors implement it. This RFC is an unofficial part of the standard by sheer use and implementation. This RFC is based on the

LDAP v2 standard. There is work in progress to produce a re-placement RFC that covers LDAP v3.

The function calls specified in RFC 1823 mostly map to the basic LDAP operations. For example, consider the server operation used to add entries. There is a standard API function called `ldap_add()` that a client program would use to ask the server to perform the add operation.

API calls mostly map to the standard server operations

For each function, there are usually two versions. A synchronous version blocks until all results are available. The program calling a synchronous version doesn't get control until the server finishes replying to the request. The asynchronous version immediately returns a message ID. The program can then use other functions (supplying the message ID) to determine when the server has returned results for the operation. The synchronous versions are easier to use, but the asynchronous versions give your program greater efficiency and freedom at the cost of managing multiple requests/replies. The synchronous versions have a "_s" appended to the end of the function name, while the asynchronous versions do not. For example the synchronous version of the add operation is `ldap_add_s()`, whereas the asynchronous version is `ldap_add()`.

Each function has a real-time version and a version that combines results into a single response

Several of the functions have more than just the synchronous and asynchronous versions. Some of the functions support slightly different functionality. Each set of versions of a function is loosely called a family, or friends of the primary function.

Additional versions of functions offer other functionality

Results or errors from the primary operation function calls are returned via a special data structure called the *LDAPMessage*. The results in this structure can then be accessed by function calls that do not map to the primary LDAP operations. These other functions allow you to step through results or errors as you see fit. For example, one such function, `ldap_first_entry()`, calls the first entry returned in the LDAPMessage. This

The LDAPMessage structure holds the results of the client's request, and it can be manipulated by functions

entry can then be stepped through with functions like `ldap_first_attribute()`. The functions `ldap_next_entry()` and `ldap_next_attribute()` allow you to step to the next entry and attribute, respectively.

LDAP API functions are flexible and easy to use

For a list of the functions defined in the LDAP API, see Appendix A. All the functions are included to highlight the flexibility available, should your organization want to develop applications that use their LDAP directory. In addition, the complete listing serves as a quick reference for developers getting started with the LDAP API. Each function is accompanied by a short description. More details on these functions can be found in the RFC, and programmers will want to consult vendor-specific API implementations for differences or significant additional functions.

API libraries in almost every language and platform are available

There are many different implementations of LDAP APIs in a multitude of languages. Netscape's LDAP SDK provides APIs in C, perl, and Java. Sun provides JNDI, a Java API. The PerLDAP SDK uses the perl language. Microsoft provides the ADSI SDK, which can be used with any COM-compliant language, such as C, C+, Visual Basic, Java, and VBScript. Many other APIs exist, including ones for PHP, ODBC, server-side JavaScript, ColdFusion, and others. Books on using the APIs and online resources should make it easy for a programmer to locate and learn whatever is needed.

Summary

LDAP operational functionality benefits from a unique blend of standardization and entrepreneurship

The client-server operational functionality of LDAP directories is largely standardized across every vendor's product. This provides a baseline of interoperability that is critical to LDAP's success. You will find this baseline invaluable when you want to centralize directory information. However, the operational functionality is not fixed or limited by the standards. Both the extended operation and LDAP controls provide a means for operational extension. This allows vendors to create unique and powerful enhancements that advance the usefulness of LDAP directories. Not all the operational functionality of LDAP directories is tied to the client-server interaction. In fact, the standard is largely silent about server-to-server interactions. For more detail on this topic, see Chapter 5.

Appendix Material

Appendix A contains reference information on the LDAP API functions, as well as the draft controls mentioned.

4

LDAP Schema

Chapter 1 introduced the schema and its importance. The schema defines the rules that govern much of what the LDAP directory can do. When you change the rules of a game, the game can change significantly. The nice thing about the schema is that users interacting with the directory usually don't need to be aware of it, and certainly they don't need to understand how it works.

The schema holds a central importance, which is hidden from users

But the schema defines more than just the rules of interaction; it defines what kinds of entries can be created in the directory. It defines what information the directory can store. So modifying the schema can greatly increase the value of the LDAP directory and its flexibility.

The schema determines the type of data a directory holds

You modify the schema to allow new types of objects or to create a new attribute type. The impact of creating a new type of entry can add greatly to the functionality of a directory. You can also add to the attribute-matching rules and, by doing so, change how the LDAP directory resolves search operations. I

Modifying the schema can extend the functionality of a directory

discuss some interesting examples of schema modifications at the end of this chapter.

The schema components are highly interdependent

The schema consists of several components. Figure 4-1 represents how each of these schema elements relates in the context of the schema. You can use it to visualize each of these elements as it is explained. There is quite a bit of interdependency between each of the elements; in fact, each schema element might depend on several other schema elements. Complex elements such as object classes and attributes are built from simpler elements such as syntaxes and matching rules. Figure 4-1 shows this dependency among elements.

Object classes and attributes are the top level of the schema

An *object class* defines the kind of entry allowed in the directory. An object class definition consists of content rules, struc-

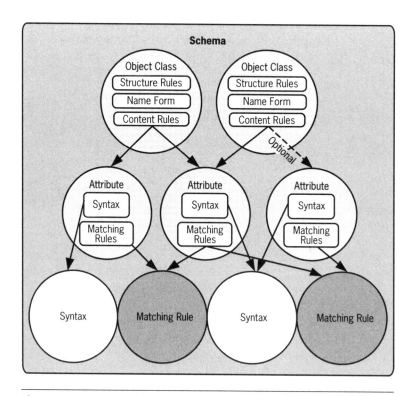

Figure 4-1   Conceptual diagram of schema

ture rules, the name form, and additional operational information. *Content rules* within the object class definition detail the attributes that an object class contains. *Structure rules* define how each object class participates in the namespace, in other words, where entries of the object class can reside. The *name form* defines what attribute(s) can be used to name entries of the object class. An attribute defines the kind of information associated with each of these object classes, and therefore in the entries. The *attribute type* is the definition of the attribute. An attribute type is defined by syntax, matching rules, and other operational information about the attribute. The *syntax* determines how data values are represented. *Matching rules* determine how to compare these data values in an LDAP operation.

Syntax defines the kind and form of the data allowed in the attribute value. An example of syntax is a Boolean value. For a value to fit the Boolean syntax, it must be either FALSE or TRUE. Other syntaxes allow for data to be represented in the directory in a variety of forms. Matching rules also use syntax and are included in the attribute type definition.

Syntax is the building block of matching rules and attribute types

Chapter 1 introduced the concept of *schema checking*. On every add, modify, or modifyRDN operation, the attribute values must be checked to see whether they meet the schema requirements for the object class and attribute type. If these checks fail, the operation fails. The schema-checking process is concerned primarily with ensuring that the data structure of a directory is consistent. This process is analogous to the work of a referee or official, who makes sure the game is played according to the rule book.

Schema checking maintains the integrity of the directory

The default schema that an LDAP directory begins with is defined by several documents. RFC 2252 describes the framework for the LDAP schema, in other words, the portion of the schema that supports the internal directory functions and allows you to define specific components in the schema. This framework includes a set of syntaxes, matching rules, and attribute types.

Several documents define the recommended LDAP schema

RFC 2252 also describes the encoding rules that should be used to represent the data in attribute values during LDAP operations. Including a description of the encoding method ensures that LDAP will interoperate across implementations. RFC 2256 describes the user schema, in other words, the portion of the schema with which clients regularly interact. There are only two requirements in this RFC that every LDAP server must implement. But the RFC contains many recommendations on object classes and attributes, and nearly all vendors implement these recommendations.

X.500 schema definitions are valid for LDAP

The LDAP schema uses the same schema definitions developed for X.500 directories because X.500 was LDAP's predecessor. For example, the RFCs noted previously draw heavily on definitions established in standards for X.501, X.520, and X.521, as documented by the ITU, which is an international standards organization. This close tie to X.500 directories provides a convenient pool of historically tested definitions to build upon, while also allowing vendors to implement a directory that supports both LDAP and X.500.

How Does X.500 Affect the LDAP Schema?

X.500 is a set of standards that define directory structure and services, whereas LDAP is a protocol used to interact with directory structures and services. LDAP was initially intended as a gateway service to X.500 directories, so clients didn't need to implement the hefty set of directory access protocols (DAPs) required for X.500. LDAP therefore never focused on directory structure or services; the X.500 standard and model were assumed. But as LDAP has developed, vendors have begun implementing LDAP without X.500 support. This trend has spurred debate concerning whether LDAP should include directory structure and service models in its definition. If you examine the LDAP schema, you will see frequent references to this relationship to X.500 standards.

The lack of a required default schema means that Mycompany has a great deal of flexibility when implementing its directory. Vendors can also take advantage of this flexibility to create functionality for their purposes, and individual organizations can pick and choose schema modifications as they design their directories. Extensions to the schema can be made after implementation to extend the functionality of a directory.

The LDAP schema is flexible

LDAP v3 requires that the schema be published in a subschema entry that can be found by querying the value of the `subschemaSubentry` attribute of any directory entry. The value of this entry is the DN of the subschema entry that holds the published schema. By publishing the schema, the client can be made aware of functionality that the server supports. This also can simplify schema maintenance both by making the schema easier to modify, and by leveraging any other maintenance the directory supports, such as replication.

LDAP v3 publicizes its schema to clients

Object Classes

Object classes define what entries are possible in an LDAP directory. Every entry in an LDAP directory has an attribute named `objectclass`, and the `objectclass` attribute value(s) corresponds to an object class definition in the schema. Object classes define what attributes are required and which are optionally available for use with a directory entry. They also provide a convenient way for a user to query for all the entries with a particular `objectclass` attribute. For example, I might want to find all the entries with `objectclass=user` so I can identify all the user accounts in a Microsoft Active Directory.

An object class defines the types of entries in a directory

There are three categories of object classes: abstract classes, auxiliary classes, and structural classes. Every entry in the directory has at least one structural class and one abstract class, and it may have auxiliary classes. Some vendor implementations of LDAP do not distinguish between these categories of

Three categories of object classes create a template for building object classes

object classes, but this doesn't mean that these categories aren't used by the underlying schema. Any particular object class may build on another object class definition or pick the attractive parts of another object class definition; object class categories are what enable this functionality, even if they aren't formally acknowledged by the vendor. Object classes can either include or inherit existing definitions, thereby forming relationships between object classes. These relationships mean that one object class has a whole set of object classes depending on it, so a hierarchy is formed. The purpose of each of the categories of object classes, and how each helps you build new object classes, is discussed shortly.

Elements of an Object Class

The object class definition contains several key fields that help to define an entry of the object class and what rules that entry follows. The following fields are part of the object class definition:

- **OID**—The unique object identifier for this object class.

- **Name**—The name used to refer to the object class.

- **Description**—Brief description of what the object class represents.

- **Inactive status**—Indicated by OBSOLETE, which means the object class is inactive.

- **Superior class**—Lists the object class(es) on which this object class is based. Some schema formats label this field SUP while others call it SUBCLASS OF.

- **Category of object class**—Specified with the presence of abstract, auxiliary, or structural. By default, structural is assumed. The categories indicate to the schema-checking process how to create an entry of that object class, and what attributes are required or allowed.

- **Mandatory attributes**—Usually noted by a MUST field, which lists all the attributes that must have values for an entry of this object class to exist.

- **Optional attributes**—Usually noted by a MAY field, which lists all the attributes that are allowed on an entry of this object class.

Although the following object class fields are not defined in RFC 2252, many LDAP directories also support them:

- **Naming attribute**—Designates which attribute or attributes are used for naming (RDN) of entries of this object class. You can designate more than one attribute to form multivalued RDNs.

- **Superior rules**—Designate which object classes can contain entries of this object class.

To illustrate, here is an example of the subschema object class definition:

```
subschema OBJECT-CLASS ::= {
    SUBCLASS OF { top }
    KIND auxiliary
    MAY CONTAIN { dITStructureRules | nameForms |
        ditContentRules | objectClasses |
    attributeTypes | matchingRules |matchingRuleUse }
    ID 2.5.20.1}
```

Most directory products use a text file to store the schema definitions. This text file can be modified to include new definitions or change existing ones. Many products require that the LDAP server be restarted for changes to be recognized. The subschema object class definition uses the ASN.1 schema format. Definitions follow a special format that is dependent on the vendor. Appendix B examines the common schema formats.

Most products store the schema in a text file

Some products allow schema modifications via LDAP operations

Some directories represent the schema object classes and attributes as directory entries, allowing LDAP clients to search and modify the schema definitions via LDAP operations. For example, the `person` object class might exist as an entry at `cn=person,ou=Schema,dc=mycompany,dc=com`. In this fictitious example, the mandatory attributes are listed in a special attribute called `must`, and the optional attributes in a special attribute called `may`. An LDAP client with the proper access control can modify the definitions. Although it doesn't follow the details of this fictitious example, Microsoft's Active Directory product is an example of a product that allows users to add or modify the schema via LDAP operations.

Creating the Entry You Want

Creating the entry you want may require using multiple object classes

Object class definitions let you create entries that have the attributes, content rules, and name form you want. Let's say you want to create an entry with a particular profile in Mycompany's directory. But among the existing object classes, there is no single class that fits the profile you want. You have two choices. Either you pick and choose from among the existing object classes, and create an entry that has several object classes. Or you design a new object class.

You may have to build a new object class to get the entry you want

Let's further suppose that there isn't any combination of existing object classes that fits the profile you want, because an attribute is missing or the combination of content rules from multiple classes is too restrictive. But an existing object class does have some of the elements you need. You must create a new object class, and it would be easier if you could build on that existing object class. The following two sections explore your options.

Option 1: Use Inheritance and Object Class Relationships

Object class inheritance allows content and structure rules to be shared

Your new object class can inherit name form, content rules, and structure rules from another object class. When a new object class builds on an existing object class, the new object class is said to be a *subclass* of the original, and it *inherits* the traits of the existing object class. We'll look at what inheritance means shortly. The original class is called the *superior class* or *super-class* of the new object class. This relationship is included in the definition of the new object class in the superior field.

This relationship between object classes is similar to the relationships that scientists observe in biological classifications. There is a hierarchy among life form classes, just as there is a hierarchy among object classes. If a life form is classified as human, it is also classified as an animal, a mammal, and a primate. A human shares some characteristics with all other animals, mammals, and primates, but it also has other unique characteristics. Figure 4-2 shows a concrete example of the

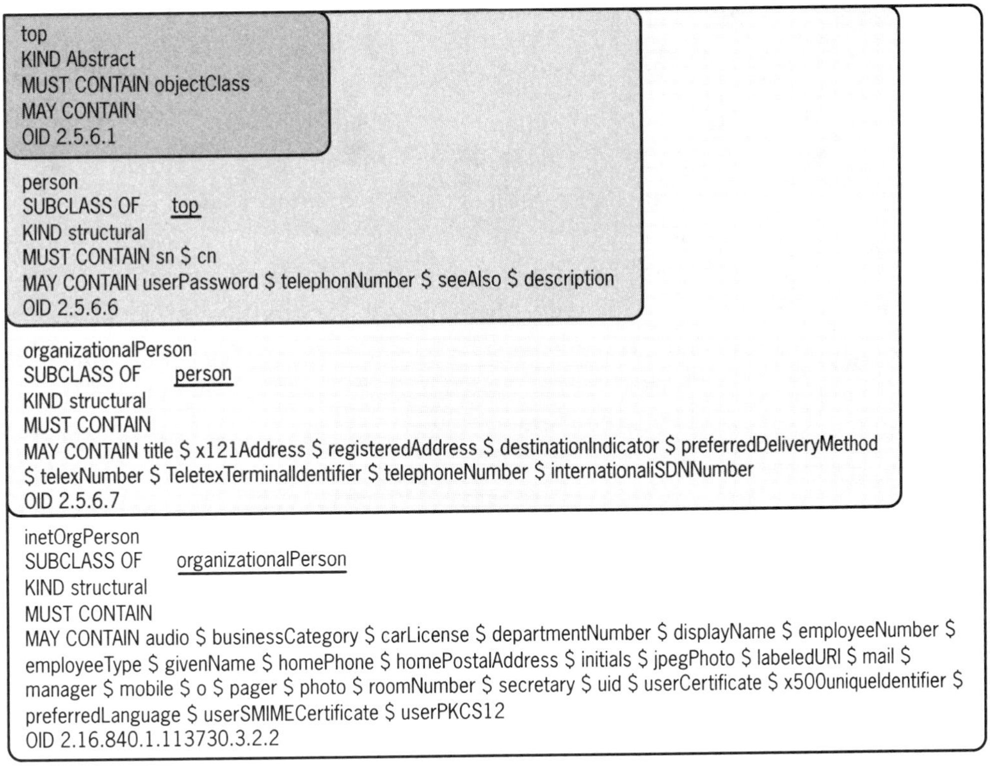

A hierarchical relationship of object classes is created when you use inheritance

```
top
KIND Abstract
MUST CONTAIN objectClass
MAY CONTAIN
OID 2.5.6.1

person
SUBCLASS OF      top
KIND structural
MUST CONTAIN sn $ cn
MAY CONTAIN userPassword $ telephonNumber $ seeAlso $ description
OID 2.5.6.6

organizationalPerson
SUBCLASS OF      person
KIND structural
MUST CONTAIN
MAY CONTAIN title $ x121Address $ registeredAddress $ destinationIndicator $ preferredDeliveryMethod
$ telexNumber $ TeletexTerminalIdentifier $ telephoneNumber $ internationaliSDNNumber
OID 2.5.6.7

inetOrgPerson
SUBCLASS OF      organizationalPerson
KIND structural
MUST CONTAIN
MAY CONTAIN audio $ businessCategory $ carLicense $ departmentNumber $ displayName $ employeeNumber $
employeeType $ givenName $ homePhone $ homePostalAddress $ initials $ jpegPhoto $ labeledURI $ mail $
manager $ mobile $ o $ pager $ photo $ roomNumber $ secretary $ uid $ userCertificate $ x500uniqueIdentifier $
preferredLanguage $ userSMIMECertificate $ userPKCS12
OID 2.16.840.1.113730.3.2.2
```

Figure 4-2   Building object classes using inheritance

hierarchical relationship between object classes. The ASN.1 schema format is used to represent the object class definitions.

Inheritance allows entries of one object class to take the traits of another object class

If I call you human, I don't also need to call you a mammal; everyone assumes that you are a mammal. In a similar fashion, if you create an entry with an object class that is the subclass of another, you do not need to indicate all the superior classes. The directory assumes those other classes and automatically includes them in the entry. When you create an entry of the new subclass, the `objectclass` attribute value of the new entry will have both the new object class name and the names of any object classes noted in the `SUP` field. The new entry is required to follow the rules and requirements defined in the schema for all these object classes.

Inheritance results in simpler schema definitions

Note that the new subclass does not explicitly include the schema definitions for any of its superclasses. It doesn't need to. The requirements, rules, and definitions are all inherited when you create the entry. The directory takes care of these details. Building inheritance into entry creation results in elegant and efficient object class definitions, as well as a simplified process for creating an entry. Figure 4-3 shows how the elements of object classes are used to create an entry of a subclass. On the entry, the italicized attributes are optional, the bolded attributes must be supplied by the client request, and the single attribute shown in regular font is automatically supplied by the directory itself.

An example of creating an entry using an inherited object class

An example of how inheritance works will illustrate this concept. Using the definitions shown in Figure 4-2, I send an add operation to Mycompany's directory with the following parameters:

DN: `cn=Boba Fett,ou=People,dc=mycompany,dc=com`
Attributes: `cn=Boba Fett;sn=Fett;objectclass=inetOrgPerson;`

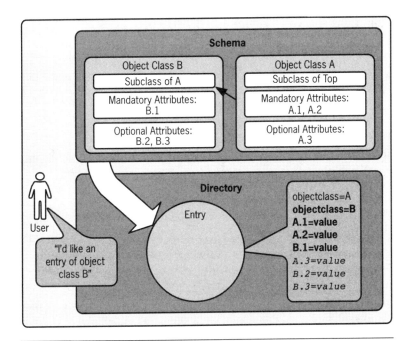

Figure 4-3   How elements of inherited object classes are used to create an entry

An entry with the following information is created:

```
DN: cn=Boba Fett,ou=People,dc=mycompany,dc=com
    cn=Boba Fett
    sn=Fett
    objectclass=inetOrgPerson
    objectclass=OrganizationalPerson
    objectclass=person
    objectclass=top
```

Note that three additional `objectclass` values were automatically added. Had I left off the `sn` attribute in the add operation parameters, the operation would have failed. Even though I'm creating an entry of `inetOrgPerson`, I must meet all the requirements of every superclass of `inetOrgPerson`, and `sn` is a requirement of the object class `person`. I might have added any of the optional attributes in any of the four object class definitions shown in Figure 4-2. So `inetOrgPerson` gives me four object classes even though I have to specify only one.

You use abstract classes to build other object classes

Abstract classes form the building blocks of other object classes. You use an *abstract class* as a template via inheritance to build other object classes. There is a special abstract class called `top` that is the ultimate superclass of all object classes. To build an object class that doesn't inherit anything, you build an object class that is a direct subclass of `top`. The abstract class is the least frequently used, and it is typically used to support internal LDAP operations as opposed to building a data structure for an entry.

Structural classes are used in every directory entry

Each directory entry must contain one *structural class*. A structural class always uses inheritance, and it must be a subclass of another object class. Conversely, only structural classes can use inheritance; abstract classes and auxiliary classes cannot use inheritance. A structural class can be a superclass of another object class.

Option 2: Use an Auxiliary Class

Instead of using inheritance to create the entry you need in Mycompany's directory, you might use an auxiliary class. The combination of an existing object class that has some of the elements you require plus a newly defined auxiliary class would result in the entry you need. To create your entry, you'd need to explicitly add both the existing object class and the auxiliary class.

You use auxiliary classes to mix and match

An *auxiliary class* augments the other object classes of an entry without the costs tied to inheritance. The auxiliary class is never involved in inheritance because an auxiliary class is never the superclass for a structural or abstract class. Instead, auxiliary classes are explicitly included in an entry rather than included implicitly via inheritance. You use auxiliary classes to add specific functionality to a standard object class without modifying the original object class definition. The same auxiliary class may be added to entries with different object classes. This is the most significant advantage of the auxiliary class. In other words, the auxiliary class is not part of a chain of inheritance, and you can use it with entries of differing classes. Figure 4-4 shows how the elements of auxiliary classes are combined with other classes in the creation of an entry. The attributes shown in italics are optional, and the attributes shown in bold must be supplied by the client request.

Many LDAP directories allow an object class to inherit from only a single class, so only one superclass is allowed for any particular object class. This constraint leads to a dependent chain of object classes that inherit the characteristics of all the superclasses in the chain. You might want some of the characteristics (usually attributes), but not others. This chain

Auxiliary classes are outside of class inheritance chains

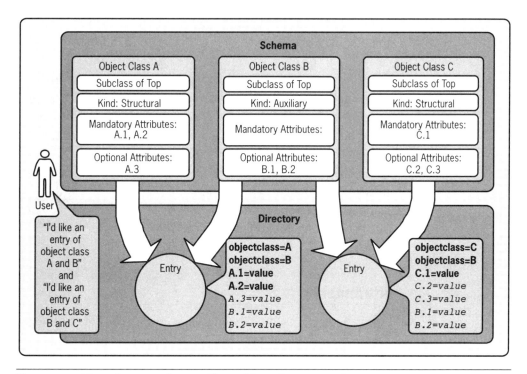

Figure 4-4   How elements of an auxiliary object class are used to create an entry

of dependencies is why the auxiliary class is important; the auxiliary class doesn't participate in an inheritance chain. The auxiliary classes that maximize this benefit have no mandatory attributes and include only optional attributes, thus truly allowing the class to extend functionality. You use the features of the auxiliary class to augment object classes that don't (and shouldn't) have a hierarchical relationship to one another.

For example, Mycompany may want to attach a globally unique identifier (`guid`) to each group (`objectclass=groupOfUnique Names`) and user (`objectclass=inetOrgPerson`) entry in the directory. The `guid` is defined as an attribute. An auxiliary object class `guidClass` is defined with the `guid` attribute as an optional attribute. Then the `guidClass` object class can be added to each of the group and user entries. We would do this via a modify request that added `objectclass=guidClass`. Finally, `guid` values can be added to all the entries. These values could be added via the same modify request that added the auxiliary class.

Consider the alternative, assuming a directory that supports only single inheritance. The alternative using class inheritance would require that you define two distinct object classes that are subclasses of `groupOfUniqueNames` and `inetOrgPerson`, respectively. Call each of these subclasses `guidgroupOfUniqueNames` and `guidinetOrgPerson`. Each of these would effectively have the same purpose—to add the same single optional attribute—but you would have to provide both definitions to circumvent the single inheritance issue.

Attributes

An attribute type is described in what is called the AttributeType-Description in RFC 2252, and the AttributeType in RFC 2251.

So Which Is a Better Strategy: Inheritance or Auxiliary Class?

Given my description, you might think that auxiliary classes are a more efficient way to design a new object class. But consider things from the perspective of users who want to create an entry. They must explicitly include both object classes. If they use inheritance instead, they need to include only one object class. With the auxiliary option, problems can occur if a user forgets one of the object classes. The best strategy really depends on who the users are of the object class. Of course, if you have an LDAP-enabled interface that hides these details, it may not matter.

Ultimately, this is not an either/or choice. You will find both options useful. In fact, you may have noticed that the code shown in Figure 4-4 uses both inheritance and an auxiliary class to create entries. You may not have noticed this fact because the inherited object class is the top class (which has no mandatory or optional attributes). Tricky, huh? Whichever approach you take, be clear on what you want and aware of any potential liabilities.

An attribute type contains several key fields. These fields help to define the attribute as well as what rules that attribute follows. The critical fields define the syntax and matching rules for the attribute. The syntax defines the kind and form of the data allowed in the attribute value. The matching rules define how the directory can determine whether an asserted value matches an attribute value during an LDAP operation. As noted earlier, matching rules also use syntax. The attribute type also specifies whether multiple attribute values are acceptable. By default, an attribute is *multivalued,* meaning that an attribute can have multiple values on each entry.

An attribute is defined by an attribute type, which is composed primarily of syntax and matching rules

Elements of an Attribute Type

The following fields are part of the AttributeTypeDescription:

- **OID**—Unique object identifier for this attribute type.

- **Name**—Usually specified with the NAME label, which is the name used to refer to the attribute type.

- **Description**—Usually indicated with the DESC label, which is a brief description of what the attribute type represents.

- **Inactive status**—Usually specified with the presence of the OBSOLETE label, which means the attribute type is inactive.

- **Superior class**—Lists the attribute type on which this attribute type is based.

- **Equality matching rule**—Matching rule used to determine whether an asserted value matches an attribute value.

- **Order matching rule**—Matching rule used to determine whether an asserted value is ordered before or after an attribute value.

- **Substring matching rule**—Matching rule used to determine whether an asserted string value with a wildcard character matches an attribute value.

- **Syntax**—The kind and form of the data allowed in the attribute value.

- **Number of allowed values**—Whether only a single value or multiple values are allowed. By default, multiple values are assumed. The presence of SINGLE-VALUE indicates only a single value is allowed.

- **Collective**—By default, not collective is assumed.

- **Modifiable**—Whether the attribute value can be modified by user-initiated LDAP operations. By default, the attribute value is user modifiable.

- **Usage**—Type of operations for which the attribute is used. By default, `userApplications` is assumed. `userApplications`, `directoryOperation`, `distributedOperation`, and `dSAOperation` are all valid values; however, many vendor implementations throw out these values and replace them with only two values: `user` or `application` and `operational`. Attributes that are not marked `userApplications` are not returned by default on a search operation, because they are considered information that only the internal directory needs to support internal operations.

To illustrate, here is an example of the `createTimestamp` attribute definition:

```
( 2.5.18.1 NAME 'createTimestamp' EQUALITY
    generalizedTimeMatch
    ORDERING generalizedTimeOrderingMatch
    SYNTAX 1.3.6.1.4.1.1466.115.121.1.24
    SINGLE-VALUE NO-USER-MODIFICATION USAGE
        directoryOperation )
```

This definition is given in the BNF schema format, which is different from the format used for the example object class earlier in this chapter. For more details on schema formats, see Appendix B.

Any particular attribute type can have more than a single name. These names are synonyms for each other. For example, the attribute `facsimiletelephonenumber` might have `fax` as a *synonymous name*. Or `cn` might have `commonName` as a synonym. The synonymous names are included in the NAME field of an attribute type definition. The first name in the NAME field of an attribute type definition is called the *canonical attribute name*. Within a directory that shares a common schema, a user can generally

Attributes can have more than one name

employ these synonyms interchangeably, but this doesn't necessarily hold true between directories with different schemas.

How synonymous names are handled is not standardized, which is problematic

Usually LDAP directories prefer to return attribute names in the canonical form, replacing any synonymous name used in a request. For example, I might ask for `fax`, but get back `facsimiletelephonenumber`. Attribute name synonyms are not governed by the LDAP standards, and how any particular vendor or organization implements them is unregulated. When Mycompany needs to integrate multiple LDAP directories, the attribute name that one directory allows or prefers may be different from that of another directory. This difference can cause serious integration problems. Hopefully this oversight in the standard will be addressed in the future.

Attribute Subtypes

Subtyping is not defined in the LDAP standard, yet it is mentioned as a feature

The existing standards (in RFC 2256, Section 5.50) mention the possibility of *subtyping* but don't explain it. *Subtypes* are common in X.500; and because LDAP was originally thought to be an extension of X.500, the definition was implied. Now that LDAP directories are being implemented without X.500 support, this omission in the standard presents a problem.

An attribute subtype builds on an existing attribute definition

As you might expect, the concept of subtypes is similar to that of subclasses. Subtypes are for attributes what subclasses are for object classes. You can extend an existing attribute type into a subtype. The attribute subtype inherits the syntax and matching rules of its supertype. For example, the `cn` attribute type is derived from the `name` attribute type. `cn` is therefore a subtype of `name`. And `name` would be a *supertype* of `cn`. The `cn` attribute description doesn't include any syntax or matching rules because it inherits these elements from the `name` attribute definition. Figure 4-5 shows this relationship.

Subtypes change how the search operation operates

Subtypes extend the functionality of the directory. Searches that ask for the `name` attribute will return `name` values as well as values from all subtypes of `name`. For example, a search for all

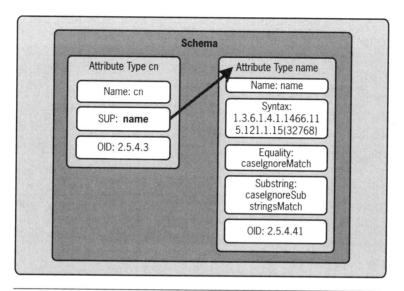

Figure 4-5   Conceptual example of attribute subtypes

the entries with any value present in the `name` attribute (in other words, (`name=*`)) will return all the entries with values in `name` or `cn` (and the many other subtypes of `name`).

As noted already, subtypes are only a possibility in LDAP, not a requirement. Few LDAP implementations include this functionality, and these implementations usually include X.500 functionality as well. Subtypes can be a powerful addition, but they change many of the basic assumptions, so Mycompany will be cautious when using them.

Subtypes are usually seen only in LDAP products with X.500 support

Attribute Options

The AttributeDescription is defined in RFC 2251 as a superset of the attribute type definition. This is not the attribute type, but a slightly larger definition. The AttributeDescription encapsulates the attribute type definition, allowing special *attribute options* to be specified. These attribute options are largely undefined in terms of their purpose. Historically they have been used to

An Attribute-Description associates special attribute options with an attribute type

change the format of the attribute value that is communicated to the client.

Figure 4-6 shows how the AttributeDescription and attribute options relate to an entry in a directory and a client that might use that attribute option. In the figure, the client would like attribute A of entry Y to be returned with the `munge` option. Attribute A's schema definition includes the `munge` option, so this request is allowed. The directory looks up the value of attribute A and then reformats that value based on the syntax defined for the `munge` option. The directory reports to the client the attribute value seen through this `munge` reformatting.

The `binary` option changes the format of the attribute value communicated to the client

For example, RFC 2251 gives an example of the `binary` option in which you can force the server to change the syntax

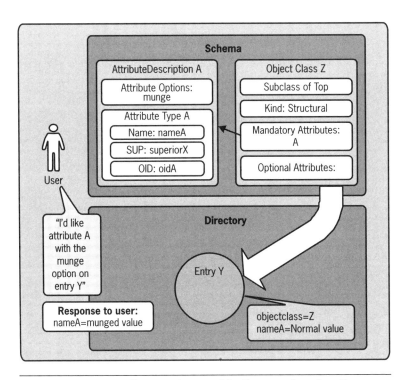

Figure 4-6   How attribute options enable directory functionality

format of the attribute value that is communicated to the client to a binary format instead of the typical string-based syntax. This does not necessarily mean the server must store the attribute value in the binary format, just that it must communicate the value in a binary format to the client.

You can also use attribute options to indicate the language in the attribute value. This approach doesn't change the format of the value, but rather indicates that the value is stored in a specific language. For details on language support via attribute options, see the following section, Language Support.

Options do not have to change the format

Users specify the attribute option(s) they want by appending a semicolon and the name of the option to the end of the attribute type in the relevant search or compare operation parameter. For example, the `binary` option with the `cn` attribute would be specified `cn;binary`. You could use this approach in a compare operation in which you want to compare a data value in binary form but the attribute value has a string syntax. You can specify multiple options at once. Servers that don't recognize a requested option should treat the request as an unrecognized attribute type and the operation will fail. The only common use of the binary option is with digital certificates, for example, `userCertificate:binary`. Here it is used to correct an invalid assumption made in the early days of LDAP about how digital certificates are represented. You should never search for digital certificates without the binary option.

Clients specify attribute options by appending them to the attribute type

Language Support

LDAP supports the possibility of international language support, based on Unicode. LDAP v3 specifically uses Unicode Transformation Format-8 (UTF-8), which is a character set that can be used to represent virtually all written languages. Because LDAP uses Unicode, you don't need to specially denote what language an attribute value takes. Using multi-valued attributes, several languages could be supported at

LDAP supports multiple languages in data format, but further support is needed

once. However, special syntaxes and matching rules that support a specific language might be required in a multiple-language directory, so a user of a particular language could search and receive results using the rules of that language.

Attribute-based language code suffixes are used to extend support

The approach to this issue has been standardized somewhat in RFC 2596. For this purpose, the RFC proposes to specially designate language codes that are associated with an attribute type definition via the attribute option portion of the AttributeDescription. The attribute option functionality noted in RFC 2251 was intended as a way to allow extensions to the framework of the LDAP directory.

The language code desired is added to the option field of the attribute type in the schema

In terms of the schema, each attribute type definition can be extended with the desired language codes. RFC 1766 specifies the language code suffix to be used. So for example, Mycompany might choose to extend the `description` attribute type with the Spanish language. Mycompany would modify the description AttributeDescription in the schema, adding `lang-es` to the option portion of the definition. Then users could specify this option during a search request. In this example, `description; lang-es` would be specified as the full attribute type designation, meaning the `description` attribute type using the Spanish language.

Entries with the extended attribute option can have a value both for the option format and for the default format

The entries in the directory that have an attribute with a language option defined can have values for both the language option and the base attribute type. For example, if the description attribute type were extended with the Spanish language as noted already, the following entry would be valid:

```
objectClass=person
cn=Brian Arkills
sn=Arkills
description=He is very crazy.
description;lang-es=Está muy loco.
```

Each language option desired would have to be individually set because the server does not automatically translate the value from the default format to the language option format.

Directory administrators can modify the AttributeDescription to support many language options; then users can set an attribute value for each of the language options for that attribute type. The syntax of each attribute doesn't need to change, because UTF-8 supports multiple character sets. Also the data that is communicated to the user is not transformed in any way, as it is with the binary option.

Multiple language options can be set

In terms of search behavior, you can consider each language option a subtype of the attribute type. Just as you can expect that a search on the attribute supertype will return a match for all the attribute subtypes, so a search on an attribute type will return a match on that type and all the language options for that type. With attribute subtypes, the reverse is not true; a search for a specific language option of an attribute type does not return values of the attribute type without a language option. You can find specific examples that illustrate this behavior in the RFC. Despite this search behavior, the language option extensions are not subtypes defining a new attribute type; they are options.

Searches on attribute options work like they do for attribute subtypes

RFC 2596 does not supply a complete solution in every case. As mentioned earlier, matching rules that support the cultural rules specific to a language are needed for full functionality. Matching rules are needed to define many issues of syntax that are often taken for granted. Examples include:

Matching rules that support language and cultural rules are needed

- The order of characters in the language's alphabet

- Issues of language type, such as what is a number and what is an alphabetic character

- The cultural formats for common data types like time, money, and date

We'll look at matching rules shortly. Mycompany will want to carefully review language support in a potential product if this is a critical requirement.

Operational Attributes

Operational attributes support internal directory operations

Operational attributes are used by the directory to support internal directory operations, and they are the attributes not marked with a usage of `userApplications`. Several of these operational attributes are required by LDAP v3 in the `rootDSE` entry and the `subschema` entry. Other operational attributes can be of value to the client because they contain information that can reveal what an LDAP server supports, what rules might be used, and even information of critical importance, such as the last modified time for an entry.

Operational attributes are noteworthy enough to list

The only way to get a handle on the operational attributes is to peruse the standards and your vendor documentation. In Tables 4-1 and 4-2, the operational attributes from the standard are listed by the type distinction noted in RFC 2252. The OID, syntax, matching rules, and other information are not listed, so you can focus on the description and intended function. You can easily obtain this information in RFC 2252, Sections 5.1 through 5.4.3. More detail is outside the scope of this book and may be dependent on the specific vendor implementation.

Subschema and directoryOperation Attributes

The subschema publishes the schema to clients

The `subschema` object class is a required element of the LDAP v3 standard; it is one of only two required object classes. The subschema is used to advertise the supported schema in an LDAP directory. The `subschema` entry (there can be more than one in each directory) is used by clients to determine what rules they can expect when interacting with that specific LDAP directory.

What Exactly Is the Definition of the Subschema?

For the definition of the subschema object class, see RFC 2252. This definition omits the mandatory attributes required on the subschema entry noted in RFC 2251. RFC 2251 uses language that allows implementation of additional mandatory and optional attributes, whereas RFC 2252 does not use the same inclusive language. RFC 2251 is talking about a subschema entry, whereas RFC 2252 is talking about the subschema object class. Although a subschema entry and a subschema definition are not semantically identical, the omission can only be viewed as a mistake. Fortunately, the standard does outline what attributes can be in a subschema entry.

Table 4-1   directoryOperation attributes

Attribute Name	Description
createTimestamp	Keeps track of when an entry was created.
modifyTimestamp	Keeps track of when an entry was last modified.
creatorsName	Keeps track of who created an entry.
modifiersName	Keeps track of who last modified an entry.
subschemaSubentry	Contains the DN of a subschema entry.
attributeTypes	Contains a list of the supported attribute types; is located in the subschema entry.
objectClasses	Contains a list of the supported object classes; is located in the subschema entry.
matchingRules	Contains a list of the supported matching rules; is located in the subschema entry.
matchingRuleUse	Contains a list of the supported matching rules that are available via the extended match filter described in Chapter 3. This attribute is located in the subschema entry.
dITStructureRules	Contains the structure rules that this server supports.
nameForms	Contains the name forms that this server supports.
ditContentRules	Contains the content rules that this server supports.

Table 4-2   dSAOperation Attributes

Attribute Name	Description
namingContexts	Identifies the naming contexts that this server supports directly or indirectly. An empty string value indicates that this server should contain the entire directory namespace. The client can use this attribute to find a suitable namespace to search.
altServer	Refers to another LDAP server that is equally capable of providing a response. The value is in an LDAP URL format. LDAP clients can cache this information so if the server becomes unavailable, the client can continue operation with the other server(s).
supportedExtension	Contains OIDs for the extended operations that the server supports.
supportedControl	Contains OIDs for the controls that the server supports.
supportedSASLMechanisms	Contains OIDs for the supported SASL mechanisms that the server supports.
supportedLDAPVersion	Contains the version of the LDAP protocol that the server supports.

The `subschema` entry has at least four mandatory attributes and many optional attributes. The mandatory attributes include `cn`, `objectClass`, `objectClasses`, and `attributeTypes`. `objectClasses` contains a list of all the supported object classes in the directory. `attributeTypes` contains a list of all the supported attributes in the directory. The optional, operational attributes of the `subschema` entry are known as the `directoryOperation` attributes. See Table 4-1 for these attributes and a short description. You find the `subschema` entry by asking for the value of the operational attribute `subschemaSubentry`, which is on the `rootDSE` entry as well as every entry in the directory. The value is the DN of the `subschema` entry.

rootDSE Entry and dSAOperation Attributes

The `rootDSE` entry provides basic information about a directory server. The `rootDSE` entry has no defined object class in the standard. It must, however, exist and allow the `dSAOperation` operational attributes listed in Table 4-2. Additional attributes may be located in the `rootDSE` entry to support vendor-specific functionality. The `dSAOperation` operational attributes can also be included in other object class definitions.

Syntaxes

A syntax defines the data format used by an attribute type or matching rule. A special system called Abstract Syntax Notation One (ASN.1) is used to convey the definition of a syntax. ASN.1 is defined by X.209 and is similar to the BNF notation (defined in RFC 822). ASN.1 is a flexible system that can be used to define a variety of data types, from integers and strings to complex sets and sequences of a variety of data types. It is used to build type definitions from what you might call a predefined toolbox. This toolbox consists of a small set of simple types like integer, IA5string (ASCII), or bit string (binary), along with special operators to denote ways to combine these simple types, using sequences, sets, and multiple choice. Complex type definitions can be built by referencing less complex definitions via substitution.

ASN.1 is commonly used to build syntax

ASN.1 has several advantages. One is that ASN.1 has special encoding rules called BER and DER that define how content represented in ASN.1 can be put in messages fit for transmission. LDAP uses BER encoding, specifically a simplified subset of BER. ASN.1 messages are placed in a format it calls octet strings. *Octet strings* are arbitrarily long strings of 8-byte data. So an octet string's length should always have a factor of 8. Incidentally, ASN.1 is used by many standards, including X.509 certificates used by SSL and Kerberos version 5, which make those technologies easier to integrate with LDAP.

ASN.1 helps to provide cross-platform interoperability

RFC 2252 lists 58 default syntaxes for LDAP servers, but only defines 33 of those listed. Vendor implementations are under no obligation to implement any of these syntaxes, and they may implement new ones. This is an area of possible extensibility, but it could be at the cost of breaking interoperability with

There are no default syntaxes in the standard, only commonly used ones

other clients or servers. For the most common of these syntaxes, see Appendix B.

The syntaxes that an LDAP server supports may be published in the `subschema` entry in an attribute called `ldapSyntaxes`. Unfortunately, including this attribute and the information it contains is not required by the standard.

Matching Rules

Matching rules are used to compare data values

Matching rules are used by the LDAP server to compare an attribute value with an assertion value supplied by the LDAP client search or compare operations. The server also uses matching rules to transform the client assertion value to an attribute value in add or modify operations. Finally, the server uses matching rules to compare asserted DN names with the DNs of entries in the directory. Pretty much every LDAP operation uses a matching rule, and many times a single operation will use matching rules more than once. Matching rules have a simple definition that link a name and OID with a syntax. Attributes then include the matching rules in their definitions so at least equality matches are supported for each attribute type.

Extended operations employ matching rule use definitions for the attributes specified in the definition

Matching rule use definitions are slightly different from matching rule definitions. A matching rule use definition links a matching rule definition with specific attribute types for use in extended search filters. You employ this type of definition to associate a matching rule with an attribute type outside the attribute type definition. Values of the `matchingRuleUse` attribute, listed earlier in the chapter, denote the matching rules used by the directory. Each value denotes a matching rule use definition that tells the directory which matching rules to use with specific attribute types in extended search filter operations.

Both matching rule definitions and matching rule use definitions are dependent on syntax definitions. The syntaxes
`Matching Rule Description` and `Matching Rule Use
Description` are used to build the matching rules. Syntaxes are
also defined for matching rules whose assertion value syntax is
different from the attribute value syntax. The basic matching
rules noted in RFC 2252 are listed in Table B-1 in Appendix B.

*Syntaxes are used
to build matching
rules*

OIDs

An *OID* is a special number designed to uniquely identify some
object, regardless of the technology. Object classes, attribute
types, syntaxes, matching rules, and controls use them. In fact,
an OID is required for every object definition. OIDs are used
outside directory technology in areas in which guaranteeing
uniqueness is important. For example, Management Information
Base modules (MIBs) use them. A MIB is commonly used by
management software to understand the status of each entity.
One common use of MIBs is monitoring and managing networked computers. An OID is an arbitrarily long string of integers separated by periods. For example, `1.4.23.98740` is a
valid OID. An OID can be used in place of the object's name.

*An OID is a string
of numbers that
guarantees the
uniqueness of an
object*

The Internet Assigned Numbers Authority (IANA) governs the
OID space and gives out OIDs by request. Once an organization has an OID, it owns all extensions of that OID space. If
Mycompany were granted the OID `1.4.23.98740`, it would also
own `1.4.23.98740.1` and `1.4.23.98740.2` and so on. Extending an OID is called *creating an arc*. Common convention is to
organize each type of object into a separate arc. Mycompany
might put its object classes under `1.4.23.98740.1`, attributes
under `1.4.23.98740.2`, syntaxes under `1.4.23.98740.3`,
matching rules under `1.4.23.98740.4`, controls under
`1.4.23.98740.5`, and so on. But there are no rules about
this. Mycompany can delegate an arc to you, for example

*OIDs are centrally
governed, with
delegated authority*

OIDs Are Problematic

OIDs are ugly and hard to use, and their length can be problematic if they need to be used in place of a named object. To further complicate matters, no one actively manages OID use or associated definitions. Therefore, you and I might give an object the exact same definition, but with different OIDs. When our directories interoperated, they wouldn't be able to treat those objects as the same. One of the directories would have to have its schema definition modified. The only good thing about OIDs is that they guarantee uniqueness. The IETF should take a serious look at revising how they are used by LDAP.

1.4.23.98740.6, but Mycompany better not also use that arc, or you and Mycompany may run into problems with the objects in that space have any interoperation. The Web site http://www.alvestrand.no/objectid/top.html is the only public listing of OIDs. It is an informal attempt to provide a mapping between the OID space and definitions.

OIDs aren't special, but they are required

In summary, OIDs don't enable any special functionality, but they do uniquely identify the definition of objects. Fortunately, users never have to know about OIDs; only administrators and those who design schema definitions need to work with them.

Schema Checking

Schema checking ensures that an operation doesn't violate the schema definitions

The schema holds definitions, but the directory must ensure that all requested operations follow those definitions. To do so, it uses a process called *schema checking*. Schema checking, which isn't mentioned in the LDAP standard, is another of the concepts borrowed from X.500. Vendors therefore choose how (and whether) to implement schema checking. In general, a schema-checking process will ensure that

- All attribute values conform to the syntax noted in the schema definitions.

- All mandatory attributes for an entry's defined object classes are present.

- DN syntax is used properly.

For example, the DN syntax is verified by checking the attribute(s) designated in the name form to see whether the values meet the DN syntax rules. The DN is not usually an attribute of the entry so it must be checked independently.

If the schema-checking process finds a violation of the schema definitions, it will return an error to the client that requested the operation. The entire operation will fail to ensure that partially completed operations do not result in a state that is undesirable to the user.

Schema violations cause the entire operation to fail

Is Turning Off Schema Checking a Good Idea?

If schema checking is turned off by the administrator, inconsistent data in the directory can result. This lack of consistency creates major problems when your organization needs the directory data to implement an enterprise application. The cost of cleaning up data is higher than that of keeping schema checking on. A better approach would be to leave schema checking on and work through the problems that prompted turning it off.

You may find what you think is a good reason to turn off schema checking. For example, the vendor implements an object class in a manner that is inconsistent with your organization's requirements (or the standards), but doesn't allow any modification to that object class definition. Turning off schema checking affects all the schema definitions, so you should make every effort to find an alternate solution.

Extended Schema Definitions

The following interesting definitions are not mentioned in the LDAP standard. As noted earlier, the schema is one of the primary places where the directory can be extended and the directory functionality increased. This makes new schema definitions valuable. Because incongruities in the schema between LDAP directories can create integration issues, standardization of new schema definitions is even more important. The following definitions are all noted in standards documents or in documents that are in the process of becoming standardized.

DNS Extensions

DNS namespace mapping is supported via RFC 2247

RFC 2247 describes the `dc` attribute as well as the `dcObject` and `domain` object classes. These schema elements are used to allow the use of DNS names within the DN syntax. The `dc` attribute makes it clear which part of the DN maps to a DNS name. The `dc` attribute maps directly to a DNS name, either the name of a zone or a hostname. It is the naming attribute for entries of both the `dcObject` and `domain` object classes. Values of the `dc` attribute are not case sensitive, which matches the DNS standard. Nearly every LDAP vendor implements this RFC.

The `dcObject` is used to attach a DNS name to an existing container object class

The `dcObject` object class is an auxiliary object class, and it can be used to extend the definition of existing entries that are being used as containers, like organizational units, to support a clear mapping to the DNS namespace. The `dc` attribute is a mandatory attribute of the `dcObject` object class.

You use the domain to create objects with DNS names

The `domain` object class is a structural object class. You use it to represent new entries that do not need to be based on an existing object class definition. The `dc` attribute is a mandatory attribute, and there are several useful optional attributes.

extensibleObject Object Class

The `extensibleObject` object class is very interesting indeed. Entries of the `extensibleObject` object class allow you to use any attribute type. You might use this flexibility to represent objects that do not conform to a tidy classification or to give an entry maximum functionality without the hassle of carefully designing an object class. You can see one such use in Chapter 8.

The `extensibleObject` includes every attribute type as an optional attribute

The `extensibleObject` object class is auxiliary, and you can add it to another object class definition to extend its functionality. Mandatory attributes of the other object class are still required. The definition of the `extensibleObject` object class does not literally include the hundreds of available attributes in the list of optional attributes; instead, it implicitly includes them. You can use this object class to avoid turning off the schema-checking process, because it allows all the optional attributes within the rules of the schema.

You can use `extensibleObject` to extend an existing object class

dynamicObject Object Class

RFC 2589 describes the `dynamicObject` object class and the extended operations needed to support it. You use the `dynamicObject` object class to represent a dynamic entry that expires if the entry is not updated periodically. This object class is appropriate for representing data that is time dependent. Meetings and temporary employees are two common examples of short-lived data suited to this object class. The directory administrator can use this object class to automatically maintain data whose accuracy is guaranteed only for a certain period of time.

Use the `dynamicObject` for transient data

The dynamic functionality is accomplished via a time-to-live attribute that automatically decrements, unless a client operation intervenes to reset the attribute value. The `dynamicObject` object class is auxiliary. An entry that is dynamic can't become static, and vice versa. There are structural rules imposed on

A time-to-live attribute establishes when the object will be deleted, unless a client operation intervenes

entries of the object class, to prevent the loss of static entries below a dynamic entry, should the dynamic entry expire.

Java

Java object schema allows Java code to be stored in LDAP

One exciting development is the opportunity to store Java objects in an LDAP directory. Combined with the Java LDAP API, which is in the process of being standardized, this enables Java applications at your organization to access common sets of code as well as other directory information. RFC 2713 specifies a standardized way to store a Java object. It includes schema definitions for object classes and attribute types to represent this data.

inetOrgPerson Object Class

inetOrgPerson is a contemporary definition for a person entry

The common user object classes listed in RFC 2256 don't fully address the type of information associated with a person. The `inetOrgPerson` object class defined in RFC 2798 is an attempt to provide a closer definition. It includes definitions for the following new attribute types: vehicle license number, department

Why Does Java Get This Special Accommodation?

It isn't really a special accommodation. In fact, if you think there is something useful to add to the LDAP protocol, you should talk with the folks at the IETF and submit your idea. RFCs are simply suggestions that are watertight enough to be considered worthy of publication. Many of them don't have any special status; and in the case of LDAP, there are some RFCs that are considered part of the core protocol definition, and others that are just good ideas. As an example, there are RFCs (RFC 2549 and 1149) that describe how to implement TCP/IP via carrier pigeons. Look it up if you don't believe me. But just because you've got an RFC doesn't mean it is useful or implemented in any widespread fashion. For example, no network products claim to be compliant with the carrier pigeon RFC (that I know of), and if they were compliant—would you buy them?

number, display name, employee number, employee type, JPEG photograph, preferred language, MIME certificate, and PKCS certificate. This object class is implemented in almost all contemporary vendor implementations, and you may want to find out more about it by reading RFC 2798.

Still in Development

Significant extensions to LDAP are constantly being developed. A wise LDAP administrator pays attention to the public efforts to standardize extensions by participating in IETF proceedings. Table 4-3 lists significant examples of efforts under development at the time of this book's publication that will probably result in a published standard.

Table 4-3   Interesting LDAP schema Internet drafts

Internet-Draft Title	Description
LDAP Schema for DHCP	Defines a schema for DHCP configuration. Entries can represent DHCP configurations for an entire network. This in turn enables centralized management of DHCP services.
Kerberos KDC LDAP Schema	Includes definitions for attributes defining a realm, a realm policy, principals, and principal policies. This enables central management of Kerberos services, as well as allowing for the possibility of interoperability between different Kerberos implementations.
Definition of an object class to hold LDAP change records	Used to efficiently support replication.

Summary

In summary, the schema employed by an LDAP product is one of the biggest factors contributing to the functionality of that product. Although the LDAP standard specifies very little of the schema or even the model employed by a vendor, vendors have followed the X.500 schema model with few deviations.

The schema determines directory functionality

The object classes, attributes, syntaxes, and matching rules control the behavior of the directory and diversity of information it can hold. A directory that doesn't support a specific syntax or allow Mycompany to create its own will prevent Mycompany from creating some special attribute that will either give it an advantage over its competitors or provide a way to integrate an application or standalone directory.

Understanding the details of the schema is not required, but it can further the usefulness of a directory

Understanding of what the schema does and how to extend it is important for directory administrators, but most users do not need to know anything about these topics. Users that create many entries may need to have some understanding of object classes, inheritance, and interesting attributes. Some directory administrators may not need to know much detail about the schema, if the vendor supplies a comprehensive schema. But ultimately understanding of the schema will lead to further use of Mycompany's directory and extend the value it provides.

Appendix Material

For tables of common syntaxes and matching rules, see Appendix B. An overview of the syntax for the different schema formats, together with examples, is also included.

5

Directory Management

Consolidating information into a directory is the primary reason for implementing LDAP. Administrative controls that allow a directory administrator to more easily manage that LDAP directory are therefore relevant to the business value LDAP provides. This type of operational functionality differs from the client-server operations I examined in Chapter 3.

This chapter addresses directory management topics. Of these topics, most are not included in the LDAP standard yet. Some of the topics are addressed by RFC documents but are not formally associated with the standard. The first half of the chapter explains advanced LDAP namespace concepts, including replication, referrals, and aliases. This discussion leads to the management issues surrounding multiple LDAP servers. Special attention is given to a distributed directory service and the effort required to integrate independent directories to centralize management. Directory security concepts and recommendations are next, followed by some of the common server parameters and maintenance tools that you can use with LDAP.

Replication

Centralizing information into an LDAP directory raises the need for fault tolerance

Mycompany's decision to implement an LDAP directory may be stressful. Mycompany will centralize critical information into a single repository and integrate key business processes with this directory. The implications of the central directory being unavailable are greater than when the information was in several nonintegrated directories. How can Mycompany have any peace of mind that its directory will be available if a directory server fails?

Directory replication can provide fault tolerance, but it isn't part of the LDAP standard yet

Replication is the simplest solution. With replication, you deploy more than a single directory server. The information in the directory is then *replicated* between multiple directory servers, and the replicated information can be accessed from several points of distribution. However, LDAP has no specifications on how replication should be accomplished. Implementation of this feature is left to vendors. Almost every vendor does implement this feature, though. Fortunately, there is ongoing IETF discussion about what type of replication model should be used to distribute directory information from one LDAP server to another. An LDAP replication standard should emerge in the future. Mycompany will need to closely compare how each vendor implements directory replication before choosing a product.

Partitions

A partition is the portion of the directory that is replicated to other servers

A *partition* is the portion of the directory that is replicated to other servers. The partition is a naming context (or directory suffix) that forms the element of replication. Some vendors allow flexibility with respect to the portion of the directory that can be a partition. The directory partition is replicated (by some means chosen by the vendor) to other directory servers. Usually (but not always), the administrator has some choice of how often replication occurs and can designate which partition is replicated to which server. The term "partition" designates a unit of the directory that is being replicated. This unit is usually the same as a naming context, but it might be a smaller or larger portion of the directory.

Replicas

A *replica* is a copy of a directory partition. The term "replica" refers to the subservient copies of the master partition. The difference between a partition and a replica is subtle. A replica is the replicated unit of the directory.

A replica is a replicated copy of directory information

Figure 5-1 shows examples of replication used by Mycompany. In the figure, we see part of the Mycompany directory as well as a separate directory for Mycompany's network operating system directory. The two directories have different base DNs and even different directory structures. The Accounts and Computers naming contexts of the Mycompany directory are being replicated to the NOS directory because the Mycompany directory is the primary source of information to make authoritative changes. The Accounts and Computers naming contexts (of either directory) can be referred to as partitions because they are the units of replication. You might simply call the Accounts naming context the Accounts partition and not designate which directory or server it is on, because replication makes the content identical. Each of the Accounts partitions can also be referred to as replicas because both directories are the destination of replication. The Computers partition of the NOS directory is also a replica. However, the Computers partition of the Mycompany directory is not a replica, because it is not the destination of replication, but only a source.

Some replication models suggest a *single-master model*, in which one directory server holds the *authoritative* (writable) version of any particular partition, and the other servers have this version replicated to them. In the single-master model, all modifications of data must be made on the single authoritative server and the other servers are read-only replicas. In Figure 5-1, the Computers partition is being replicated in a single-master

In single-master models, directory information must flow from one server; in multimaster models, there are multiple directions of flow

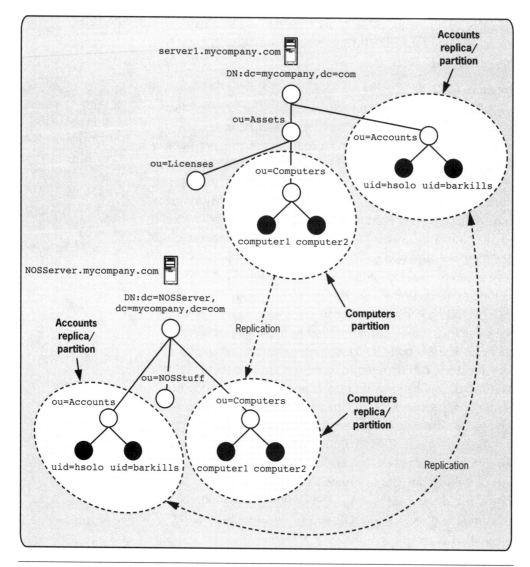

Figure 5-1   Example of replication, partitions, and replicas

model from the Mycompany directory to the NOS directory. In a *multimaster model*, all the servers hold an equally authoritative version that can each be modified. Sometimes a ring topology is used to limit the replication connections, but not always. In Figure 5-1, the Accounts partition is being replicated in a multimaster model between both servers, so that changes can be made on either server and propagated to the other. The multimaster model makes the replica and partition terminology much harder to distinguish, because replication is being done in multiple directions. Therefore, it shouldn't be surprising that the terms "partition" and "replica" can frequently be used interchangeably in contexts in which they can't be distinguished.

The NOSServer.mycompany.com server has the Computers container replicated to it. The network operating system can then make use of the authoritative ownership and location information that the Assets department must own. Server1.mycompany.com is the authoritative server for computer entries.

Which Is Better: Single or Multimaster?

At first glance, a multimaster model seems clearly superior. You are distributing the write operations that perform poorly on an LDAP server. You also might control the use of WAN links for geographically dispersed locations. But it really depends on how the multimaster scheme is implemented. For example, many implementations still have a single point of failure. In most cases, the point of failure has a smaller impact, but it is still there. Another issue that the multimaster model introduces is the concept of a loosely synchronized partition. Multiple servers hold the data, and each can have that data changed. Because no single server is the authority for a given partition, at any given moment in time you can't be sure that the value you get from an entry is the authoritative value. Still another issue is what happens when the same entry (or same attribute on the same entry) is changed on two different servers at the same time. This is called a *collision*. Obviously, the multimaster model introduces a greater level of complexity. Whether the multimaster model is truly better really depends on whether the vendor has implemented it well, and what your requirements are. Are there still points of failure? Does a loosely synchronized directory affect your business? When a problem happens, is it easy to troubleshoot? I personally prefer the multimaster model, because it helps reduce the reliance on a single point of failure.

Server1 is authoritative because new computers are first known about by the Assets department at Mycompany, and because Mycompany considers the Assets department primarily responsible for computers. The people in the Assets department create a computer entry for a computer and enter any asset tag numbers, ownership information, physical location, and any other information they need to track the computer as an asset. The Assets department has given NOS administrators access to the NOS-specific attributes on the computer entries in the central directory so they can do their work. Note that administrators of the NOSServer shouldn't make any changes to the Computers replica because they would be overwritten by replication.

Generally speaking, most vendors support only a single-master replication model. A read-only server (in other words, a server that contains only replicas) will usually generate a referral to the master server when a modification is attempted. This eliminates client confusion and simplifies management.

Referrals

LDAP v3 implements referrals to provide cross-reference to other LDAP directories

LDAP v2 had problems garnering widespread support because a centralized directory was limited to a single server. This single server could become a bottleneck or a single point of failure. LDAP v3 provides considerably more structural flexibility with referrals. A *referral* is a response returned to the LDAP client that instructs the client to contact another LDAP server to perform the operation the client requested. The client then automatically contacts the other LDAP server. Typically, referrals are encountered during search operations, but modify, delete, and all the other operations can follow referrals as well. The process of contacting a second LDAP server to follow a referral is called *chasing the referral*. All LDAP client software should support this functionality to be in compliance with the LDAP standard. Referrals will cause a greater latency in response time because the client must do additional work by contacting the second server after receiving the referral response from the first server. This additional complexity for the client was initially given great weight in designing the standard, and it was one of the reasons LDAP v2 didn't have much support for referrals. But this gain of functionality at what is a small cost of client complexity has become one of the most significant features of LDAP v3.

By using referrals, you can create a cohesive structure of LDAP servers with different namespaces, as demonstrated in Figure 5-2. Each individual LDAP server may contain referrals to the other servers at the appropriate place within the internal directory structure. This allows Mycompany to break up a namespace into contiguous pieces on several servers or connect two independent directory servers. Referrals can help overcome scaling problems, in which a single server's response is poor, but multiple servers could handle the capacity for millions of entries.

Referrals allow greater flexibility in directory architecture

Referral Resolution

The client must replace any host, port, and base DN components of the original LDAP operation with components supplied by the referral. If the referral contains a different base DN, the base DN of the referral is used, and the original base DN is dis-

The client must resolve referrals

What About a Referral Loop?

Can a referral on one server trigger a referral (directly or via a search with a subtree scope) back to the originating referral? Isn't this a critical flaw in referrals? Yes, this is possible. However, the LDAP standard addresses this issue. LDAP clients must not repeatedly query a server with the same base DN, scope, and filter. However, experience shows that vendors pay lots of attention to the LDAP standard with respect to server code, and not a lot of attention when it comes to client code. You might want to test this case out yourself with the software your organization implements so you know what to expect.

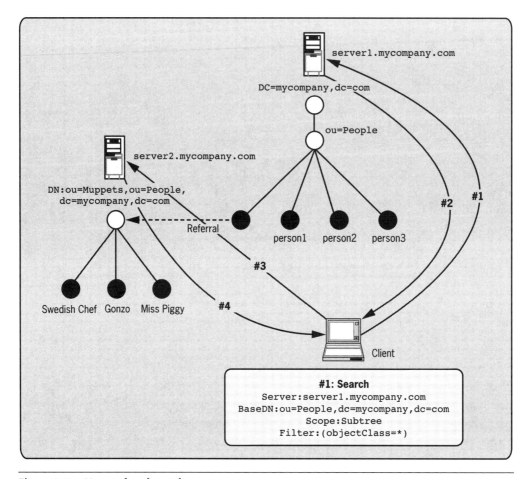

Figure 5-2   How referrals work

carded for the purpose of chasing the referral. Similarly, if a search filter is designated in the referral, it is used. But if a component isn't designated in the referral, the component from the original request is used. The client forms a new composite request from the merging of the original request and the referral, and then acts on this request.

Figure 5-2 demonstrates the client-server interaction when referrals are involved. The client requests the search operation noted in message #1. The server replies with message #2, which includes the entries for person1, person2, person3, and a referral to the server2.mycompany.com servers, with a specific DN, in the URL format covered earlier. The client then automatically chases this referral with a new request in message #3. This request simply replaces the BaseDN parameter of the original request. The second server replies with message #4, which includes Gonzo, Miss Piggy, and the Swedish Chef. Finally, the client reports all six entries as the results of the original request. In some cases, the results are reported in real time as they return.

Incidentally, some LDAP client implementations can be configured to not chase referrals. In some cases, this ability extends to designating which kinds of referrals should or shouldn't be chased. For example, you might want to stop the client from chasing external referrals or from chasing subordinate referrals. The ability to designate this choice can either be a persistent setting for all subsequent searches or a parameter for single searches.

You can turn off referral chasing

Referrals that point to DN locations that are contiguous with the server's directory namespace are called *subordinate* or *superior referrals* depending on whether they point up or down in the namespace. You can even use a referral to point to any place on the same directory server. More importantly, you can also connect directory servers with disparate namespaces. Referrals that point to DN locations outside the server's directory namespace are called *external referrals*. You can also specify *default referrals*, which are returned on all requests for entries that aren't located within the directory's local namespace and for which the directory has no other name resolution information. The variety of referral types supports an incredible amount of flexibility in directory design, interoperation, and integration. Later in the chapter, we will examine the usefulness of referrals in the context of directory integration solutions.

A variety of referral types provide a means of directory integration and organization

If an LDAP directory contacted by a client doesn't know about an attribute used in the DN and the entry holds a subordinate referral, the referral will fail. In this case, the attribute's OID can be substituted for the attribute type, and the referral will be successfully generated. This rare situation might happen if all the LDAP servers involved didn't have the same schema definitions.

Referral Syntax

Referrals are represented with the LDAP URL syntax

LDAP referrals follow the syntax of the LDAP URL format. Each referral must have at least a single URL, and it can have more than one. But if there is more than one URL, each must be equally capable of completing the operation. In other words, if multiple URLs are listed in a referral, each of the destinations must return the same results. By following the LDAP URL format, the hostname, port, base DN, and search filter are easily communicated to the LDAP client. An interesting side note is that a referral doesn't need to designate the LDAP protocol, and it might designate another protocol operation. But the LDAP client would need to support such an operation.

The Real Meaning of Referrals

LDAP operations with a scope of one level or subtree never return referrals, according to the LDAP standard as specified in RFC 2251. Instead, *continuation references* are used and returned to the client when these scopes are used. So technically speaking, only what I've called default referrals are really referrals. However, continuation references are identical in type and syntax to referrals. For this reason, almost all literature (including the most popular vendor implementation documentation) dealing with referrals and continuation references simply calls both referrals. The terminology introduced here in the text is commonly accepted, and I will follow this precedent and ignore the unused term. Anyone interested in the full details can refer to Sections 4.1.11 and 4.5.3 of RFC 2251.

Referral Examples

Figure 5-3 shows examples of subordinate, external, and default referrals. In the example, mycompany.com has a subordinate referral in the People container to the Muppets container on the server2.mycompany.com server. The namespace on server2.mycompany.com extends the namespace on server1.mycompany.com, with an additional container (ou=Muppets) that isn't present on the server1.mycompany.com server. The example also shows an external referral to the deathstar.net server. Again, the People container in the

Using a variety of referrals can produce a distributed directory with greater functionality

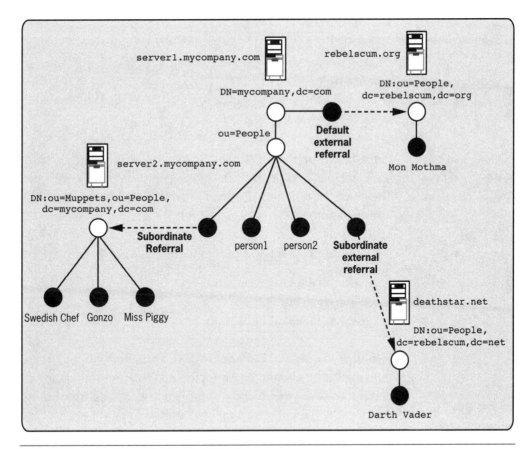

Figure 5-3   Distributed directories connected by referrals

mycompany.com directory holds the referral, but this time it is a referral external to the directory namespace. Note how the namespace on deathstar.net is not contiguous with the namespace on mycompany.com. Finally, the example shows a default referral in the root of the mycompany.com directory to the People container in the rebelscum.org directory. The default referral is external to the directory namespace.

An LDAP client might have the following searches:

1. Server: server1.mycompany.com
   Base DN: cn=Mon Mothma,dc=rebelscum,dc=org
   Scope: one
   Search Filter: (objectclass=person)

2. Server: server1.mycompany.com
   Base DN: cn=People,dc=mycompany,dc=com
   Scope: subtree
   Search Filter: (objectclass=person)

Example of default referral in URL form

In the first search, server1.mycompany.com would find that the base DN was outside the namespace contained on the server. The server would then check all referrals within the scope to locate the appropriate namespace. In this case, it happens to have a default referral to the namespace in question, and it will pass this referral back to the client. The referral will take the following form:

```
ldap://rebelscum.org/ou=People,dc=rebelscum,dc=org??
    one?objectclass=person
```

Note that the referral is passed in URL form. This format allows both the hostname and other pertinent LDAP information to be communicated. Note that the same scope is carried forward on the referral. The client will use this referral to search rebelscum.org. The Mon Mothma person entry should be returned as a result of this process. Had the original base DN been `cn=Fred Flintstone,dc=Bedrock,dc=gov`, the default referral to the rebelscum.org server still would have been passed to the client. The client would fail to find Fred's entry, but the referral would still be passed. The default referral is the last resort, so to speak, and is passed when the directory doesn't have any valid reference to the namespace desired.

In the second search, the client has contacted server1.mycompany.com and would like all person entries below the People container in the mycompany.com namespace. The server responds with a list of the two person entries contained on the server (person1 and person2), as well as two separate referrals:

Example of multiple referrals on a search

```
ldap://deathstar.net/ou=People,dc=deathstar,dc=net??
    sub?objectclass=person
ldap://server2.mycompany.com/ou=People,dc=mycompany,
    dc=domain,dc=com??sub?objectclass=person
```

The LDAP client then chases these referrals. The server2.mycompany.com server reports three person entries (Miss Piggy, Gonzo, and Swedish Chef), while the deathstar.net server reports one entry (Darth Vader). The LDAP client reports the results (six entries) from all three servers in a response and indicates successful completion after all the referrals have been chased, and there are no outstanding server responses.

Chaining

Chaining can also provide a way to connect LDAP servers together. *Chaining* is similar to referrals, except that the server initially contacted by the client chases the referrals for the client and provides a complete response to the client, instead of making the client chase referrals and compose this complete response. This approach results in a more efficient response time for the client, but it places additional burden on the server. Chaining is not part of the LDAP standard, and it is not widely implemented by vendors. The chaining concept comes from the

With chaining, the server chases the referrals

Referral Usage

You should carefully think out use of referrals. As you might realize by this point, you could create a complex web of referrals, adding administrative headaches and poor client response. A referral loop in which a client chases a referral back to the originating namespace is just one of the possible snares that could be deadly. A wise directory administrator limits referrals to the root of other directory servers, or at least to significant naming contexts. To avoid referral problems, devote the effort to fully understand the architecture of the external directory. It may also be beneficial to have a similar structural architecture in all the directories that are connected by referrals. Other facilities exist to redirect searches to the same directory server, so resist using referrals for this purpose. Finally, don't forget that external directories probably employ different methods of access control. In general, most LDAP clients use the same bind credentials provided in the originating search when chasing referrals. The architecture you hope to use should be well planned out, so your user community won't be bothered with cryptic authentication errors and slow response.

Extending LDAP Beyond the Norm

One example of work to extend the usefulness of LDAP is the European-based project group DESIRE. DESIRE completed a software toolkit in the year 2000 that enables independent LDAP directories to be integrated into regional (or political) LDAP index servers. The index servers are an entry point for all LDAP clients in that region, holding just the name of each entry and a referral to the server holding that entry. Furthermore, the index servers are fully integrated with the Web, extending the accessibility of the data to Web search engines. This work solves two issues: unifying disparate directory namespaces, and simplifying the problem of how a client finds information in directory servers. However, adoption of this solution hasn't been impressive—probably because these issues aren't seen as critical problems in need of solutions. For a different approach to the same problems, see Chapter 6.

X.500 directory standard, and you may find that LDAP directory implementations that are also X.500 compliant may support chaining. Some LDAP vendors implemented chaining support during the LDAP v2 timeframe, and this support was called *server-side referral handling.*

Aliases

Aliases are another concept inherited from the X.500 standards. An *alias* is a special type of entry that provides a redirection mechanism to an entry in the same directory. The alias is a "dummy" record that simply points to a "real" record, which is called the target of the alias. An alias differs from a referral conceptually in three ways. First, an alias can point at only another entry within the same directory. A referral can do this as well, but it can also point to other directories (or any valid URL destination). Second, an alias can point at only a single entry. In contrast, a referral can point at a single entry, an entire directory, or something between. A referral can be very complex when a filter is used. Third, the server resolves the alias, while a client must chase referrals. There are a few other differences between a referral and alias that I'll cover later, but these are the primary ones. So an alias is simple in contrast, but still useful.

An alias provides a means to refer to a single entry

An alias provides a useful means of placing an entry in two or more locations in the directory. The LDAP namespace prohibits a Web-like structure; but by using an alias, you can circumvent this restriction for a single entry. This functionality can help to eliminate problems that a structure introduces. For example, Luke Skywalker's person entry might belong in both the Sales and Marketing OUs because he fills two functional roles for Mycompany. But these functional roles are not under the same branch in the directory, so this isn't possible. The alias solves this problem; an alias could be placed in one of the OUs and the real entry placed in the other OU. Aliases are not specifically documented in the LDAP RFC standards. The LDAP RFC

Aliases allow an entry to be in two places at once

standards refer to the possibility of their use but do not require that an LDAP server implementation support them. The LDAP standards also reference the X.500 documentation regarding aliases. Mycompany will keep alias support on its list of items to check when examining LDAP vendor implementations.

The alias name is different from the target name

An alias entry can have a different RDN than the target entry. This provides a layer of abstraction for protecting names that require privacy. The alias with an abstracted name can be located in a container with public access, while the entry with a private name resides in another hidden container. The user never knows about the real entry's private name and assumes the alias's public name is the real thing.

Aliases are good only for searches

Aliases redirect the client only on the LDAP search operation. Modify and delete operations are performed on the alias entry itself to allow you to make changes to it. The add operation also does not redirect aliases. This setup may sound like nonsense, but an example will illustrate the point. If an add operation created an entry beneath an alias that targeted a container, the operation would place the new entry not in the targeted container, but instead beneath the alias.

Should I Use an Alias or a Referral?

The fact that add, modify, and delete operations do not follow aliases is significant when you consider whether to use an alias or a referral to implement a redirection. Referrals are preferred in almost all cases. You should always use referrals for containers, and only consider aliases for entries that will be searched and not changed in any way. Aliases are primarily useful for situations like the Luke Skywalker example. An alias lets you circumvent a structural limitation of LDAP, so an entry can seem to have relationships that aren't normally allowed. For example, an entry with an alias seems to have two parents, one for the real entry and one for the alias.

The LDAP server resolves aliases differently depending on the client configuration. The client must also specify whether the server should *dereference* the alias. One of the LDAP search parameters designates the behavior the server should use in handling aliases. These parameters are covered in Chapter 3. You should be aware of the default setting of this parameter for the client implementation deployed, so the desired behavior is taken without the need to manually designate the parameter on each search operation.

Alias behavior is influenced by client search parameters

Distributed Directory

A *distributed directory* service employs more than a single server to provide service to clients. These multiple directory servers can contain identical information, or only part of the whole directory. The reasons to distribute an LDAP directory across multiple servers are many and varied. This design allows regional specific directory entries to be placed on a server local to the region and supports physically separate servers for management by different political departments within the same organization. You can achieve a distributed directory with referrals or with replication.

A distributed directory can improve service

Figure 5-4 shows a distributed directory with people entries based in distinct regions as well as political departments divided across different servers. Recall that Mycompany had a reorganization that placed the Customer Contact information managed by the Sales department under the People information managed by the Human Resources department. After this reorganization, the Sales department received a separate directory server (customers.mycompany.com) for the customer contact information. The directory implementation with this new server is shown in Figure 5-4. Additionally, the people at Muppet headquarters are all on the server2.mycompany.com server, to consolidate the administration duties at Muppet headquarters to a single server.

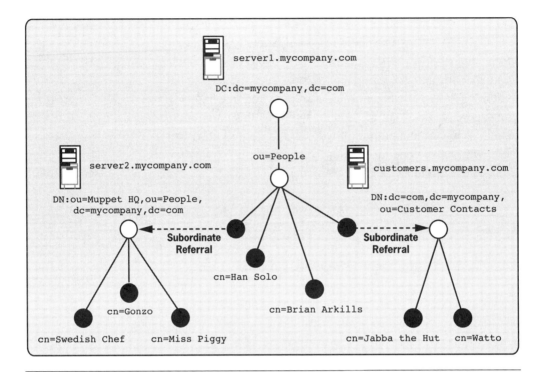

Figure 5-4   Distributed directory by region and political division

Reliability

A distributed direc-
tory increases ser-
vice reliability

Distribution across multiple servers can improve the client's perception of availability and reliability by distributing the operational load. Distribution of the directory can also decrease the risk of service outage or data loss by replicating the entire directory partition to multiple servers. For example, the people located at Muppet headquarters might see improved directory performance because their directory data is kept on a server local to their site.

Replication
achieves distribu-
tion with a
minimum of
administrative
overhead

In most cases, distributing an LDAP directory across multiple servers is preferable because of the associated management benefits. Centralization of resources increases the impact of service outages, but distributing the service across multiple servers can decrease this overall risk. In particular, replication of the di-

rectory is valuable because it distributes the points of failure
while keeping management of the directory simple.

Replication Topology

Figures 5-5 and 5-6 show distributed directories with single-
master and multimaster replication, respectively.

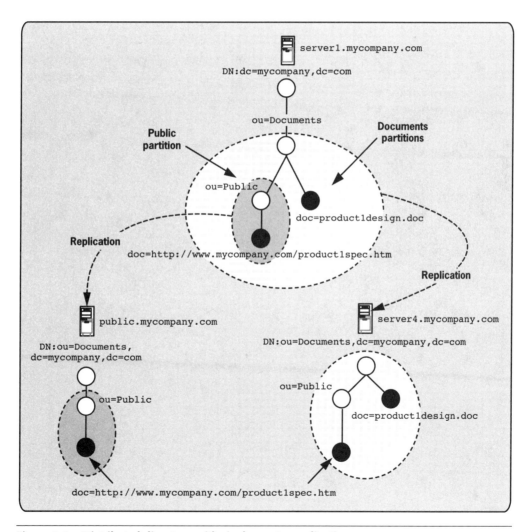

Figure 5-5   Distributed directory with single-master replication

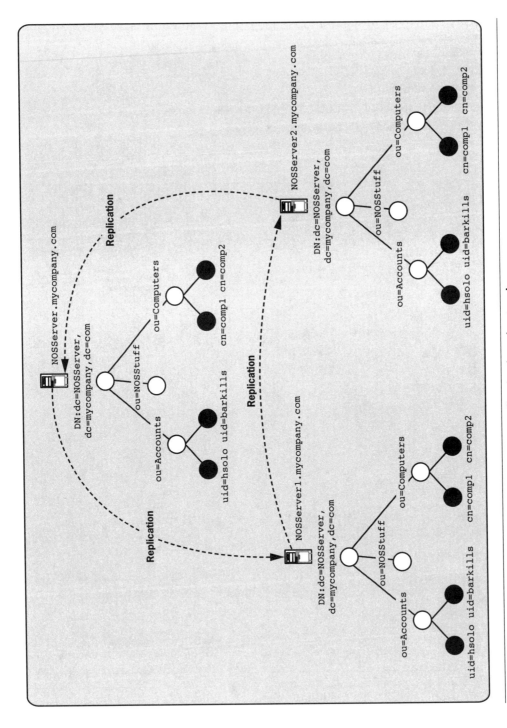

Figure 5-6   Distributed directory with multimaster replication in a ring topology

You can more easily accomplish server and directory maintenance if the directory is distributed via replication. Distribution
across multiple servers can also happen because of organizational circumstances such as the merger of two companies. The
issues associated with integrating two initially disparate LDAP
directories with one another are addressed later in the chapter.

*Replication makes
distribution easy*

The flexibility of the directory namespace means that replication
can be creatively used to distribute information. In Figure 5-5, the
Documents naming context on server1.mycompany.com is used
as a partition in a single-master replication model to two different
directory servers. The two replica servers serve different purposes
and have slightly different partitions replicated. The entire
Documents partition is replicated to server4.mycompany.com to
provide load balancing for company employees who use the directory heavily to work with documents. The Public partition is
replicated to the public.mycompany.com server. This server allows anonymous access to public clients, and all public information, such as the public documents, can be replicated to it. Other
public information, such as public calendar events, might also be
replicated to it even though this isn't shown in Figure 5-5. If public calendar events were replicated to this server, the best approach would be to have a second top-level naming context for
these entries. Although all the examples so far have only a single
top-level naming context, more than one top-level naming context can exist. For example, the directory products discussed in
the last three chapters (Part II) all have multiple top-level naming
contexts. Also note that the top-level naming context on the public server is not identical to the other server namespaces. There is
no requirement that all distributed directory servers have an identical top-level namespace.

*The directory
namespace flexibil-
ity plus replication
can combine into
creative solutions*

In Figure 5-6, the Mycompany's NOS directory (see Figure 5-1)
is shown in more detail. There are three directory servers in a
ring replication topology in the NOS directory, which means
that changes made at any of the servers will be propagated to
the others. This arrangement provides load balancing for the

NOS directory that is heavily used daily to support computer services, authentication, and other infrastructure at Mycompany. There is a brief lag before a change is propagated across all the servers, and a vendor-specific change-tracking system ensures that the last change made to any particular entry is the one that wins. You may recall that portions of the NOS directory have replication relationships with the Mycompany central directory. As a refresher, the Computers naming context in the NOS directory is a replica of the Computers partition in the central directory, whereas the Accounts naming context shares a multimaster replication relationship with the central directory. These replication relationships help to ensure that the relevant information in the NOS directory is integrated with other business systems at Mycompany. What is noteworthy about the replication between the NOS directory and the central Mycompany directory is that replication can occur across directories with different topologies and partitions employed.

Maintenance

Sometimes replication creates greater maintenance requirements

In some instances, replicating a directory across multiple servers is not a good thing. These instances typically are related to protecting the access and integrity of directory data. For example, if your directory data includes security information such as account passwords or private certificate keys, you may want to limit the number of servers this critical information is stored on, especially if the physical security of the directory servers can't be guaranteed. The security of distributed directory servers should not be ignored. Another example of when replication wouldn't be a good idea is when connectivity between directory servers is poor or bandwidth is low. The value of the directory depends on the quality and timeliness of the data it holds. When replication cannot complete in a timely manner, users will complain.

Maintenance on a distributed directory may have additional costs

A directory that is distributed in a nonreplicated manner may have additional maintenance costs. A good example of such a situation is a directory with distributed naming contexts based on the geographical location. This directory may require data maintenance tasks that affect all these regional directory servers. For example, a schema modification that affects the entire directory might require a modification on each directory server. Coordination and implementation of these tasks would be more challenging.

Integrating Independent Directories

LDAP provides a directory standard that cuts across platform divisions and seems to provide an interoperable panacea for your enterprise. But in actual implementation, this is messier than it seems. Frequently, vendors implement a product that makes use of LDAP, but in a very narrow way. For example, a vendor product might run only in a proprietary directory or with a specific nonstandard schema. There are network operating system directories based on LDAP that are designed to support only a single operating system or with key functionality that works only if the directory is on a specific platform, as well as application products with a standalone application directory that is designed for that application's use. The examples are numerous and annoy the practical nature in all of us.

Vendors create management problems when they implement standalone LDAP directories

Because we want our directories to be centralized so data is consistent and up-to-date, managing these disparate directories poses a problem. This is the problem that the *metadirectory* products try to solve; and regardless of whether you use metadirectories, you need good approaches to solving this integration problem.

Disparate directories pose a problem of management

The following section on integration addresses practical implementation concerns instead of analyzing how the technology works, as the rest of the book does. Here I focus on the abstract approach and concepts behind directory integration instead of trying to cover every possible permutation of integration scenarios. This section looks at the roles involved in directory integration, forms a set of questions about directory data usage that will be invaluable to you as you design a real-world architecture, looks briefly at metadirectories as a possible instant solution, and finally examines the common approaches used to integrate disparate directories. Appendix C includes the real-world example of Stanford University's existing directory integration, which illustrates most, if not all, of the concepts introduced here.

Data Architecture Management

You can employ many different products to meet the business needs of your organization. Weaving these products together into a distributed directory service so the data each product uses is shared and consistent is the ultimate goal of integration. Distinguishing sets of data, the source of each set, uses of each set, and any special concerns is critical to finding successful solutions. This process of creating a *data architecture* for a distributed directory may involve more than finding just technical solutions, because the data sets may have political or legal issues that govern their use. Business policies about the use of some data may be needed, as well as development or purchase of software solutions to help manage data consistency. Figure 5-7 shows a directory at the center of an enterprise data architecture at Mycompany. The following sections refer to this diagram.

Sources and Owners

Where does the data come from?

Consider carefully the *source* of the data to be managed. The data may come from several different sources. Some data may come from a Human Resources system. Other data may come from a certificate authority. Mycompany may have multiple suborganizations that are sources of data for the directory. The source of data is critical to the design of an integrated solution.

Who "owns" the data?

A person or division within Mycompany may be given the responsibility of handling a set of data. Noting ownership of sets of data is critical to an integrated design, because the *owner* may

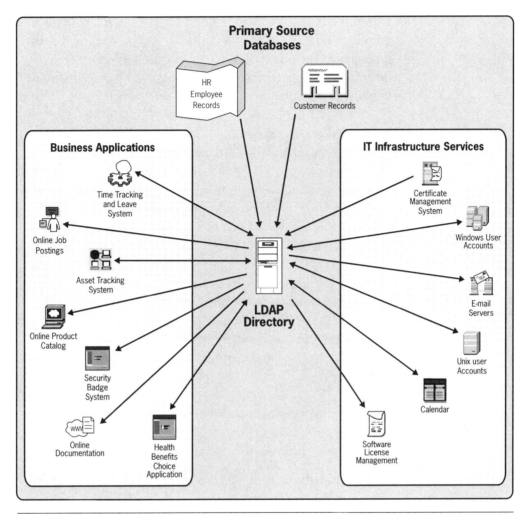

Figure 5-7   Directory at center of enterprise data architecture

want to restrict where that data is replicated, and how it can be accessed. The owner may also have special privacy concerns about access to the data. In cases of overlapping data sources, the owner is the arbiter of what information is authoritative.

Sometimes the nature of the data determines whether it can be distributed across multiple servers. For example, distributing

What is the data?

shared secret key information or passwords has many implications regarding the level of security needed on each of the distributed servers. Some data related to people is considered private. For example, users would complain if salary information were distributed across directory servers needlessly.

Subscribers and Consumers

Who/what needs the data?

Consumers of data can be services, users, or business systems that provide a critical administrative task. The consumer needs access to data and performs actions based on that data. For example, an HR application at Mycompany might query the directory for all the person entries and print a physical phone book. In contrast, a *subscriber* is another directory service or application that other consumers use to access the data that is passed to the subscriber. For example, an e-mail service at Mycompany might offer an organization-wide address book. This address book service might periodically pull person entry information from the directory to republish this information to e-mail clients. But the difference between consumers and subscribers is slight.

Evaluating the needs of consumers includes examining

- How consumers use the data

- What access controls consumers use on any subsequent products or data

- How to manage authoritative data modification

An example of this evaluation process illustrates the interdependencies that are involved. The basic questions that an administrator at Mycompany might ask are noted in italics.

What products or systems need to have access to which data sets? Let's say an e-mail system needs access to portions of the human resource data, including the person's name, contact information, and particularly e-mail address.

How will a consumer service or product use the data that it has access to? Specifically, how does the e-mail system use this data? It might publish an e-mail address book, and by doing so expose users to undesirable spam or violate privacy policies. Clearly this use needs to be accounted for, and you need to ask the following:

Will a consumer service apply a consistent level of access control to the data? Some access controls might limit who can view this address book, or whether someone is put into the address book at all.

Will the consumer service want to make changes to the data? Specifically, what if users of the e-mail system want to update their e-mail address data via the e-mail system? Changes to the local copy of data need to be reconciled with the authoritative source.

How does the consumer service manage data modification? Does the service redirect the user's changes directly to the source, or are local changes reconciled somehow with the directory service? If the e-mail service uses LDAP, we might be able to use a referral to redirect client modifications to the source; but otherwise, we may need to disallow direct modifications within the address book or design our own process to push changes back to the source directory. Clearly, the consumers of data are also critical to the design of an integrated solution.

Privacy Concerns

Many organizations have privacy statements about personal information, legal regulations on certain information, or critical business reasons that necessitate protecting data in their directory. Governments, hospitals, and educational institutions all have federal restrictions (some with jail time for offenses) for publishing sensitive data that might be stored in a directory. The *Family Educational Rights* and *Privacy Act of 1974 (FERPA)* and *Health Insurance Portability and Accountability Act of 1996*

The privacy of data in a directory can be a legal issue

(HIPAA) are two examples of legislation that mandates privacy protections on some personal data. These types of restrictions typically allow sensitive data to be used to support business functions, but not beyond these functions.

Some vendors disregard privacy legal issues

A vendor implementation might make the establishment of privacy protection more difficult. Some vendors design the default schema in a way that undermines modifications that would support privacy. Others assume that some information is public that your organization (or the federal government via legislation) considers private. Imagine that the RDN for a person entry is forced to be the person's name and this attribute is assumed to be public in order for the product to work successfully. In other words, the directory doesn't allow access controls that restrict naming attributes. This design is clearly unacceptable, and Mycompany will avoid products with such privacy issues.

Metadirectories: Glue Together Your Directories

Metadirectories promise to seamlessly integrate these standalone directories, but they may not stand the test of time

Metadirectories promise to solve the issue of managing many disparate directories by seamlessly integrating the data among them. Products take diverse approaches to this task. This area is still in the early stages of maturity, despite several years of product launches. The challenge of integrating standalone directories involves complex issues that are not simple to solve.

Tread Lightly as a Directory Administrator

Determining where to draw the line and establishing clear access controls to implement privacy restrictions are tasks sometimes left to the directory administrator when the organization's leadership doesn't address privacy in a clear and specific policy. The directory administrator should therefore be cognizant of privacy issues and push for a business policy to govern what is implemented. Take implementation of privacy controls seriously or your organization will be embarrassed.

Learning a metadirectory product is not simple and in most cases requires special training. Most metadirectories require additional custom extension via scripts to deal with the business rules needed. Because of all these factors, metadirectory products may fail completely, and the basic approaches employed by metadirectories may instead become the common solution deployed by organizations. In other words, some organizations may choose to develop their own custom metadirectory that uses many of the same approaches.

Many of the companies that offered these products a few years ago are now out of business, and more may follow. Therefore, this discussion focuses on the basic concepts and architectures used by metadirectories rather than on specific products. You can use these concepts when your organization looks at metadirectory products to solve your directory integration problems. You should realize that no standard currently addresses this area, and there is very little public information available. The alternative to buying a metadirectory product is to develop and maintain a custom solution to meet your needs.

Metadirectories aren't standardized, but the discussion here should help you understand the products

Master Directory

This approach involves taking each existing directory service and integrating it as a part of a *master directory* service. The master directory might be one of the existing directories, based on some choice by your organization, perhaps the one that is most used or with the best integration functionality. Or the master directory might be a new directory with no data of its own. The end result is that all the directory services can be accessed from the master directory, and from the user standpoint the directories are merged into one. A master directory that supports both X.500 and LDAP will accommodate the widest range of technology. Existing standalone directories are integrated with LDAP referrals and chaining. The master directory server returns LDAP referrals to the client, directing the client to the correct directory server for the question being asked. Figure 5-8 shows

Referrals and chaining can glue standalone directories together into a master directory

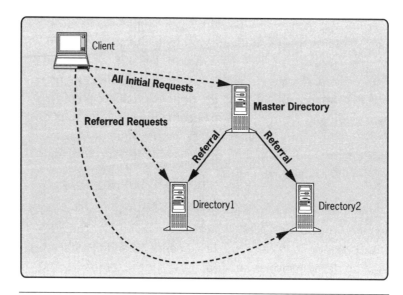

Figure 5-8   Master directory architecture

how this configuration works conceptually. Alternatively, with chaining the master directory server connects to the LDAP server on behalf of the client.

Index directories only hold referrals and become a single entry point for many directories

Some organizations and indeed some countries go a step further and implement what are called directory index servers. These index servers hold referrals to many independent directories rather than data. Clients can use these index servers to find information across all the linked directories. In other words, each entry in an independent directory has a corresponding referral entry in the index server, in an identical hierarchy to that of the independent directory. The index server then becomes a one-stop destination for many directories. Index servers represent the same idea as a master directory, but they may implement additional functionality, such as a gateway for the Web so search engines can access the data in all the indexed directories.

Implementing a master directory is not trivial

Creating a master directory or index directory can require quite a bit of work. The independent directories must support some common authentication method so clients are not required to authenticate multiple times. Additionally, the authorization model employed on each directory should be similar, so a user doesn't have widely different experiences while being redirected.

Earlier in this chapter I referred to the Dante DESIRE project that provided resources to implement an index server with these types of functionality. Additionally, some vendors are beginning to implement this type of functionality. Microsoft, for example, implements a simple version of an index server (which they call a global catalog) with Active Directory.

There are resources available to help implement an index server

Directory Synchronization

This approach allows the multiple directories to exist but works to share the information between them via *directory synchronization.* In other words, the directory entries or the data in those entries is copied from one directory to another. You can employ different techniques to share data between directory services, but generally there is duplication of data. It doesn't matter that there are multiple directories because the data in each is centrally available. The end result of this approach is that the multiple directory services share common data. The user perception is that each of the directories contains the same information. Figure 5-9 demonstrates how this approach is configured. When the business needs that mandate the different directory servers (or vendors) evaporate, eliminating the unnecessary server is simple with this approach because the data has been duplicated already.

Synchronization can glue stand-alone directories together into a master directory

Creating a directory synchronization mechanism can be simple if a common schema is shared. Both directories should also share a common method of synchronization. For example, replication, LDIF, or DSML can be used as a method of synchronization. If both directories support a common way to move directory data between them, some automation can be

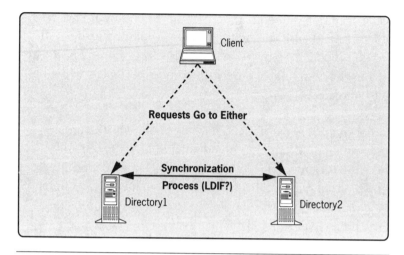

Figure 5-9   Directory synchronization

introduced, which makes management much easier. The topic of moving data across directories is discussed later in this chapter.

Loose Directory Interconnection

Clever user inter-faces can make users unaware of multiple directories

A loose directory interconnection approach leaves multiple directories with different information in place and provides the user with a convenient mechanism to access each of these independent services via a single interface (see Figure 5-10). The LDAP-enabled Web interface discussed in Chapter 3 is a good example of such an approach. *Loose directory interconnection* focuses on providing a common user interface to multiple directories. This approach is sometimes called a *gateway* or *proxy*. Many problems are left by this approach if it is used alone, as it doesn't unify the data in the separate directories into a consistent version. Providing only a common client interface to the independent data sets may be useful, though. Elimination of the work involved in integrating the disparate directories is usually at the cost of integration with client applications and services. However, the cost of educating users on multiple directories is reduced.

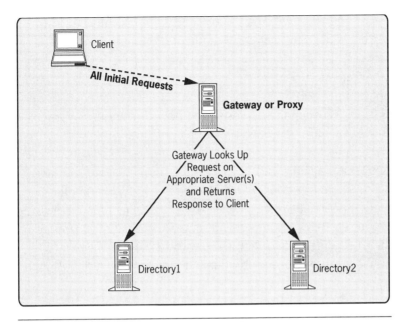

Figure 5-10   Loose directory interconnection

Harvesting Data (Connectors)

The data harvester approach is often used in conjunction with the prior approaches to build the specific architecture desired. The idea is to have LDAP-enabled software that *harvests* data from one directory to another. By harvest, I mean both a pull and push of data—a pull from one source directory and a push to a subscriber directory. This approach is also called *data brokering*, with the software agent called a *broker*.

I call this software a harvester because its primary function is to harvest data. Harvesters have only a slightly different effect than replication. Replication pushes an entire partition of data within a directory, whereas a harvester copies only a very specific subset of data. For example, a harvester might copy (or harvest) all entries with `objectclass=user` or entries in a specific container. Replication also differs from harvesting in that replication is initiated by one of the directory servers and is a server-to-

A harvester moves a specified set of data from one directory to another, but this is not replication

server operation. Whereas harvesting is intrinsically a client-server model, the harvester is a client of both directories. The software usually resides on a computer separate from the two LDAP directory servers it connects, which means an additional point of failure. Another implication is the need to encrypt the sessions between the harvester and both directories. Figure 5-11 shows how this approach might be configured.

Metadirectory products have harvesters called connectors, but you can build your own harvester

Almost all metadirectory products use a similar approach and call the software *connectors*. The term "connector" implies more functionality than the harvester, and in fact metadirectory products usually do implement more functionality—therefore the slight difference in terminology. A typical metadirectory connector provides the additional ability to map attributes with

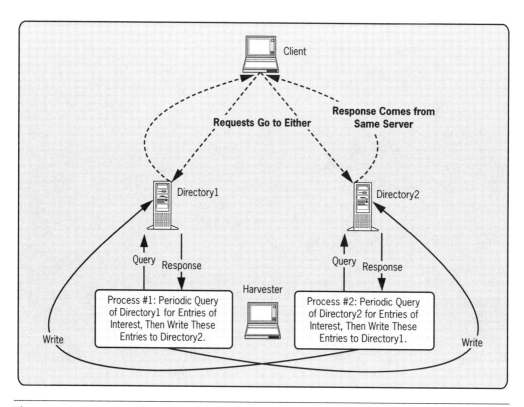

Figure 5-11   Harvester directory connection

different names between the two directories. Mycompany can build its own custom software to provide all this functionality, and creating a simple version isn't difficult. More complex functionality provided by a metadirectory might modify the attribute values to make them conform to a specific limitation between the two directories. The advantage of using a harvester or connector is that it is more configurable than replication, but it has the same disadvantage as replication in that it is time dependent and collisions are possible.

A harvester uses the LDAP operations to search for data in one directory and push it to another directory. This reliance on existing functions eases the creation of a custom harvester. This is also why a harvester is considerably more flexible than replication. The harvester can specify distinct sets of data by using complex search filters and base DNs that aren't the same as a partition. However, if either the source or subscriber is not an LDAP directory, building a harvester is obviously more complex.

Harvesters use the LDAP APIs and are more flexible than replication

A harvester has one critical problem. It is time dependent. A harvester can copy data between directories, but it needs either some intelligent way to determine when to harvest or notification that the data it is interested in has changed. There are several solutions to this problem, depending on the sophistication needed.

The harvester must solve the problem of getting notified of changes

One solution is to simply harvest on a periodic basis. Mycompany must live with the possibility that data could be inconsistent and unreliable between these periodic updates. This approach is the same as the most basic replication technologies. Another solution is to use an LDAP control. Chapter 3 describes three LDAP controls—PSEARCH, TSEARCH, and DIRSYNC—that can be used to notify the harvester of directory changes. Some of these controls have the added benefit of being able to distinguish important information about directory changes. Some products support one of these controls. In the future, the IETF LCUP effort should produce a standard that helps address this issue.

Three solutions lend themselves to this problem

Another solution involves implementing an event database to track changes. This solution is applicable only in an environment in which all changes to the master directory are tracked. For more detail on this kind of solution, see Appendix C, which describes the directory architecture and harvesters at Stanford University.

Moving Data Between Directories

Aside from using a connector or harvester to move data between directories, you can take advantage of two file format standards that enable bulk importation and exportation of directory data or bulk modifications of existing directory data. Almost all LDAP directories provide support for LDIF, and an overwhelming majority of vendors have committed to supporting DSML. Both these standards define file formats for representing the directory data in an easily transmittable format. Neither of these standards addresses how an LDAP directory should provide support for operations that import or export these formats. For these formats to be truly valuable in automating directory integration across vendors, some standardization of the operational aspect of these formats is needed.

LDIF

LDIF is a file format for LDAP directory entries

LDIF stands for the LDAP Data Interchange Format. LDIF is used to represent the entries of an LDAP directory or a set of changes to an LDAP directory in a text-based file format. You can use LDIF for a variety of management functions, including directory backup, replication, schema modifications, and bulk import or modifications of directory information.

LDIF allows complex manipulations on large sets of entries

Manipulation of directory information while it is in the LDIF format is much easier than in an LDAP directory. Text manipulation programming languages such as perl can be used to do

LDIF Standard

RFC 2849 standardizes the LDIF specification, but it doesn't address several points that I consider critical. For example, why isn't there a definition of the process for an LDAP server to import or export to this format? How should the directory treat error conditions that arise from an imported LDIF file? Can a client present an LDIF file? If so, how? Or is this considered an unacceptable security risk? Another basic, but unaddressed issue is whether an LDAP server should advertise support for LDIF. Allowing for flexibility in vendor implementations is good, but these omissions are disconcerting when you consider that LDIF is a key component in moving directory information between servers.

more complex operations and perform bulk modifications on many directory entries while they are in a text-based file format. The LDIF format lends itself to simplifying changes to data sets that would be more difficult without it. For example, imagine that Mycompany has moved to a new city. As the administrator, you need to modify the `postalCode` attribute of employees to `87345`, which is the postal code at the new site. Without LDIF, you could find all the entries with the `postalCode` set by using a presence filter (`postalCode=*`), but modifying all the entries would require painstaking work. With LDIF, you could dump all the entries to a file. Using perl or even a text editor like Microsoft Word, you could search and replace using the `postalCode` string as a match phrase.

The LDIF file format is specified in RFC 2849, and it is used to define an operation on an entry and the data elements needed for such operations. Each LDIF file can describe either LDAP directory entries or a set of changes to LDAP directory entries, but not both. If the LDIF file describes directory changes, each entry is preceded by a `changerecord` statement that indicates the LDAP operation associated with the entry that follows. Entries

The LDIF format can be used to request LDAP operations

are separated by a line separator, and comment lines are permitted. Controls can be specified in LDIF.

LDIF Examples

The easiest way to become familiar with LDIF is to view a few examples. As a point of reference, most of the example entries used in this book are represented in the LDIF format without the `changerecord` statement. For your convenience, some explanatory comments are interspersed in Examples 5-1 and 5-2.

Example 5-1   LDIF entry with folding and encoding in both base64 and UTF-8

```
version: 1
dn: cn=Han Solo, ou=People, dc=myserver, dc=domain, dc=com
objectclass: top
objectclass: person
objectclass: organizationalPerson
cn: Han Solo
sn: Solo
uid: hsolo
telephonenumber: +1 650 555 1212
# Comment lines are marked with a pound character
# Note that the postalAddress value is base64 encoded.
# This is noted by the double colon between type and value.
postalAddress:: NzIyLTM0MyBOZXJmaGVyZGVyIERpc3RyaWN0LCBDb3J1c2hhbnQ=
# Note the folding of a line that is too long, with a space to
# denote a continuation of the previous line.
description:Mister Solo is a retired smuggler, who loves to take
    unnecessary risks.
# Note the language code use, as well as the UTF8 encoding of the
# value. Spanish largely uses the ascii character set, but the ñ
# character in Señor is notably translated.
description;lang-es:: SeÃ±or el Solo es un contrabandista jubilado,
    que ama de tomar los riesgos innecesarios.
```

Example 5-2   LDIF file containing a series of change records including use of a control

```
version: 1
# Add an entry
dn: cn=Mara Skywalker, ou=People, dc=myserver, dc=domain, dc=com
changetype: add
objectclass: top
objectclass: person
```

```
objectclass: organizationalPerson
cn: Mara Skywalker
sn: Skywalker
sn: Jade
uid: mara
jpegphoto:[left] file:///bin/photos/mara.jpg
# Note that URLs are supported

# Delete an entry
dn: cn=Chewbacca, ou=People, dc=myserver, dc=domain, dc=com
changetype: delete

# Modify a relative distinguished name
dn: cn=Part2, ou=Xwing Parts, ou=Parts, dc=myserver, dc=domain, dc=com
changetype: modrdn
newrdn: cn=Hyperdrive spanner
deleteoldrdn: 1

# Rename an entry and move all of its children to a new location
dn: ou=Droid Parts, ou=Xwing Parts, ou=Parts, dc=myserver, dc=domain,
    dc=com
changetype: modrdn
newrdn: ou=Droids
deleteoldrdn: 0
newsuperior: ou=People, dc=myserver, dc=domain, dc=com

# Modify an entry: add an additional value to the postaladdress
# attribute, completely delete the description attribute, and
# delete a specific value from the organization attribute
dn: cn=Luke Skywalker, ou=People, dc=myserver, dc=domain, dc=com
changetype: modify
add: postaladdress
postaladdress: 1 Jedi Academy $ Old Temple $ Yavin 4
-
delete: description
-
replace: title
title: Jedi Knight
title: Jedi Master
-
delete: o
o: Rebel Alliance

# Delete a container and all subordinate entries with the
# Tree Delete control. The criticality field is "true" so the
# operation will fail if the control isn't supported.
dn: ou=Xwing Parts ou=Parts, dc=myserver, dc=domain, dc=com
control: 1.2.840.113556.1.4.805 true
changetype: delete
```

DSML

DSML represents directory data in an XML language intended for browsers

Directory Services Markup Language (DSML) is the proposed XML open standard for directories. *XML* is a metalanguage used to represent data in a text-based format. The format is very similar to HTML, because they both use tags, but it is not HTML. XML is not meant for human consumption; rather, it is code. XML is generally more readable than typical code, but its power lies in its flexibility. DSML is simply a specific set of recommendations that translate an XML document into something meaningful to a directory. And a directory might create an XML document as output to a client or in a batch dump like LDIF.

DSML has widespread vendor support

DSML is supported by significant software companies like IBM, Microsoft, Novell, Oracle, and Netscape, which also happen to be the leading LDAP directory vendors. DSML seeks to represent not only directory data in terms of XML but also LDAP directory operations. DSML v1 defines the directory data structures that can be employed, and DSML v2 defines the LDAP operations.

Directory operations can also be represented in DSML

Representing directory operations in a textual format is not unique, as the LDIF standard also represents directory operations in this format. In fact, the approach taken is strikingly similar to LDIF, except DSML has a clear operational model whereas LDIF does not. DSML uses the HTTP protocol for operation, whereas LDIF has nothing. DSML v2 lets you send one or more operations in a single request document, and a single response document returns the results of these operations. Two bindings (or transport mechanisms) have been defined for DSML v2 so far: Simple Object Access Protocol (SOAP) and files. SOAP uses an XML encoding of a request and response to deliver a message over a protocol such as HTTP.

DSML enables organizations to easily build Web-based applications that leverage the directory

DSML allows Web-based applications to easily integrate with a directory. As a result, Web developers don't have to find a way to represent or format directory data. Using the XML language, they can take advantage of the DSML components to represent directory data within their Web-based applications. Users see a consistent data format, and they don't have to wait for a more lengthy development process. DSML should open another way for disparate directories to easily communicate and represent data in each other. Novell's eDirectory already has an XML interface that allows XML-based LDAP operations, and several other vendors have incorporated support in their SDKs or via gateway products that act as a middle-tier interface. It will be only a matter of time before all the directories adopt DSML functionality.

Note that DSML is only a language, and as such it is only a tool that can be used with one of the approaches just described. But clearly, DSML should eventually make the job of a metadirectory, whether it be a product or a custom solution, much easier. You can find out more about DSML at http://www.dsml.org and http://www.oasis-open.org/committees/dsml/. Keep your eye on this technology and on how it affects directory functionality. Clearly the potential to make a directory interoperate better with other technology is significant.

DSML requires programming to be used

Directory Security

Securing an LDAP directory is a significant concern. It was such a significant concern for the IETF that the existing LDAP v3 standards were "marred" with a warning note indicating that the standard did not address security. Fortunately, several LDAP v3 standard documents have emerged since then to address this oversight. RFC 3377 removed the warning by revising the standard to include these later documents that address security.

The LDAP v3 standard was marred by lack of security

Computer security is concerned with several primary concepts. One is the idea of proving who you are. This is called *authentication*, and usually there are two parties involved with a third party of mutual trust. Another is the idea of assigning certain access rights or privileges to someone, and requiring certain rights to access resources or perform actions on resources. This is

Authentication, authorization, and encryption are common ways to provide security

called *authorization*, and it usually involves something called the *ACL*, or *access control list*, which holds the authorization information. Another is the idea of transmitting or storing data securely so it is kept private. This is called *encryption*, and it usually involves a *public-private key technology*.

RFCs 2829 and 2830 standardize security recommendations for LDAP

These basic security concepts are addressed in two RFCs: RFC 2829 and RFC 2830. RFC 2830 addresses the specifics of data encryption issues via the Transport Layer Security (TLS) standard, while RFC 2829 standardizes a minimum set of requirements for authentication, authorization, and encryption depending on the intended use of an LDAP directory. Because RFC 2829 comes late in the development of the LDAP standard, it is understandably more abstract as it seeks to maintain interoperability between existing implementations, while establishing a minimum set of security standards. The RFC does an excellent job of addressing these issues, and it is successful in providing some specific recommendations.

Authentication

Authentication establishes identity

Authentication is the process of asserting and proving that you are who you say you are. In other words, it establishes the identity of a client. This identity in general terms is known as the *authentication identity*, but in practice it is usually a username, user identity (uid), ticket, or certificate. Authentication is a fairly complex process, because it involves multiple parties and those parties generally must trust a third party as the authority for establishing (in other words, verifying) identity. The verification stage usually involves a password, but different authentication schemes use the password in different ways.

Password-based authentication methods are generally less secure

The less secure authentication methods communicate the password in some form to the party that is verifying identity. The basic authentication method (known as cleartext) does this, as do several other methods that use an encryption algorithm to make the password harder for malicious listeners to decode. These types of methods are less secure because a malicious listener can capture the password even if it is encrypted and eventually decode it for personal use.

Some methods of shared secret authentication methods don't transmit the password on the wire. These authentication methods are considered secure, because it is much harder to steal someone else's identity. Kerberos is one example of this type of authentication method, as is DIGEST-MD5. Generally speaking, the party that verifies identity and the user share a secret (a password). The user enters the password, but the process on his computer doesn't send this password. Instead, it uses the password to encrypt and decrypt a challenge and response from the party that verifies identity. This party has assurance that only someone who knows the shared secret can pass the challenge.

Some password-based authentications are more secure by design

Public-private key authentication methods are considered more secure, because they do not subject a password to transport. These methods protect the password by using an encryption algorithm that uses the password as the private key to encode and decode nonsensitive information that is communicated. In this way, the password is never exposed because the server-authority doesn't know it (it knows the public key) and the local client never communicates the password.

Public key authentication methods are more secure

RFC 2829 proposes specific authentication requirements for specific circumstances. Public directories that allow only read operations can use anonymous authentication. *Anonymous authentication* occurs when a client has not successfully completed an LDAP bind operation or has completed one using empty credentials. Nonpublic directories that support the range of LDAP client operations should support both TLS data encryption as well as SASL authentication.

Both SASL and TLS are recommended by RFC 2829

However, supporting these technologies does not mean that access requires their use, or that trivial encryption is what is employed. For example, there is an anonymous SASL mechanism

You should use a strong authentication method

that provides no better protection than no authentication at all. To address this, RFC 2829 imposes the following authentication requirements. Directories that support password-based authentication must support the DIGEST-MD5-SASL mechanism described in RFC 2831, and are encouraged to require this mechanism or a stronger one for access. This guideline helps to ensure that malicious intermediaries must spend a substantial amount of effort to compromise a password.

Authorization

Authorization determines access to a resource

Authorization is the process of establishing whether a client is authorized to access resources. Authorization can be determined by a combination of *access control factors* like authentication identity, source IP address, encryption strength, authentication method, operation requested, and resource requested.

Access control factors help determine the access control policy

An *access control policy* defines the restrictions on a resource. The access control policy is expressed in terms of the access control factors and the resources that are restricted. The common *access rights* available can vary from implementation to implementation, but Table 5-1 lists the typical rights employed. The rights listed apply to an entry, but most directories support setting access rights at the attribute or container level as well.

Inheritance makes access control management easier

It is also common for access control to be inherited by subordinate resources. In the context of a directory, access control inheritance would mean that access controls applied to a container would apply to all the entries under that container, including other containers and their subordinate entries. Applying access control to the logical root of a directory with inheritance would affect all the directory entries.

LDAP operations are easily linked to access control rights

One can see how applying the typical access rights listed in Table 5-1 to entries would affect how client operation requests were handled. An authorization identity (in other words, client user) might be permitted to read entries, and therefore success-

Table 5-1   Typical directory access rights

Access Right	Description
No Access	No access is allowed to this entry.
List	Enumerate name(s) of entry.
Read	Read attribute value of entry.
Add	Add a new entry or add new attributes to existing entry.
Modify	Modify the existing attributes of an entry.
Rename	Rename entry.
Delete	Delete entry.
Admin	Change the ACL of the entry.

fully complete an LDAP search operation; but that identity might not be permitted to modify entries and might fail to complete an LDAP modify operation. The typical access rights map fairly directly to LDAP operations.

A common implementation of the access control policy is the ACL. An ACL is associated with a resource to provide an access control policy. An ACL usually consists of a list of *access control entries (ACEs)*. Each ACE designates an authorization identity and access rights. An access control list is associated with a specific resource, and therefore the ACEs within that access control list designate what level of access any authorization identity has to that resource.

Access control lists link specific identities to specific access rights to a resource

Generally, an authorization identity is mapped to the authentication identity. This makes the most sense—if you are going to go to the trouble of authenticating a user, you might as well use that authentication identity. Usually the authentication identity is mapped to the DN of an entry that represents the person. RFC 2829 requires that an LDAP directory support DN mapping if a password or credentials are stored in the directory. However, the implementation doesn't have to actually do this mapping; it

The authentication identity is usually the authorization identity

just must support it. The mapping is usually a one-to-one relationship: one authentication identity to one DN. But it can be a
many-to-one relationship, with many authentication identities
mapping to a single DN.

The authorization identity can be many other access control factors

However, the authorization identity doesn't have to correspond
to the authentication identity at all. Other access factors, like
source IP, authentication method, encryption level, or membership in a group, can be used as the authorization identity.
Source IP as an authorization factor uses the IP of the client to
allow or deny the operation requested. This is less sophisticated
than using an authentication identity, because client IP addresses are easily spoofed, and IP addresses are not authenticated. Authentication method as an authorization factor uses
the method requested by the client to help determine whether
to allow an operation. For example, if a client uses cleartext authentication, the client might not be allowed to access any entries because of the poor security employed by the client. This
approach would help prevent malicious users impersonating
the client from accessing sensitive directory entries. Encryption
level is used as an authorization factor in a similar manner, if
you want some resources or operations to be more highly protected via encryption. When group membership is used as an
authorization identity, the DN that maps to the authentication
identity must be listed in the membership attribute of the group
entry. These methods are less commonly employed, but are
valuable factors in helping to secure resources. Sometimes they
are used in combination to provide a much more robust authorization control.

RFC 2829 recommends a few authorization requirements

RFC 2829 recommends very few authorization requirements.
RFC 2829 requires that the root DSE be available to anonymous
clients. Additionally, the RFC recommends that idle connections should be timed out, and expensive requests from unau-
thenticated clients should fail. The scarcity of authorization
requirements in the standard should not be considered poor,
because almost no authorization factors are required by the

standard, and more abstract recommendations allow different implementations to address authorization in the manner deemed most appropriate to the vendor. The standard does require that the authorization identity be supported by all implementations via the SASL authentication mechanism, and this provides for a clear point of interoperability between implementations.

Encryption

Encryption is the process of making the information passed between two parties private by use of a transformation of the information. This encryption protects all the data passed between these parties from snooping, and it provides a level of privacy. The value of this privacy is directly proportional to the strength of the encryption technology employed, and the algorithm used. The basics of encryption are presented here.

Encryption provides privacy

Any encryption is based on two elements, namely an algorithm and a key. The algorithm is a special mathematical function that transforms the data into an unintelligible form. There are many common algorithms that are publicly known and used. The fact that these algorithms are known does not affect the strength of the encryption, because the key forms the basis of the encryption strength.

Encryption strength is based on the algorithm used and the length of the key employed

The key is a special string that is used by the algorithm in the transformation process. The key can usually be used to transform the data both ways, but this isn't always true. The length of the key determines how many possible keys can be used with the encryption. For example, encryption with a key of 4-bit length would have only 16 possible keys. The length of the key determines the strength of the encryption. An encryption with a 4-bit key length would be considered so trivial that not even a calculator would be needed to break it. The recommended key length for a minimum strength is dependent on the processing power available. Several years ago a key length of

The key length is the basis of encryption strength

40 bits was considered strong enough, but no longer. You should choose the longest key length supported, taking the extra processing time to support encryption with a longer key into account. 128 bits is a common choice.

How Encryption Relates to LDAP Management

The encryption technologies described here relate to LDAP in two primary ways. First, LDAP client-server sessions transmit data across public wires. To ensure privacy of directory data, SSL or TLS must be employed. This implies that certificates for the LDAP directory must be supported and maintained on an ongoing basis. Optimally, you would also require that clients have their own certificates as well. In some instances, depending on the vendor product, this requirement may require implementing a certificate authority to provide the LDAP directory certificate. Second, certificate authorities need a place to store and publish certificates and certificate revocation lists. The LDAP directory fits this need very well. Encryption underlies any authentication that the directory requires for access. A good grasp of encryption will help guide implementation decisions that ensure the integrity of the directory data is reasonably protected.

For these reasons, LDAP directory administrators usually are familiar with the organization's encryption policies and PKI (public key infrastructure) architecture. Additionally, the directory administrator is likely to be in charge of managing certificates. In any event, a familiarity with encryption is worthwhile so the administrator has a sense of the strength of the privacy and access control LDAP can provide.

Shared Secret Key Encryption

Both parties share the same key in secret key encryption

Encryption in which the key can be used to both encrypt data and decrypt it is called *shared secret key encryption*. The key in this instance is known as a shared secret key. Shared secret key encryption generally requires very little processing time, which makes it attractive for encrypting large amounts of data.

We were talking about shared secret encryption when we discussed Kerberos and DIGEST-MD5 in the previous section, Authorization.

However, secret key encryption has a problem. How do the two parties decide on and communicate the shared secret key to each other? Without some prior encryption protecting their communication, it is difficult to share a secret key. This problem gets worse as one imagines all the parties one might wish to communicate with, and the number of different secret keys needed to support encrypted communication between all these parties. Usually scalability isn't a problem because a single authority holds all the shared secret keys, and everyone agrees to trust that single authority. However, that single authority and the party still must somehow communicate the secret they share. Public key encryption handles this issue.

Secret keys must be communicated safely and stored safely

Public Key Encryption

Public key encryption uses a pair of keys with an algorithm that has a special feature. The pair of keys consists of a public key and a private key. The *public key* is published for anyone to know, whereas the *private key* is kept secret from everyone but the user. Only the private key can decrypt data that is encrypted with the algorithm and the public key. Similarly, only the public key can decrypt data that is encrypted with the private key. Attempts to decrypt an encrypted message without the opposite paired key will fail. This technique solves the problem of distributing and choosing a key for the two parties, because the two parties don't share the same key. It doesn't matter who knows your public key, because the public key can't be used to impersonate you. Figure 5-12 shows the relationship of the pair of keys to the encryption process. All the arrows in Figure 5-12 going in a clockwise direction could just as easily go in a counterclockwise direction.

A pair of specially linked keys is used with public key encryption

Let's say I want to send a shared secret to you. I would encrypt the shared secret using my private key. This would indicate that

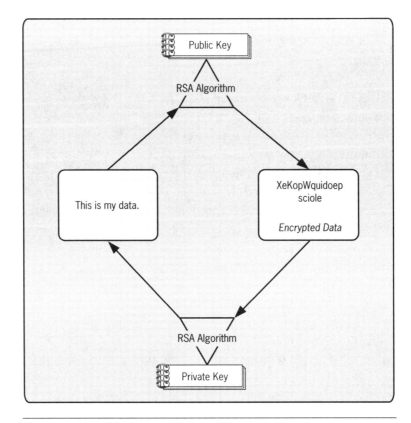

Figure 5-12   Public key encryption

the shared secret came from me. Then I'd encrypt the results of that with your public key. This would guarantee that only you could decrypt the shared secret.

Public key encryption is slower and requires an outside authority to verify identity

Public key encryption, however, has a few problems. It requires more significant processing time, so it is not ideal for encrypting large amounts of data. There is also an issue of authentication that is somewhat outside the scope of the problem it is designed to solve. Say I get an encrypted message from Bill Gates along with a public key. I decrypt it with the public key, and this proves that the person who sent it has the private key that corresponds to the public key. But it doesn't prove that the message was sent by Bill Gates. This problem is solved by certificates, which I discuss after looking at one particular use of public key encryption.

Digital Signatures

A digital signature for me connotes a picture of my signature scanned in a computer. Because my signature is illegible, I'm glad this isn't what digital signatures really are. A *digital signature* is a specific application of public key encryption. The idea is to encrypt a representation of the message and append it to the message to provide a measure of authentication, as well as proof that the message wasn't altered in transit.

Digital signatures provide authentication and data integrity to data messages

A special algorithm called a *hash function* takes the message and computes a brief string that is based on the message body. This string of characters is called a *message digest* or *checksum*. For example, one commonly used hash using SHA-1 results in a 20-byte message digest. The message digest is then encrypted with the private key and the result is appended to the end of the message. The recipient can use your public key to decrypt the appended message digest, compute a personal message digest of the body of the message, and compare the two results. Assuming they match, the recipient knows that you sent the message and that no one has tampered with the message in transit.

The encrypted message digest is the digital signature

Note that a digital signature does not encrypt the message. It does not provide privacy, but it is a way to provide message authentication and data integrity. However, there are several problems with digital signatures. For example, let's say the CEO of Mycompany sends an e-mail to Han Solo that says, "You're fired!" The CEO attaches his digital signature to verify that he sent it. Luke Skywalker just happens to intercept this e-mail. He saves the e-mail and later sends it to several other employees to trick them into thinking they have been fired. Unless the checksum protects the message header that includes the recipient and time, this scenario could happen. Also note that if the public

A digital signature does not provide privacy, nor does it prove identity without an outside authority source

key is sent along with the message, there still is no real verification of the identity of the sender. This is what certificates are
about. A digital signature is designed to provide authentication,
but one still needs a trusted authority to reliably associate the
key pair with a specific person.

Certificates and Certificate Authority

*Certificates map a
public key to an
identity. A CA is the
authority other par-
ties can trust*

Certificates associate a public key with an identity. To learn
more about certificates, review RFC 2459. As described in the
previous section, you need a trusted authority to manage these
certificates and assert that the certificate is valid, in other
words, that the public key is really associated with the identity.
This authority is called a *certificate authority* or *CA*.

*The CA issues cer-
tificates and places
its signature on
each as a mark of
authenticity*

Figure 5-13 shows a simplified representation of a CA and a
certificate. The CA issues certificates. The CA is in turn referenced as the source of authority in all certificates that the CA
has issued. A user can know that a CA really issued a certificate
because the CA puts its digital signature on each certificate it issues. You verify that a certificate is valid by checking this digital
signature, which requires getting the public key (and certificate)
of the CA. A certificate usually has a time period for which it is
valid.

*CAs have a hierar-
chy of authority,
but ultimately the
user decides
whether to trust
each CA*

A CA's certificate in turn references other CAs as the source of
authority. This hierarchy of authority helps the user and applications check how authentic the certificate might be. Additionally,
each CA provides a list of certificates that have been revoked.
You are probably now wondering how you know whether to
trust the identity of a CA. After all, anyone might bring up a CA
and have it create a certificate with Bill Gates's name on it. This
doesn't mean that messages that use this certificate really are
from Bill Gates, because the CA isn't necessarily trustworthy.
There are several public CAs, such as VeriSign, that are fairly
well trusted by organizations. But ultimately, you must decide
to trust the chain of CAs listed for any given certificate, just as
you must decide to trust authorities in other systems of authenti-

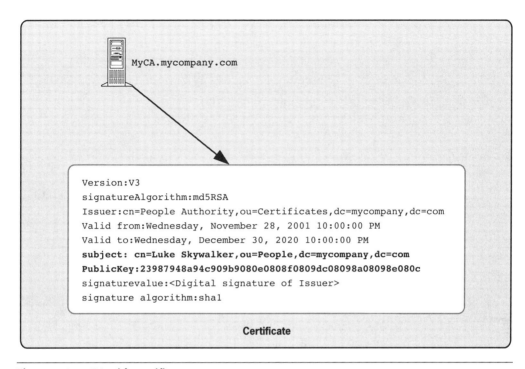

```
Version:V3
signatureAlgorithm:md5RSA
Issuer:cn=People Authority,ou=Certificates,dc=mycompany,dc=com
Valid from:Wednesday, November 28, 2001 10:00:00 PM
Valid to:Wednesday, December 30, 2020 10:00:00 PM
subject: cn=Luke Skywalker,ou=People,dc=mycompany,dc=com
PublicKey:23987948a94c909b9080e0808f0809dc08098a08098e080c
signaturevalue:<Digital signature of Issuer>
signature algorithm:sha1
```

Certificate

Figure 5-13   CA with certificate

cation. This element of trusting a third party (and that party's security of their CAs and policies verifying identity before issuing
a certificate) is one of the reasons certificates haven't completely replaced other technologies yet. Other reasons include
solving how to easily deploy the certificate to users, and how
the certificate can physically follow the user. It is important to
note that solutions to these issues are sometimes included with
the software or operating system deployed. For example, it is
fairly common for operating systems to trust a list of well-
known public CAs by default.

SSL and TLS

Secure Sockets Layer (SSL) is the most commonly used implementation of public key encryption. SSL is used to encrypt the
session traffic between two hosts. SSL uses public key encryption

*SSL combines pub-
lic and secret key
encryption*

to pass a shared secret key. This shared secret key is then used by both systems to implement secret key encryption on all subsequent session traffic between the two hosts. This elegant combination of both public and secret key encryption avoids the slow processing that comes with public key encryption, while solving the problem of safely distributing a secret key.

SSL can be used to encrypt a service session between any two parties

SSL is typically used to encrypt traffic to Web sites such as a commercial Web site. Browsers are passed certificates and understand how to deal with the encryption with a minimum of user intervention, while the details below the surface are fascinating and complex. However, other services make use of SSL. In fact, any service that passes data between two parties that needs to be kept private should consider using SSL.

TLS is the successor to SSL, and it is an Internet standard

SSL is not a formal standard in the sense that many other technologies are. Netscape owns the SSL standard. Transport Layer Security (TLS) is a similar technology that is a formal standard. RFC 2246 describes the TLS standard in detail and briefly outlines the relationship between SSL and TLS. Basically, TLS is a successor to SSL, and it will likely subsume SSL. TLS implementations can downgrade to act like SSL.

Administrative Server Parameters

Server-based parameters help control directory operations

Most LDAP vendors implement server-side configuration parameters that allow the directory administrator to control some of the behavior of the server. In almost every case, the LDAP client options noted in Chapter 3 are also implemented on the server as a global control. Recall that client options apply only to the client's session. In this case, these server parameters would affect all client sessions and override client options when there is disagreement. Some vendors include additional parameters that provide help to control directory behavior and maintenance. The following section discusses the more common parameters, but again these parameters are not necessarily in all implementations and are certainly not required by the LDAP standard.

The *session timeout parameter* controls the maximum period of time the server will process an operation for a client. The *search query limit* controls the maximum number of entries to return on any operation. These two limits can help in limiting the effectiveness of a denial-of-service attack based on resource consumption. *Anonymous user controls* can be used to limit what operations a server will perform for a client that hasn't completed a bind operation successfully. *Allowed authentication methods* denote which authentication methods clients can use with the bind operation. Administrators should follow the security recommendations noted in this chapter and, in particular, pay close attention to the lowest strength authentication method allowed. *IP restrictions* can be used as an access control factor in denying or allowing a client access to the directory server. A *referral chaining parameter* controls whether the directory server should chase referrals for the client. This parameter has implications on server resources when referrals are used widely.

Server-based parameters also indirectly affect directory security

Other Directory Management Tasks

There are a multitude of other management tasks associated with a directory. Although it is not useful to address the specifics of all those tasks here, mentioning the common ones is worthwhile so you are familiar with some of the tasks directory administrators and technical managers should be prepared to support. Use this list as a useful starting point for further research and implementation planning.

- **Certificate authority management**—Management of certificates, revocation lists, and the certificates used to establish trust between CAs is a critical function.

- **User account management**—People have to log in, and LDAP directories often store the organization's user accounts. Providing account management is a common task.

- **Directory server storage management**—The directory must have space to grow.

- **DNS records**—The records that provide access to the directory are a critical dependency. There is no maintenance needed; but should the records break, you will want to know how to fix them quickly.

- **Schema maintenance**—The initial implementation will require an in-depth examination of your needs and will translate these needs into the specific schema elements that support your goals. The need to store new types of data in the directory will be an ongoing process, and having a clear methodology on how to propose and evaluate schema changes will be useful. Failure to deal with the schema usually results in the need for a lengthy data cleanup effort later.

- **Replication troubleshooting**—If there are collisions or failures in the replication process, you will need to intervene.

- **Bulk modifications**—The directory administrator may be called on to make bulk modifications to the directory data.

- **Performance monitoring**—Perception is everything. Performance monitoring will help you provide a reliable directory that doesn't seem slow to users. It will help you gauge when to upgrade or add additional servers, and maybe help detect a problem before users do.

- **Backups**—Loss of data is still far too common an occurrence. Have a backup system in place before bringing up a directory.

■ **Documentation**—People have to use what is designed. You need up-to-date user documentation, in-depth developer documentation, internal directory administrator documentation that addresses architecture, maintenance, and management, and probably one high-level overview for managers explaining how the directory can be used to enable other technical projects.

Summary

Distributing LDAP directories across multiple servers increases reliability and makes maintenance more manageable. Replication, referrals, chaining, aliases, and LDIF are all critical functionality for providing distribution. These same functionalities also provide the means for integrating both distributed and disparate directories. But the problem of integration can be very difficult, and it may require extensive development or an expensive metadirectory product. Fortunately, DSML may provide some critical relief in the near future.

Distribution and integration of LDAP directories relies on several critical functionalities

Directory security is an area in which products differ widely. Access control factors, authentication methods, and encryption strength provide some key areas to investigate when you are comparing products. LDAP directories can also provide a convenient distribution and storage mechanism for PKI.

Directory security differs between products and will require investigation

How Vendors Have Implemented LDAP

6

OpenLDAP

OpenLDAP is a directory solution that is rapidly being adopted. However, the reasons for this rapid adoption are quite different from the reasons Active Directory was rapidly adopted. OpenLDAP embraces the open source philosophy of software development. In addition, development of OpenLDAP is on a volunteer basis, and the software is available free of charge. This combination of philosophical differences appeals to many organizations, and it has rapidly made OpenLDAP a major contender in the directory space.

OpenLDAP embraces the open source philosophy

The OpenLDAP Server is unlike Active Directory in another way. OpenLDAP is not oriented or even tied to a specific network operating system. Because the OpenLDAP code base is open source, anyone is welcome to port the code to an operating system, compile, and implement it. This kind of operating system independence represents a movement within the directory space that other vendors, including traditional NOS vendors like Novell, are embracing.

The OpenLDAP directory server is OS independent

Open or Closed Source?

A debate is raging on whether software should be open or closed source. One of the issues in this argument is whether seeing the source code results in more security and stability. Being able to see the code lets people find problems and fix them proactively, instead of being dependent on the vendor. This preference sounds reasonable, but there are also drawbacks to this approach. Opening the source code means that a company might lose valuable intellectual property and open the code to people with malicious intent. When a company loses business because people take or attack its code, it is less able to provide dedicated support for it. This is only one topic in the larger debate, which is likely to be with us for a long time.

OpenLDAP targets general functionality, which appeals to a wider audience

Although some vendors implement an LDAP directory primarily to support a NOS, this is not the primary aim of OpenLDAP. OpenLDAP is focused on implementing the LDAP standard and directory features that are useful to a wide audience, instead of enabling platform-specific technology. This approach may be especially relevant for organizations in which a significant portion of the clients of the directory don't interoperate well with specific network operating system features. In addition, directory implementation features are simpler to understand and explain.

The OpenLDAP code has a positive history, and it lends itself to flexibility

The OpenLDAP server code base comes out of the open source University of Michigan code that pioneered the LDAP standard. Some organizations still run this University of Michigan code. Migration to OpenLDAP will be appealing to these organizations because of the larger customer base and contemporary development. Additionally, the OpenLDAP server code has a high degree of component interchangeability. Having interchangeable components supports a higher degree of flexibility. For example, being able to select the authentication module or database of your choice, instead of being limited to your vendor's choice, is a valuable benefit.

OpenLDAP has two special processes—slapd and slurpd—that are central to understanding how the directory server functions. Both these special processes come from the University of Michigan code; and because the Michigan code came first, several other LDAP directory servers also have them. This similarity might be considered a benefit by directory administrators who are familiar with LDAP.

Two processes are at the heart of the OpenLDAP server

The slapd process runs the DSA and processes client operations. The behavior of the slapd process is easily controlled via a text configuration file. The slapd configuration file holds a great deal of importance for operation of the OpenLDAP server.

The slapd process handles the LDAP operations

The slurpd process is used to replicate partitions between two servers running the slapd process. The slurpd process works in conjunction with the local slapd process, reading all changes that the slapd process commits out of a special log file, and sends corresponding modify operations to the remote slapd

The slurpd process handles replication

What Is the DSA?

DSA stands for Directory System Agent, a term that comes from X.500. X.500 defined what we understand as the LDAP server process as the DSA, and what we think of the LDAP client as the DUA or Directory Service Agent. These terms are confusing and out of date, though they are still occasionally used. You will see these terms in literature about replication, such as a reference to "a DSA to DSA operation." If you also see the term "DSP" or "Directory Service Protocol," the document is referring to an X.500 directory; but otherwise, it is likely to be an LDAP directory.

process. One way of thinking of the slurpd process is as a harvester that uses a log file.

The client library is popular because it is openly developed

In addition to the OpenLDAP server software, the OpenLDAP client library is becoming a rising star among LDAP client libraries. This is largely because open feedback and development generates a greater amount of active development and peer use. The OpenLDAP effort is also known for adhering closely to the LDAP standards and not implementing proprietary additions. Using the OpenLDAP client library to create a piece of code means that it should work with any LDAP server.

Version releases are frequent

The OpenLDAP solution is a constantly moving target because the latest version is sometimes released on a weekly or monthly basis. This frequency makes it difficult to cover the feature set without being outdated by press time. To accommodate this timing issue, I've taken a little liberty in mentioning functionality that hasn't been implemented yet but is planned in the near future at the time of writing. The OpenLDAP group tests each release for stability and also announces the latest stable release, so instable releases can be avoided.

Namespace

OpenLDAP supports using DNS for directory service location

Thankfully, by default OpenLDAP does not implement a complex namespace. The OpenLDAP namespace follows the existing LDAP standards described earlier. OpenLDAP leverages DNS in its namespace per RFC 2247 and supports using DNS SRV records to locate directory servers.

OpenLDAP hosts a root server to provide referrals for LDAP service location

In fact, OpenLDAP has taken the DNS SRV record functionality to its logical conclusion, in RFC 3088. RFC 3088 provides a mechanism to begin tying together all the LDAP servers on the Internet. OpenLDAP runs a special root server, root.openldap.org, which, given an RFC 2247 DN string, will determine whether there is a DNS SRV record for the server indicated by the string.

If so, the root server returns an LDAP URL directed to this server.

Obviously, this service works correctly only when the destination LDAP server has the appropriate SRV record. So for example, assume you submitted a DN of `dc=mycompany,dc=com` to the special root server. The root server would generate a DNS query for the SRV record `_ldap._tcp.mycompany.com`. If the DNS query returned a valid record that pointed at server1.mycompany.com, the root server would generate an LDAP URL of `ldap://server1.mycompany.com/`. An administrator for an LDAP server can direct its default external referral reference to this special server and know that requests for an entry outside the namespace of the local LDAP server will be properly referred to the correct LDAP server.

Your directory can use the OpenLDAP root server

Naming Contexts and Partitions

An OpenLDAP server can have multiple naming contexts. Generally speaking, each naming context has a separate database. In reality, multiple suffixes can be associated with a single database, but the OpenLDAP team discourages this practice. You can potentially use different kinds of databases on the same OpenLDAP server, but there is little practical reason to do so.

Multiple naming contexts are allowed, and each corresponds to a separate database

Something for Free?

You don't often get something for nothing. But OpenLDAP is providing more than just the software for free, the movement is also providing the root namespace service for free. I think this choice reflects the classy nature of the folks in the OpenLDAP community. You may wonder where the money comes from. OpenLDAP receives some support from Sourceforge, Net Boolean, and Internet Software Consortium, but support is largely on a volunteer basis. Hopefully the IETF will formally embrace this idea of tying together directory namespaces.

Design flexibility is created by separating each naming context into a separate database

Because each naming context is a separate database, greater design flexibility is possible. For example, each naming context can have different configuration settings, including different replication topology, attribute indexing, or forcing the naming context to be read-only. These different configuration settings are set in the slapd configuration file under the appropriate database directive section. Alternative maintenance and optimization configurations for each naming context are also possible, which may be useful depending on the type of data in each naming context. For example, one naming context might contain data that is accessed frequently and needs a great deal of indexing for optimal performance. Another naming context might contain highly confidential data that is accessed infrequently and requires more frequent backups.

Distributed Directory Functionality

OpenLDAP supports subordinate and external referrals

As you might have gathered already, OpenLDAP supports referrals. Both subordinate and superior referrals are supported, and the referrals can be internal or external to the directory namespace.

Subordinate referrals and a control to provide maintenance are supported

You can create subordinate referrals by creating an `object-class=referral` entry in the appropriate location within the namespace. OpenLDAP supports the `ManageDsaIT` control with the add, modify, and delete operations to allow changes to referral entries. This control allows an administrator to suppress the usual behavior of the referral entry to return a client referral to another location.

Superior referrals are created outside the LDAP directory

Superior referrals are created in the slapd configuration file as a directive. A superior referral to the OpenLDAP root server noted above would consist of the following line:

```
referral        ldap://root.openldap.org/
```

OpenLDAP's referral support allows the creation of a directory distributed across multiple servers. Each server might host a separate portion of the namespace, depending on the needs of the organization. As noted in Chapter 5, there are many possible reasons for such a design, including segmenting data to a specific location or segregating client groups to a specific server.

Referral support enables the possibility of a distributed directory

As noted earlier, OpenLDAP supports directory replication across multiple servers. The slurpd process performs this functionality. OpenLDAP supports only single-master replication at this time. Multimaster replication is possible with the existing versions, but it is considered experimental and is poorly documented.

OpenLDAP supports single-master replication via the slurpd process

The slurpd process works closely with the slapd process running on the same server. The slapd configuration file controls much of the behavior of the slurpd process. Two things are needed in the master server's slapd configuration file. First, a replica directive is needed that specifies what server the replication should be directed toward as well as the authentication method and credentials that should be used in the LDAP session with this other server. The slurpd process uses the LDAP operations to perform the replication. Second, a replogfile directive is needed to instruct the slapd process to log all changes to file. This file is in turn used by the slurpd process to determine what operations need to be replicated. You may have wondered how the portion of directory to be replicated is specified in this scheme. The replication directives are placed in the same database section as the naming context that you want to replicate. You are really replicating a database via LDAP operations, and the databases on the server represent the partitions you can replicate. You'll notice this same approach to replication in many other LDAP products. In fact, Chapter 8 describes something remarkably similar with slight improvements.

The slapd configuration file controls the replication behavior

Database Functionality

OpenLDAP has special support features for the LDBM database type

OpenLDAP gives administrators a choice of databases to support the directory functionality. OpenLDAP favors the LDBM database type, and it has built-in configuration options for this database type.

You can use other databases with OpenLDAP

However, OpenLDAP can use other types of databases, including SQL. OpenLDAP accomplishes this functionality via what it calls the Shell backend database type. The Shell backend is really just the basic interface that OpenLDAP supports to interact with other types of databases. In the slapd configuration file, you would specify an external database command for each of the ten LDAP operations. After this configuration, the OpenLDAP directory would be able to use the external database. In this case, database configuration, indexing, and optimization would all be external to OpenLDAP.

Database support customization is possible

For more integrated database support, you can write your own backend. A backend is code that redirects LDAP operations to a database, thus acting as a proxy. By writing your own backend, you can allow any special database functionality to interoperate more closely with the LDAP configuration.

Indexing

Determining what attributes to index is at the heart of optimization

Indexing is an important consideration as a directory grows. When the commonly searched attributes are indexed, performance is better. Indexing all the attributes would require more resources and performance would suffer, so you should index only those attributes that are frequently used in search filters.

Indexing support is provided for LDBM, but other databases must provide their own

The level of indexing support OpenLDAP provides is dependent on the database employed. OpenLDAP favors the LDBM database type, and you can include indexing directives in the slapd configuration file only when you are using this type of database. The indexing directives for an LDBM database are specific and support a higher degree of optimization than LDAP servers from other vendors.

The OpenLDAP indexing directives let you optimize the indexing to the type of search filter match operator that is most relevant. For example, imagine a directory with the following frequently used search filters:

Which match operators are indexed is important

```
(st=CA)
(userCertificate=*)
```

The following indexing directives would optimize the indexing:

```
index st eq
index userCertificate pres
```

The first directive indexes the `st` attribute for the equality operator, which means that the DN of every entry that has a `st` value needs to be kept in the index, and further that every value of the `st` attribute must be kept in the index so each value can be quickly matched. The second directive indexes the `userCertificate` attribute for the presence operator, which means that the DN of every entry that has a user certificate value needs to be kept in the index, but the values of that attribute are not needed.

In addition to the equality and presence index parameters, OpenLDAP supports several others. These include the approximate operator (the "sounds like" operator), attribute subtyping, and language attribute options (which OpenLDAP calls language tags).

All the standard match operators are supported for inclusion in indexing

Indexing is not the only factor in optimizing OpenLDAP performance. For example, the access controls employed can greatly affect directory performance.

Operations and Clients

OpenLDAP has fallen behind other solutions in terms of number of features

OpenLDAP has focused on performance and standards in the area of server operation functionality. This strength together with its low cost results in an attractive option. However, in comparison with other LDAP servers, OpenLDAP lags behind in terms of additional features.

OpenLDAP has im-plemented many additional LDAP RFCs, but neglected others

In its favor, OpenLDAP has implemented the password modify control (RFC 3062), strong SASL-based authentication (RFC 2829), session encryption via TLS (RFC 2830), and language tags (RFC 2596). But common features that have been imple-mented by the majority of LDAP server vendors, such as server-side sorting control (RFC 2891) and the paged search control, have yet to be implemented.

OpenLDAP got a late start

The lack of features seems to be attributed largely to OpenLDAP's late entry. The initial OpenLDAP code was taken directly from the final version of the University of Michigan's open source release in 1996. In fact, today's OpenLDAP administration guide and the Michigan administration guide are still remarkably similar. Other vendors worked for years while the code that OpenLDAP uses sat without development.

Clients

A basic set of client tools is provided

A variety of client-based tools are provided with the OpenLDAP distribution. These tools range from ones to support the basic

Intangibles Often Make a Difference

OpenLDAP hosts one of the few LDAP discussion mailing lists. Its developers are among the most active in the IETF LDAP working groups. If you follow the LDAP drafts being proposed, you'll note that many of the ideas come from someone as-sociated with OpenLDAP. All these things add up to a positive feeling about the direction and support for OpenLDAP.

LDAP operations to a few more advanced tools. Support for these tools is an integral part of the distribution, because each one uses the API library that OpenLDAP provides.

A command-line executable for a client is included in the distribution for each of the LDAP operations. The client executables include ldapdelete, ldapmodify, ldapadd, ldapmodrdn, ldapsearch, ldap_abandon, ldap_bind, and ldap_compare. Variants of each of these executables are also offered. All of the client tools are fully documented at the online OpenLDAP man pages at http://www.openldap.org/software/man.cgi, and this documentation is included in the distribution.

Client tools include all the standard LDAP operations

In addition to these basic commands, executables that support basic functionality are also included. These include operations to use the password modify control, encode elements using BER, and format the output from an entry, as well as the operations needed to step through the LDAPMessage returned by the primary operations.

A few support tools are also included

Directory-Enabled Applications

The OpenLDAP distribution comes with a few applications that closely integrate with an LDAP directory. The majority of these applications allow sendmail to query an LDAP directory (or an X.500 directory with an LDAP gateway in front) with an e-mail address. The returned message contains information regarding where to route the mail. Additional functionality includes routing resolution to mail-enabled groups via a special object class called rfc822MailGroup. There are a few other directory-enabled applications distributed with OpenLDAP, but they are unremarkable.

A couple of directory-enabled mail services are provided

Programming Support

Support for LDAP programmers using OpenLDAP is quite good. The support for OpenLDAP tools is perhaps better than with any other vendor. The support is not without quirks or

Programming support is very good

need of improvement, but it is amazing when you figure cost into the equation.

The public OpenLDAP forum provides solutions that are satisfactory to customers

Support is given primarily via online documentation, documentation distributed with the development tools, and mailing lists. As with other vendors, the online documentation is good for beginners, but it is sparse on issues of greater complexity. However, the mailing lists really fill this gap. Posts to the mailing list go to developers worldwide, and the hardest ones are regularly answered by the core programmers who volunteer their time. Most vendors filter access to their core programmers, but OpenLDAP gives you a direct and public forum to interact with them. This approach provides a real benefit to the OpenLDAP effort, because it draws new developers into donating their time to add a new feature to the code base that is shared by all.

Controls

OpenLDAP offers only a single control by default

By default, OpenLDAP supports only two LDAP controls. In addition to the aforementioned Password Modify Control, the `ManageDsaIT` control (2.16.840.1.113730.3.4.2) is supported. It allows an LDAP client to add, modify, or delete a

Is a Shared Code Base a Benefit?

Some people would argue that an openly developed code base creates the possibility that a contributor might introduce malicious code. But when you weigh this risk against your other option, you realize neither option is desirable. If you purchase your software, you will find that vendors are reluctant to add features you want because there isn't enough demand to justify their costs. So your organization is left out to dry. If only there were a middle ground. Some software products do offer a middle ground, where they expose an API that you can use, and allow you to plug your own code module into their product. Directory Server (see Chapter 8) offers something like this.

referral internal to the directory namespace. The referral must be an entry of `objectclass=referral`. External referrals cannot be modified with this control. The small number of controls implemented is indicative mostly of how long OpenLDAP has been around. After a year, I'd expect that many of the common controls will be implemented. But for the time being, the lack of control support is a weakness of OpenLDAP when compared to other offerings.

Schema

The default OpenLDAP schema includes every definition in an IETF RFC document, along with several draft and experimental definitions. Definitions follow the BNF schema format used in the RFC specifications, as described in Appendix B. The schema definitions do not follow the slapd.conf schema format, even though OpenLDAP uses a slapd.conf file like several other LDAP servers.

The OpenLDAP schema follows all the standards

The default schema definitions are in a set of nine schema files, which are included by directives in the default slapd configuration file. If desired, you can remove these directives or modify the default schema files themselves. Exactly what is included in the default definitions is documented only in the text files for the code base itself. This is an oversight that should be corrected.

Several files define the default OpenLDAP schema

In addition to the default schema definitions, directives in the slapd configuration file define schema elements. Modifications to the schema are fairly easy to make, with a short service outage required to put modifications into place. You can add schema definitions directly to the slapd configuration file, or you can place any number of schema definitions in a file(s) and include the file(s) with a directive in the slapd configuration file. Incidentally, OpenLDAP does allow you to turn off the schema-checking process, although this isn't recommended.

You can add definitions singly or in a set

*OpenLDAP sup-
ports a large num-
ber of syntaxes and
allows extension*

OpenLDAP supports 58 syntaxes by default and allows additional syntaxes to be added. OpenLDAP supports 33 matching
rules by default and allows additional matching rules to be
added. The syntaxes and matching rules are not referenced by
the slapd configuration file and are listed only in the source
code, in a file named schema_init.c. The slapd.conf man page
does list syntaxes, but the list is incomplete and the placement
of the information illogical. This poor documentation makes it
harder to use. You would use the schema_init.c file to define
additional syntaxes and matching rules. The file notes 20 additional matching rules, which may be added in future releases.
Despite the poor documentation, the number of syntaxes and
matching rules supported by default, along with the easy extensibility, represents a key benefit that OpenLDAP holds over
competitors.

Classes

*By default, 81
classes are de-
fined, each of
which corre-
sponds to a
definition in a
documented
standard*

By default, the OpenLDAP schema supports 81 classes. As
noted earlier, these classes are primarily standard classes denoted in RFC standards. In fact, there is little in the default
schema that isn't documented in an Internet standard. And unlike other vendors, OpenLDAP doesn't arbitrarily change the
standards to meet some proprietary need. The only modifications to the schema elements are minor changes to allow all the
schema elements to be implemented despite minor discrepan-
cies between the standards.

*Multiple-class
inheritance is
supported*

OpenLDAP uses a multiple-class inheritance model, in which
more than one class can be superior for any given object class.
For example, the `openLDAPperson` class has both `inetOrgPerson`
and `pilotPerson` as superior classes. This class inheritance
model provides greater flexibility than the single-class model
that most LDAP servers employ, and it is a nice feature for organizations looking to design a new class combining several existing definitions.

OpenLDAP implements the `alias` object class, which provides a level of intra-directory redirection. OpenLDAP also implements the `ref` object class, to support referral functionality. The combination of these two classes allows for any organizational hierarchy or distribution of a directory across multiple servers.

Aliases and referrals are supported

Attributes

By default, the OpenLDAP schema supports 192 attributes. As mentioned earlier, attribute subtypes are supported as well as attribute options, including language tags. This diversity of basic attribute support means that organizations can easily implement custom attributes.

OpenLDAP provides the basic level of attribute support

OpenLDAP implements several operational attributes. These include the `modifiersName`, `modifyTimestamp`, `creatorsName`, and `createTimestamp` attributes to track modifications to entries. These attributes will be automatically maintained by slapd if the `lastmod on | off` directive is set in the slapd configuration file. By default, the `lastmod` directive is on. Following the LDAP standards, the `subschemaSubentry` operational attribute is also on every entry.

Several OpenLDAP operational attributes are automatically maintained

Design Flexibility

OpenLDAP has the greatest flexibility of the products examined if you are designing your own schema elements. Lack of flexibility can be a showstopper when you have to integrate a directory into a complicated existing infrastructure. OpenLDAP gives you the ability to create any schema element from scratch, beginning from syntaxes on up. Most other products limit you to only attributes and object classes. Some products even have limitations that restrict your ability to modify default schema elements. This can be especially problematic in scenarios in which directory integration is required.

*A few unorthodox
attributes enable
access control
functionality*

There are also a few interesting attributes that OpenLDAP requires for basic functionality. Among these are the `entry` and `children` attributes. These cannot be modified by users and are maintained by the slapd process. They are used primarily to enable access control settings, but there may be secondary uses. The `entry` attribute allows access control of the modifyRDN operation, so when a client wants to change the name (RDN and DN) of an entry, there is an attribute to be used as a target in an ACL. The `children` attribute is used for a similar purpose to indicate the names of all the entries that are immediate children of the entry. How these attributes are used is covered in more detail in Appendix D.

Management

OpenLDAP provides several management tools to make administration easier. Two tools are provided to support LDIF functionality, and a third tool helps manage directory indexing.

*LDIF import is done
via slapadd*

You use the slapadd program to create the initial database (and therefore directory) along with the indexes. The slapadd command takes an LDIF file as input to create entries. The syntax of the slapadd command is

```
slapadd -l <inputfile> -f <slapdconfigfile>
    [-d <debuglevel>] [-n <integer> | -b <suffix>]
```

- `-l` is the LDIF input file.

- `-f` is the slapd configuration file.

- `-d` indicates the level of debugging desired.

- The `-n` and `-b` arguments specify which database to modify.

The arguments in brackets are optional.

You use the slapcat program to dump a database to LDIF, either to back up the directory or to have a template for changing multiple entries at the same time. For example, assume I want to change the value of the mail attribute for every person entry in the directory. The current value is in the form user@my-company.com; but for some reason, I need to change them all to the form user@mail.mycompany.com. I'd use the slapcat program to create a file. Then I might use pattern-matching software like perl to replace every instance of @mycompany.com with @mail.mycompany.com in the mail attribute. I could then clean up the file and use it with the slapadd program to modify all the entries. This solution would be quick compared to writing an LDAP-based application that did the same thing.

LDIF export is done via slapcat

The syntax of the slapcat command is

```
slapcat -l <filename> -f <slapdconfigfile> [-d
    <debuglevel>] [-n <databasenumber>|-b <suffix>]
```

The arguments are identical to those of the slapadd command.

You use the slapindex program to rebuild the indexing on a database. When the index is rebuilt, it reflects all the data in the database. Rebuilding the index is necessary when you add new attributes or operators to the indexing directives. If the index isn't rebuilt after an indexing configuration change, only new entries will reflect the changed indexing configuration. The syntax of the slapindex command is

To rebuild the index, use slapindex

```
slapindex -f <slapdconfigfile> [-d <debuglevel>] [-n
    <databasenumber>|-b <suffix>]
```

Again, the arguments match those of the slapadd command.

Special Configuration Parameters

Configuration parameters are primarily set in the slapd configuration file via directives. But because the code base is open source, motivated organizations can implement their own changes and settings as needed. We've already discussed most of the directives that can be set, except for a few omissions, which are covered here.

The backend direc-tive allows new modules to be added to slapd

Backends are a way to support databases smoothly. Backends can be any module that you want to implement to extend the functionality of the slapd process. They are not limited to new database functionality. To create a backend, you use a backend directive.

Basic limit and log settings are configurable

OpenLDAP supports the typical limit settings that most LDAP servers support. An `idletimeout` directive specifies how long slapd should wait before forcibly closing idle connections. A `sizelimit` directive specifies the maximum number of direc-tory entries that can be returned from a search operation. A di-rective called `loglevel` controls the logging performed by the slapd process and the level of detail.

Security

OpenLDAP supports all the security elements suggested by RFC 2829 and 2830. It provides a diversity of authentication meth-ods, each of which also can be used as an access control factor. The authorization support it provides is diverse, with a great number of possible access control factors, but configuration changes are subject to service interruption. Privacy support is provided, but the management features are basic. OpenLDAP takes security seriously, and future development should address some of the shortcomings.

Authentication

SASL support comes from Cyrus SASL

Carnegie Mellon University's Cyrus Project provides the SASL module used with OpenLDAP. The code is freely available and widely used. The Cyrus SASL module supports several strong authentication mechanisms. The full set of supported mechanisms consists of ANONYMOUS, CRAM-MD5, KERBEROS_V4, PLAIN, SCRAM-MD5 (deprecated), GSSAPI (MIT Kerberos 5 or Heimdal Kerberos 5), DIGEST-MD5, LOGIN, and SRP.

After installing and configuring the SASL module to support authentication, you must perform additional work to establish an authorization identity on the OpenLDAP server. When a user has successfully authenticated, the SASL module passes an authentication identity to OpenLDAP. This identity does not necessarily exist within the LDAP namespace, but it does exist within the namespace of the authentication mechanism used. Usually you will map this successful authentication identity to the DN of a directory entry. This step simplifies interaction within the directory and clearly establishes the identity of the user in the context of the LDAP namespace, so the directory entry can be used as authorization information. This step isn't strictly required, however, because you can use the native authentication identity that SASL returns in access control lists.

An authentication identity should be mapped to an authorization identity

For example, the SASL module might pass to OpenLDAP the authentication identity: `uid=barkills,cn=MYCOMPANY.COM,` `cn=KERBEROS_V4,cn=AUTH`. This identity appears to correspond to an LDAP DN, but it does not exist within the directory namespace (but it could if you just happened to use this model). The authentication identities that are passed correspond to the following format: `uid=<username>,cn=<realm>,cn=<mechanism>,` `cn=auth`. The `cn=<realm>` component is not used by all the mechanisms, and it may be absent.

To map the SASL authentication identity to a directory entry, you need to create one or more directives in the slapd configuration file that effectively transform the identity to correspond to a valid directory entry. The `saslRegexp` directives perform this transformation by using a few simple text-based pattern-matching rules to search and replace text. You must use great care in forming these directives so the wrong entry isn't mapped.

Directives in the slapd configuration file perform the authentication mapping

The Regular Expression (regex) format is used to match a pattern and substitute a DN

The regex or Regular Expression documentation is at http://www.openldap.org/software/man.cgi. This man page can be consulted for details. Regular expressions are a lengthy subject unto themselves, but a brief example will illustrate their use. I want to map the identity I noted above to the directory entry with the DN `uid=barkills,ou=People,dc=Mycompany,dc=com`. I might use the following directive to accomplish my goal:

```
saslRegexp
    uid=(.*),cn=MYCOMPANY.COM,cn=Kerberos_v4,cn=auth
    uid=$1,ou=People,dc=Mycompany,dc=com
```

The first line has the pattern match statement that must be met for the second line to be triggered. The pattern match statement uses parentheses to denote what text to save for later use. The first set of parentheses is saved to a temporary variable called $1, and additional sets of parentheses would likewise be saved to temporary numbered variables. The period character is used as a wildcard to denote any character. The asterisk character is used to denote one or more occurrences of a character. So a period followed by an asterisk could potentially match any text string, if the two were all that was used in a pattern match. The pattern-matching statement used here basically says match any identity that employs Kerberos 4 and is in the MYCOMPANY.COM realm, while saving the `uid` value. The second line has the replacement statement that maps to a directory entry. The variable $1 is used and would be replaced by `barkills`, in my example. This would yield the DN I wanted.

Complex regular expressions are supported

More complicated statements are possible, including replacement statements that use an LDAP URL with a search filter. This would be especially useful if the DN of entries in Mydirectory didn't use the `uid` attribute as the RDN, but the `uid` attribute was a mandatory attribute. An example of this might be

```
saslRegexp
uid=(.*),cn=MYCOMPANY.COM,cn=Kerberos_v4,cn=auth
ldap://server1.mycompany.com/ou=People,dc=Mycompany,
    dc=com??sub?uid=$1
```

OpenLDAP also offers an impersonation feature within its authentication support. An impersonation feature helps to simplify authorization and allows special directory services to act on behalf of other identities. The online OpenLDAP documentation calls the impersonation functionality "authorization," which is a less descriptive name than is deserved and can be confusing.

OpenLDAP supports impersonation of another authorization identity

Impersonation is directed using the same syntax as was used with the regex directive, but it is not done via the slapd configuration file. Instead, two attributes are used on the authorization entry that is mapped from the authentication identity. The attribute `saslAuthzTo` is used as a source rule, and the attribute `saslAuthzFrom` is used as a destination rule. The source rule lists what other authorization identities can impersonate this authorization entry. The destination rule lists what authorization identities this authorization identity can impersonate.

Two attributes are used to delegate impersonation authorization

You can use both source and destination rules, but only one is required. Suppose I wanted to allow my entry, DN `cn=Brian Arkills,ou=People,dc=Mycompany,dc=com`, to be able to impersonate Han Solo's entry with DN `cn=Han Solo,ou=People, dc=Mycompany,dc=com`. I could enable this impersonation in either of two ways. Using my entry, I could set `saslAuthzTo= cn=Han Solo,ou=People,dc=Mycompany,dc=com`. Using Han Solo's entry, I could set `saslAuthzFrom= cn=Brian Arkills, ou=People,dc=Mycompany,dc=com`. Either is effective and would accomplish the same end.

You can use either attribute, and each is equally effective

But impersonation is more useful than this example illustrates. For example, let's say I have a special Web site where users can change their directory entry without having to use unfriendly LDAP syntax. Users authenticate to the Web site, view their directory entry, and visually edit their information. Behind the scenes, an application service running at the Web site retrieves their entries using an LDAP search and makes modifications using LDAP operations. To do this, the application service must have an authorization entry in the directory, and that entry must

Impersonation is useful

be granted the ability to impersonate each of the users. For this purpose, its entry might have `saslAuthzTo=uid=.*,ou=People, dc=Mycompany,dc=com` or `saslAuthzTo=ldap://host/ ou=People,dc=Mycompany,dc=com??sub?objectclass=Person`. Many entries are indicated by the value. Another approach would be set the `saslAuthzFrom` attribute of every person's entry to the service's DN.

Impersonation also can enable the access controls to be simpler

Some directory administrators use the concept of impersonation in a manner similar to how security groups are used in most file systems. They set a simple set of access controls on naming contexts that give access rights to a small set of authorization identities. These authorization identities are effectively proxy accounts that are used to provide different levels of access. Then users are given impersonation rights to these special accounts depending on the level of access they need. This scheme simplifies the access controls that need to be set on the directory while also simplifying the delegation needed. But it also obscures the audit trail and makes it difficult to monitor access. This is bad security practice but optimizes performance. However, if you keep this fault in mind and minimize the impact, you can use impersonation to simplify the access controls.

Which Impersonation Approach Should I Use?

Deciding which approach to take requires investigation and an understanding of the benefits and costs involved. In the example, the first approach, with references to many entries, might cause performance problems: during the authorization context switch, each of the entries must be evaluated. The second approach is more time-consuming to initially configure and harder to maintain over a period of time. Key factors in which approach I take are the computing power of the directory server and the confidence I have in my administration.

Authorization

Speaking of access controls, it's high time to discuss how OpenLDAP provides this functionality. OpenLDAP implements an access control in the form of an open, flexible access control policy. A traditional access control list (ACL) model would place a separate ACL on each entry, possibly with inherited settings from parent entries. With OpenLDAP, there is not a separate access control list for each entry. Instead, directives in the slapd configuration file form the basis for an access control policy. The directives are set at two levels, one at the database level (in other words, the naming context level) and one at the global level. Access is determined by the first matching *access directive,* starting at the database level and proceeding to the global level. A simple example of an access directive is provided here. For more details and examples, see Appendix D.

Access control is set by a policy, using directives

The access directives themselves resemble access control entries (ACEs) with the added information of the directory entries to which the ACE applies. There are three primary elements to an access directive: <what> entries, <who> should have access, and what level of <access>. As you might expect, most of the format of these elements relies on the formatting expected by the regex command. The basic format of an access directive is:

Access control directives look like an ACE

```
access to <what> by <who> <access>
```

There can be multiple instances of the by <who> and <access> elements for each <what> element.

Here is an example access directive:

```
access to dn=_.*,ou=People,dc=Mycompany,dc=com
    by dn=_cn=Han Solo,ou=People,dc=Mycompany,dc=com
       write
    by dn=_.*,ou=People,dc=Mycompany,dc=com read
```

This directive gives control access to all the entries immediately subordinate to the People OU. The user authenticated as the Han Solo entry has write-level access, and users authenticated as one of the entries within the `People` OU have read-level access.

OpenLDAP supports many access control factors

In addition to this traditional ACL approach, OpenLDAP supports many different access control factors. These factors include wildcards (used in the example above), membership in a group, dynamic access control, the DNS domain of the client, and the IP address of the client. Multiple combinations of these factors are also supported. You can also use authentication method as an access control factor, but not as part of the access directive. With a *require directive,* a certain type of authentication method can be mandated either on a global basis or by database. For example, you might accept access only via Kerberos authentication.

A service outage is required for every access control change

There is one problem with all of these access control methods. All of them are created in the slapd configuration file, and additions require that the slapd process be stopped and restarted. This means a short directory service outage on any access control configuration, which may not be acceptable in some environments. You can minimize this problem by configuring access controls that encompass all expected situations, but there will inevitably be situations that require a change.

Service Interruption Is Expected?

Stopping a service to make a routine change is an unacceptable design weakness. Companies can't afford downtime. If OpenLDAP wants to take over a larger market share, it needs to eliminate this weakness or offer reasonable alternatives. ACI expressions suggest this problem has been recognized by the OpenLDAP community, but this functionality is still experimental and not fully supported.

OpenLDAP supports an experimental access control factor that is not subject to this problem. Experimental features in OpenLDAP are not fully supported, and assistance is on a best-effort basis. ACI expressions are considered experimental, mostly because the standard governing the definition hasn't been completed, but also because the full set of functionality in the existing definition hasn't been implemented in the code base yet. ACI expressions move the configuration and evaluation of access control from the slapd configuration file to an attribute on the entry. This approach provides a major benefit: access control changes can be made without restarting the slapd process. Appendix D includes pointers on how to find out more about ACI expressions.

An experimental feature eliminates the need for a service outage

There is a special entry called the `rootdn` that is not limited by any authorization factors. Administrators can use this account for various activities. Within the slapd configuration file, two directives are required to initially identify this account. The `rootdn` directive specifies the DN of this entry. The `rootpw` directive specifies a password for the entry specified by the `rootdn` directive. This password will work regardless of the `userPassword` attribute that is set on the entry. This password is in cleartext in the configuration file. You should take measures to restrict access to this file because it holds the key to all of your directory data.

A special entry has unrestricted access to the directory

Privacy

Transport Layer Security is provided by the OpenSSL libraries for SSL and TLS. OpenSSL is open source software, just as OpenLDAP is. You download the code, compile it for your platform, then install and configure it. The OpenSSL Web site, http://www.openssl.org/, documents common issues, as well as providing support and instructions.

Why OpenLDAP?

OpenLDAP's biggest strength compared to other LDAP server options is the fact that it can be run on any operating system

It runs on any platform and is free!

platform. This strength is tempered by the fact that the entire solution is free. Because the product is free, the support model is
not formal; but OpenLDAP provides open interaction with the
developers, which can be better than formal support.

You have an active part in what you implement, instead of being at the mercy of a cold vendor

Another key strength of OpenLDAP is an openly available code
base that you can modify. This strength lends itself to other benefits. For example, you can obtain greater control of performance because you can get closer to the code. Another
example is the high degree of interchangeable components that
OpenLDAP supports. Being able to choose components like a
database is a significant benefit. No other LDAP vendor allows
this kind of choice. Another benefit is that you can pool development resources with other organizations to get a commonly
desired feature implemented.

A diverse choice of security features is nice

The diversity of security features that OpenLDAP offers is useful. In particular, the variety of access control factors is impressive, when compared to a product that implements only a
traditional ACL model. But this strength is marred by the service interruption issue, which hopefully will be addressed in
the future.

OpenLDAP is rid-ing a wave of intangibles

A number of intangibles also fall in OpenLDAP's favor. For example, primary contributors to the code have key roles in the
current IETF LDAP working groups. OpenLDAP has a sense of
historical familiarity. The University of Michigan package was
widely used by organizations when LDAP was emerging, and
many administrators are familiar with slapd already. OpenLDAP
comes with the Red Hat Linux distribution, and many organizations are introduced to it in this way. Finally, OpenLDAP follows the standards closely, which means that long-term stability
and interoperability are more assured.

The special features don't compare well

On the negative side, the special features that OpenLDAP provides aren't at all impressive compared to those of other LDAP
servers. Some of the basic features that nearly every package

provides, such as server-side sorting of search results (RFC 2891), haven't been implemented. Inclusion of extra functionality lags behind and may continue to lag behind because of the voluntary nature of development. The adage "you get what you pay for" closely fits the comparison of feature sets.

Although it may be cheap in cost, OpenLDAP isn't cheap in quality. The package is extremely resilient and dependable. The developers are constantly looking for ways to improve performance, dependability, and security. One can check the mailing list archives and read about many large deployments that have little or no problems running over long periods of time.

OpenLDAP is a quality package that many organizations are using

7

Microsoft Active Directory

Microsoft is among several vendors who have implemented LDAP in the context of supporting a network operating system. Microsoft's Active Directory (AD) uses LDAP to support its directory technology, so a Windows enterprise network has basic directory functionality in addition to many cool management features. Active Directory is a huge step for Microsoft because it is a departure from the company's traditional model of employing proprietary technology. It is nice to see Microsoft instead use open standards as the basis of products.

Active Directory supplies primarily Windows 2000 or newer Windows platform functionality, so this chapter digresses at times to explain basic Windows concepts. This tight reliance on the Windows Server platform makes Active Directory less attractive as an LDAP server solution. Many organizations prefer to choose their server platform. After all, one of the biggest strengths of LDAP is its cross-platform integration. However, the LDAP directory underlying Active Directory does interoperate with any cross-platform client, just as it should. Non-Windows

AD requires the Windows platform

LDAP clients can still fully interact with Active Directory entries. Just the advanced features of Active Directory are limited to Windows clients.

AD offers several advanced features that promise to lower management costs

These advanced features, as well as the tight integration with Windows clients, are attractive. The ability to automate software distribution to client computers, integrate public certificate management, and have network documents intelligently synchronized for a roaming laptop user are among the features that Active Directory offers to Windows clients only. Other notable features include people-friendly LDAP client integration for Windows clients and an impressive number of extensions to the LDAP server functionality via LDAP controls.

Namespace

An NT4 domain directory offers only authentication

An NT4 domain directory consists of only user, computer, and group entries and is limited to authentication and authorization services. By participating in a Windows NT domain, a computer or user trusts the domain to provide authentication services. Belonging to the domain means you can use the entries in the NT4 domain's directory to control access to your computer and to network resources.

The flat namespace of NT4 is problematic

A Windows NT4 domain directory, which is based on the Netbios protocol, has a flat structure with only a single container. This flat namespace leads to many problems with naming conflicts, with administrators having to support both the native Netbios resolution and the Internet standard DNS resolution. Other problems include limitations on the number of objects in the directory. The NT4 domain directory also did not support LDAP, and interaction with the directory was limited to proprietary methods. This limitation meant that cross-platform integration was difficult.

In transitioning to Active Directory, Microsoft needed to drastically change much of the underlying technology while still providing backward compatibility to NT4 domains. Active Directory still offers authentication services, both the preexisting authentication services as well as Kerberos authentication. But the support for this activity is now an LDAP directory that is fully hierarchical. The directory is not limited to user, computer, and group entries. In addition to offering authentication and directory services, Active Directory can offer DNS name resolution services without Netbios support. Netbios is still supported for backward compatibility, but it isn't required if that compatibility isn't needed.

Active Directory offers authentication, directory, and name resolution services and also provides backward compatibility

DNS

With Active Directory, Microsoft implemented a DNS-based namespace along with LDAP's hierarchical namespace. RFC 2247 is implemented in Active Directory to provide a close tie between LDAP and DNS. For more details, see the following section, Directory Namespace; for now, focus on the fact that the services supporting each Active Directory domain partition require a DNS zone of their own.

Microsoft transitioned from a flat namespace to a hierarchical one by implementing RFC 2247

Can I Get Rid of Netbios?

Netbios uses an ugly name resolution standard. It is a frequent cause of administrator headaches. The typical complaint is, "I don't see such and such computer in my network neighborhood." If you are lucky, you will be able to get rid of it, but much Microsoft technology still relies on it. For example, NT4-style domain trusts require Netbios support. In order to migrate from an NT4 domain to Active Directory, you need to set up this kind of trust. Many other technologies rely on Netbios. Unfortunately there isn't a good resource to determine which technologies use Netbios. The bottom line is that you will need to do some research before turning Netbios off.

AD maps DNS domains to LDAP domains and partitions the directory on this segment

The solution Microsoft implemented, however, goes beyond being able to use DNS names in the LDAP namespace. Microsoft had to solve the problem of integrating a flat namespace (NT4 and Netbios) with a hierarchical one (AD and LDAP). To solve this problem, Microsoft defined the NT4 Netbios domains as DNS domains in Active Directory and defined each of these domains as directory partitions that are hosted separately. Each computer and user still has the older Netbios name that is unique only in the domain partition, but each one also has a new LDAP-based name (with DC components) that is unique across the entire Active Directory. This approach ensures that every computer and user entry has a unique, fully qualified name while maintaining backward compatibility with Windows NT4 network functionality. Because the Active Directory namespace is mapped so tightly to the DNS namespace, the names of entries are actually unique worldwide (at least on all networks that are connected to the Internet). In the future, Microsoft could propose linking all the Active Directory namespaces together.

DNS SRV records are used to locate an AD server

Active Directory also implements the IETF Internet draft that allows clients to locate an LDAP directory server using DNS SRV records. A client requests the LDAP SRV record for a given DNS namespace and receives the IP address of the LDAP directory server(s) that hold the directory for that namespace. Multiple directory servers can be listed in the DNS SRV record, which provides a round-robin resolution for client load-balancing.

Which Kind of Domain Do You Mean?

In general, when I use the term "domain" in this chapter, I am referring to a Windows domain. When I mean a DNS domain, I specifically label it "DNS." Fortunately, the two different meanings are beginning to converge, so confusion should lessen in the future.

Microsoft also uses several special name conventions for the SRV records so clients can be configured to request the SRV record that corresponds to the closest directory server. Windows clients automatically request the closest directory server. This extension to the Internet-draft forms a powerful solution for localizing network traffic and minimizing problems associated with network latency. Active Directory is alone among LDAP servers in providing this level of service resolution functionality.

Finally, you can configure a Microsoft DNS server to use Active Directory to store and replicate the DNS records for that service. Such a configuration integrates management, simplifies network management, and provides fault tolerance for the DNS records via directory replication.

AD integrates with DNS services

Directory Namespace

The Active Directory namespace consists of multiple naming contexts that are tied to a DNS zone. When you first create an Active Directory domain, you must pick a DNS zone for its name. This Active Directory domain is the *root domain* of what Microsoft calls a *tree* or *domain tree*. A single tree can also be called a *forest* (a forest contains one or more trees). DNS zones subordinate to the DNS zone of the root domain can become subordinate Active Directory domains in a tree. The root domain is not the same as the DNS root domain introduced in Chapter 2. A root domain is simply the first Windows domain in a tree. The first domain in a forest is called the *forest root domain*. Figure 7-1 shows a tree with a root domain and two child domains. A triangle represents a domain.

An entire AD namespace is called a forest or tree

Active Directory also supports noncontiguous DNS zones. Each noncontiguous DNS zone would be a separate tree. These multiple trees can be connected in a single directory namespace (the forest). Each tree holds a contiguous DNS zone in which each Windows child domain is a DNS child domain of the

Noncontiguous DNS zones can participate in the same forest

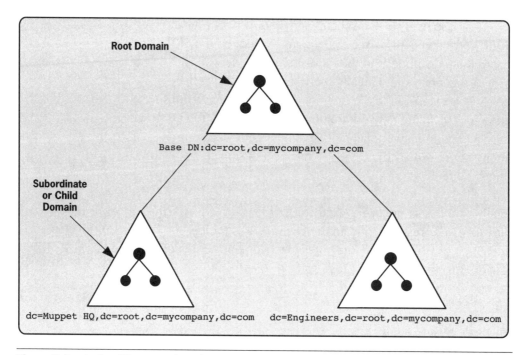

Figure 7-1   Active Directory domain tree

Windows domain immediately above it. Figure 7-2 shows a forest with two noncontiguous domain trees.

Multiple domain controllers host a single domain partition, and changes are replicated via a delta-only system

Each domain consists of an independent domain directory that is hosted by directory servers called *domain controllers*. A domain can have as many domain controllers as desired. Each domain controller replicates the domain partition to the other controllers for that domain. Client computers can join the domain by accepting it as their primary source of authentication and authorization. These client computers are also loosely considered part of the domain, because by default they share the same security context. As a result, other security principals that reside in that domain partition may have some level of access to those client computers by default. From a directory stand-

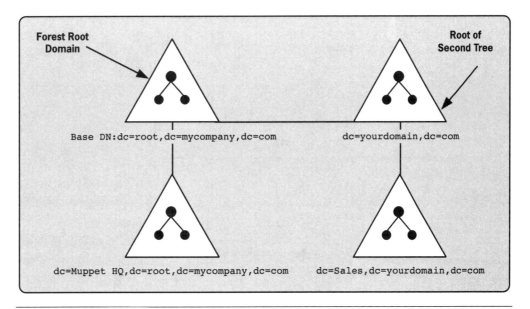

Figure 7-2   Active Directory forest with two domain trees

point, each of the client computers that joins the domain has an entry that represents it in the domain partition.

A forest has properties that are consistent across all the domain directories. For example, there can be only one schema in a forest, and it is replicated across all domain controllers. Additionally, configuration information for each of the pieces of Active Directory is replicated across all the domain controllers.

Figure 7-3 shows the logical directory namespace of the forest pictured in Figure 7-2 and how each domain relates to the partitions and overall directory namespace. Each partition is pictured as an ellipse with a tree structure to simulate the entries within that partition. Each of the partitions of this logical structure does not correspond to a single physical location. Figures 7-4 and 7-5 will illustrate how the namespace is distributed on the domain controllers.

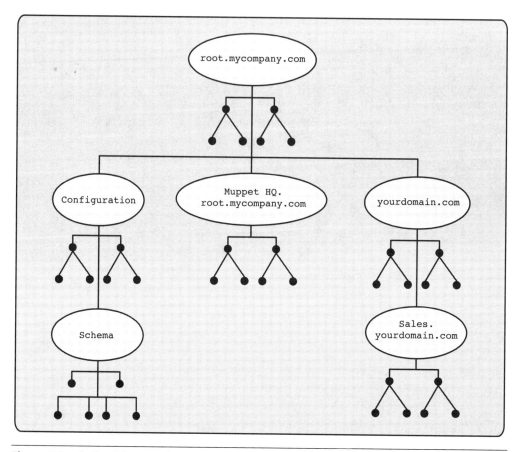

Figure 7-3   Active Directory forest namespace

Sites

Sites allow distribution of the directory with respect to physical connectivity issues

Sites are how Active Directory addresses connectivity and bandwidth issues that might affect the operations of the directory. A *site* is a network with adequate connectivity and bandwidth, as arbitrarily decided by an administrator. The site architecture has no dependencies on the directory hierarchy, and it is external to LDAP namespace design. However, site configuration information is stored in the directory, and it is a factor in determining both replication flow and which directory server any particular client uses. Every computer that participates in AD, including the domain controllers, knows the site to which it belongs. This information in turn affects the client-server interaction; the client automatically prefers to interact with domain controllers in its own site.

The administrator can create multiple sites, which are independent of the directory namespace I just described. For example, a domain might have multiple sites, with a domain controller in each site to provide localized service to clients. In Figure 7-4, the root domain illustrates this configuration (DC stands for domain controller). Alternatively, a site might contain multiple domains so controllers for different domains can provide services to clients from each domain in that site. In Figure 7-4, the Mycompany Main Site demonstrates this configuration.

Sites and domains can overlap with no restrictions

Domain controllers from the same domain in separate sites replicate the domain partition via a site bridge, according to the schedule and topology in the configuration partition. The configuration partition is conveniently stored local to each domain

Replication is scheduled between sites

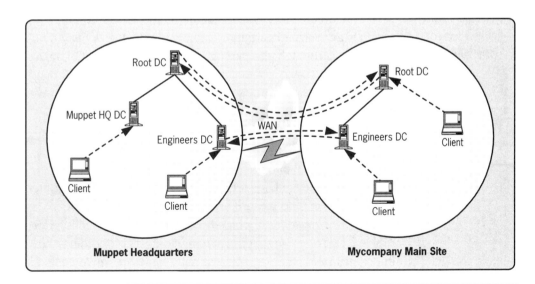

Figure 7-4   Domains distributed across sites

controller. Root domain controllers replicate the configuration and schema partitions between themselves and all other domain controllers using the site bridge when necessary. When a new domain controller is initially installed, it must be able to receive the existing configuration and schema partitions over the network. If this domain controller is across a low-bandwidth link, this requirement can be extraordinarily painful. Many companies circumvent this problem by building the new domain controller locally and shipping it to the remote site. Microsoft plans to fix this problem with .NET Server 2003 so the initial replication can be done via media.

Sites help maximize the efficiency of network traffic because of to client-server directory interactions

Sites provide useful functionality in controlling network traffic across WAN links. Clients can simply interact with domain controllers that are local, and domain controllers can replicate at times scheduled to be least disruptive. This type of functionality is uncommon among LDAP server products, and it is one of the many significant benefits in choosing Active Directory.

Naming Contexts and Partitions

Every domain controller holds exactly three partitions

Each domain directory holds three naming contexts, each of which is a replicated partition. One partition is the *domain naming context*. The domain naming context is where most of the action takes place. Most of the entries that clients need to interact with are held in this naming context. The domain naming context is replicated only to the domain controllers of that domain. Another partition is the *configuration naming context*, which is replicated to all the domain controllers in a forest. This context holds all the configuration information for Active Directory. The definitions of Active Directory architecture, replication schedules, and replication topology are held here. Finally, there is the *schema naming context*, which holds the schema definitions for Active Directory. The schema naming context is subordinate to the configuration naming context, but it has been implemented as a separate namespace. The schema partition is replicated to all the domain controllers in a forest. The following sections explore

Sites Are Out of Sight!

Sites are one of the best improvements that Microsoft brought to its network operating system with Active Directory, though the company is often not given enough credit for the change. Automatic directory location for clients and the flexibility to schedule intersite communications are major innovations that were lacking in prior Microsoft products. In fact, I'd argue that Active Directory performs these tasks better than any of its competitors. .NET Server 2003 brings more enhancements and control to this functionality.

the purpose of each of the naming contexts; for the details of replication, see the section Replication later in the chapter.

The replication topology used by AD ensures that each domain controller has a copy of the rules, the overall architectural configuration, along with the local domain partition information. No other domain's partition information is replicated to a domain controller. For example, a domain controller for the Muppet HQ domain would host the three naming contexts or partitions shown in Figure 7-5. The naming context, `dc=Muppet HQ,dc=root,dc=mycompany,dc=com`, is the domain partition that is multimaster-replicated between all Muppet HQ domain controllers. The naming context, `cn=Configuration,dc=root, dc=mycompany,dc=com`, is the configuration partition. The naming context, `cn=Schema,cn=Configuration,dc=root,dc=my-company,dc=com`, is the schema partition. The schema and configuration partitions are stored on every domain controller in every domain, and the information within them is the same throughout the forest. Also note that the container that would make these three naming contexts a contiguous namespace, `dc=root,dc=mycompany,dc=com`, is not hosted on this domain controller, but it is hosted elsewhere in the Active Directory forest.

Each domain controller can operate semi-independently of the others

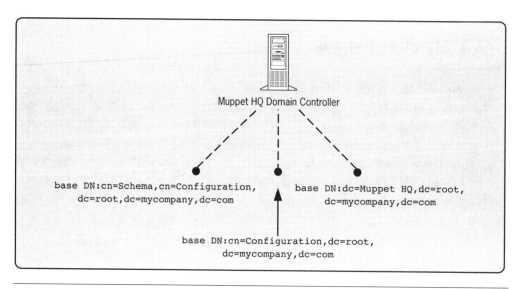

Figure 7-5   Active Directory naming contexts

Configuration Partition

*The configuration
partition holds the
directory-wide
settings*

The configuration partition contains a variety of AD configuration information. The container itself, as you can see in Figure 7-6, has several attributes (among others) that are used to keep track of the last replicated update sequence number for various directory operations.

The DisplaySpecifiers container subordinate to the configuration partition stores displaySpecifier entries for special user interface components built with the Component Object Model (COM). COM is a programming model used to simplify development of software. These entries allow object classes to be associated with graphical elements so they can be managed in a graphical user interface via the Microsoft Management Console (MMC). The MMC is a special new interface that all of Microsoft's administrative applications now use. The displaySpecifier object class, COM, and MMC are outside the scope of this book, but you can consult Microsoft's online MSDN documentation as well as Gil Kirkpatrick's *Active*

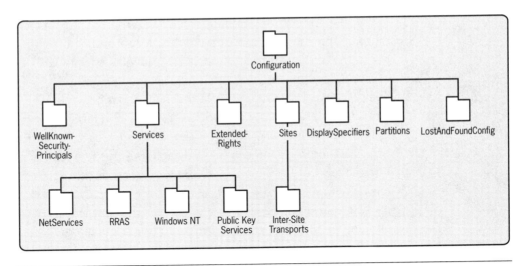

Figure 7-6   Configuration partition

Directory Programming. These resources should prove helpful for the other technical topics in this chapter too.

The `ExtendedRights` container subordinate to the configuration partition stores `controlAccessRights` entries that allow an administrator to create their own set(s) of access rights for object classes. This approach allows an administrator to extend the security functionality of a custom-designed object class in ways the AD designers didn't anticipate.

The `LostAndFoundConfig` container stores all entries received via replication that don't have an existing parent entry. The entries in this container are said to be *orphaned* because they have no parent. This situation can occur if a parent entry is created, but the replication of the parent doesn't occur prior to the creation of the child. It can also happen if a child is created prior to the replication of the deletion of the parent.

The `Partitions` container stores entries of object class `crossRef`. Each `crossRef` entry represents a naming context in the directory, an AD naming context external to the forest, or a naming context in an external directory. These entries represent the referrals present in the Active Directory topology.

Group policies are stored under the Services container

The `Services` container stores information about network services. Each service has a subordinate container. In this container the AD stores the administrative parameters, such as maximum page size, for the LDAP servers. A default forest-wide policy is stored at `cn=Default Query Policy,cn=Query-Policies,` `cn=Directory Service,cn=Windows NT,cn=Services,` `CN=Configuration,DC=Mycompany,DC=com`. The `lDAPAdminLimits` attribute on this entry stores these settings in a string format. Additional policies can be created and linked to specific domain controllers, so individual domain controllers have settings different from the default.

The `Sites` container stores information about the AD sites. Each site has its own subordinate container with objects for every domain controller in the site. These objects hold important information, such as whether the domain controller is a global catalog and links to administrative policy objects in the `Services` container. For information on global catalogs, see the following section, Global Catalog. The subordinate `Inter-Site Transports` container stores Link and Link Bridge entries that help AD know how and when to replicate between sites.

The `WellKnownSecurityPrincipals` container contains the built-in user accounts and groups that Windows uses to implement security for various types of service functionality. For example, the built-in group Authenticated Users is defined here and dynamically refers to every account in the forest. Instead of statically putting every account's unique identifier on this group's membership attribute, AD uses these special entries to apply dynamic membership at the time of access. The built-in groups and users here are the only dynamic ACL feature that

AD offers, but there are a number of useful principles here (for more details, see the section titled Security later in this chapter).

Domain Partition

The domain partition holds the most active information in AD. Everything that users will want to interact with is stored in a domain partition. The domain partition for any particular domain is held only on the domain controllers for that domain. Each domain controller can host only its own domain partition, not that of any other domain. This is a limitation built into Active Directory.

The domain partition holds the meat of the directory

Figure 7-7 shows the default entries in the Muppet HQ domain partition. The Builtins container holds the default groups that a Windows domain supports. By default, all entries in this container are of the group object class.

By default, the Computers container holds the entries of object class computer that represent computers that join the domain. These computers implicitly trust the domain to provide

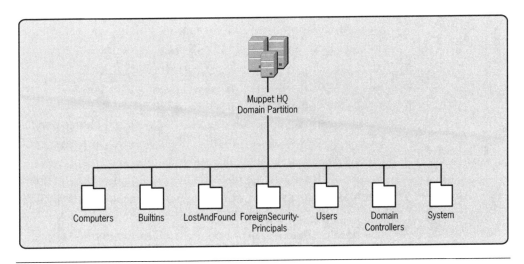

Figure 7-7   Domain partition

authentication services. Computer entries are placed by default in this container, but you can move the computer entries anywhere within the domain partition. To apply group policies to the computers, move the entries into a container that is of the `organizationalUnit` (`OU`) object class. This rearrangement lets you automatically manage the computers. The `Computers` container doesn't permit automated management; consequently, it is usually abandoned.

The `ForeignSecurityPrincipals` container holds entries of object class `foreignSecurityPrincipal`. These entries represent accounts from outside the forest. The entries are used as proxy accounts for the external accounts.

The `LostAndFound` container serves the identical function as the `LostAndFoundConfig` container in the configuration partition.

The `System` container holds a variety of containers and entries of different object classes. These entries represent configuration settings critical to the internal workings of the domain. The entries that represent these settings under this container include other trusted domains, the holders of each of the Flexible Single Master Operation (FSMO) roles, group policies internal to this domain, DNS records (if MS DNS is used and integrated with AD), and several other network services.

The `Users` container by default holds the entries of the object class `user` as well as group entries. User or group entries don't have to reside here: you can move them to an OU or other container so you can have greater automated control in applying group policies to user entries. The `Users` container doesn't permit automated management; consequently, it is usually abandoned.

The `Domain Controllers` container holds the entries of object class `computer` for the domain controllers. This container is an OU. The domain controller entries are kept separate from those of other computers because you will want to configure them with more stringent security settings.

FSMO?

FSMO is generally pronounced "fizz-mo." The Flexible Single Master Operation roles are special services that ensure the consistency of certain directory features. For example, the *Infrastructure* FSMO role is held by a single domain controller in the domain. This service checks the membership attribute of group entries in other domain partitions for all references to user account entries. The point is to ensure that the user accounts in the references still exist. If not, the value is removed to maintain consistency between partitions.

There are several other FSMO roles. The *RID Master* is a single domain controller in a domain to create unique identifiers for entries. The *Schema Master* is the single domain controller in the forest responsible for being the authoritative master for schema modifications. The *Domain Naming Master* is the single domain controller in a forest that controls which domain partitions are part of a forest (in other words, it controls the AD namespace). And the *PDC Emulator Master* is the single domain controller in a domain that provides backward compatibility with NT4 domain functionality.

I like the idea of separating the consistency-checking functionality from the core LDAP server. Separating these processes gives administrators a greater ability to troubleshoot problems as well as the ability to direct these loads onto servers that are more reliable.

Schema Partition

The schema partition holds all the schema definitions that AD uses forest-wide. Only two object classes are allowed in the schema partition. `attributeSchema` entries define attributes, while `classSchema` entries define object classes. Each entry corresponds to a class or attribute. With appropriate authority, you can modify these entries in a variety of ways. To do so, you must be a member of the special Schema Administrators group.

Entries that represent the schema definitions in AD are contained by the schema partition

By default, there are 142 classes and 863 attributes defined, but you can define new classes and attributes. Of the default classes,

14 are abstract, 4 are auxiliary, and 124 are structural. One very common extension of the AD schema is to support Exchange 2000. Exchange 2000 adds another 158 object classes and 853 attributes to the schema.

The subschema subentry for AD is in the schema partition, at DN `cn=Aggregate,cn=Schema,cn=Configuration,dc=my-company,dc=com`. The attributes of this entry hold important information about the supported object classes and attributes for clients unfamiliar with the directory.

Global Catalog

The global catalog has a copy of every entry, but with only a subset of attributes

There is another directory server role outside the FSMO roles for a domain controller called the *global catalog (GC)*. A global catalog assists the AD by holding a copy of every entry in all the domain partitions in the forest. However, each of these entries is not complete; instead, each entry is only a subset of the most interesting attributes. Some attributes are marked by default to participate in the global catalog, and you can designate additional ones in each attribute's schema definition.

A GC is read-only

A global catalog server holds a read-only partial replica of every domain partition in AD. When a global catalog–enabled attribute is changed anywhere in AD, the change must be replicated to all the global catalog servers. Information about which domain controllers are global catalog servers is stored in the configuration partition. The global catalog service is separate from the normal directory operations that a domain controller handles. The global catalog is accessible only via port 3268; whereas all operations that interact with the other partitions, including the domain partition, are accessible via the default port 389. A client can't accidentally search the global catalog; it must instead choose to search the global catalog.

The GC provides several critical functions

The global catalog performs several critical roles that integrate the distributed domain partitions in AD. Because it has a copy of all the entries in AD, it can be used as a beginning point to simplify search operations. With a GC, you can accomplish a search without a referral between domain partitions. A global catalog server provides another critical function during authentication; at least one global catalog server must be available for a user to authenticate. The global catalog locates the correct domain partition to verify user credentials, and it is required to form part of the authorization information that is placed in the authentication token when authentication is successful.

A global catalog search does not return subordinate referrals to attributes that aren't part of the GC replica. Instead, you would need to query the appropriate domain controller. However, an external referral outside the forest namespace is valid with a GC search.

Some referrals external to a GC fail

Operations and Clients

AD is compliant with the LDAP v3 standard, and it also supports the LDAP v2 standard. There are a few nonstandard choices with the schema, but the LDAP standard doesn't mandate any specific schema implementation choices. These nonstandard schema choices don't violate the standard, but they can provide a significant hurdle to interoperability.

The level of integration Microsoft has achieved with LDAP-enabled client applications is impressive. Users have more direct access to the directory and the benefits it provides, while working with a user-friendly interface. The majority of other LDAP solutions don't have anywhere near the level of integration or the user-friendly interface that Microsoft provides. This is significant because the successful adoption of any technology depends on its accessibility. Until other vendors develop well-integrated client software, Microsoft will continue to take market share in this space.

Microsoft integrates LDAP functionality into client software better than any other vendor

LDAP controls extend the functionality of AD significantly

Another strength of AD is the number of useful controls that Microsoft supports by default. AD supports more controls by default than any other directory implementation—even though Microsoft has only just brought a product to market while many other large software companies have had products for some time. Their support of controls shows that Microsoft is committed to extending the usefulness of their LDAP directory server.

Clients

Microsoft provides several LDAP-integrated clients

Microsoft distributes several LDAP-enabled applications by default that can interact with the AD in a seamless fashion. However, all of these applications run only on the Windows platform. The Address Book application supports simple search functionality through the built-in Search command on the Start menu on most Windows systems. Microsoft provides numerous administrative applications that plug into the MMC interface to support specialized LDAP functionality for accomplishing administrative tasks. Microsoft also offers a complete graphical-based LDAP client with extensive support for security, controls, and options, with all the bells and whistles you might want.

Windows strongly supports LDAP-based programming

In addition to integrated clients, Microsoft provides extensive LDAP programming support from the Windows platform. A complete LDAP API library is offered in all modern languages for Windows-based code. Microsoft has fully developed a service interface called Active Directory Services Interface (ADSI), which allows a Windows-based programmer to create abstracted code that will interact with LDAP directory implementations, including AD, NDS, and others.

Integrated Clients

The Address Book is tightly integrated with Windows and several other Microsoft products

The Address Book is installed as part of Windows 2000 or XP, and Internet Explorer 4.0 or higher also installs it. Earlier Windows operating systems have a version of Address Book with limited functionality. The Address Book is a generic search application that can bind using the existing user's credentials to a global catalog server. The Address Book can be launched manually, or it can be called by other applications. It searches primarily for contact information for people. Name, organization, and e-mail address attributes are within the scope of its search capabilities. When entries are found, the resulting information can be saved local to the client in the Address Book for later use, the contact-related attributes can be browsed, or you can take messaging actions directly from the entry. These messaging actions include sending an e-mail, dialing a phone number, browsing a home Web page, or initiating a videoconference Net meeting. The Address Book can also search other LDAP directories, and it comes preconfigured with several large public directories that hold contact information.

The built-in search functionality in the Windows platform, called the Search Assistant, enables users to search for entries of several classes. You can access the Search Assistant from several places, and the chosen location affects the types of objects that you can query. To access the Search Assistant, select Search from the Start menu, click the Search button in the Windows Explorer interface in My Network Places or the Printers folder, or click the Search button in the Internet Explorer browser. You can locate people, printers, and computers in LDAP directories from the same interface you use to perform more common searches like file or Internet searches. The search functionality lets you search a global catalog server or just a domain partition. It makes a lot of sense to integrate LDAP functionality into a client tool that is used to search for other things.

Thankfully, the Search Assistant hides the search syntax and filters

Several administrative applications allow an administrator to search and modify entries. For example, the Active Directory Users and Computers interface lets an administrator work with all the entries in a domain partition. It is designed primarily to ease the administration of users, groups, and computers, but the administrator can interact with all types of entries. There are many other interfaces, which are not covered in detail here,

Administrators have a nice interface too

that allow an administrator to focus on management of specific types of entries.

Programming Support

Microsoft has developed a set of Windows-based LDAP APIs that are part of the Windows Software Development Kit (SDK). A Windows programmer can get off the ground quickly after obtaining a few *dynamic link library (DLL)* files with the API functions from the SDK. I recommend Gil Kirkpatrick's *Active Directory Programming* for LDAP programmers who want to work with AD.

ADSI provides a layer of abstraction and an easy way to script directory changes

ADSI is a directory-independent interface for working with directories. Microsoft prefers that you use ADSI instead of using the underlying LDAP APIs. ADSI uses the COM programming model, which any modern programming language supports. ADSI helps administrators who don't want to get their hands too dirty with the lower-level LDAP API, by providing a layer of abstraction that is simpler to use. ADSI does, in fact, use the LDAP API below the surface. ADSI currently will interact with AD, its predecessor the NT4 Security Accounts Manager (SAM), Novell Directory Services (NDS), and Novell Netware 3.x binderies. It should work with any LDAP v3 directory. ADSI has interfaces to other applications such as Microsoft's Internet Information Server (IIS) that make it even more useful. System administrators should read *Inside Active Directory* by Sakari Kouti and Mika Seitsonen for many useful ADSI scripts as well as a detailed description of Active Directory.

Controls

Active Directory supports 16 LDAP controls by default. One of the default controls, called Statistics by one Microsoft source, is completely undocumented, but it will apparently be documented and supported with .NET Server 2003, the next version of AD, which will add three new controls to the default supported controls.

ADSI Was Long Overdue

ADSI is a major improvement for Windows administrators. With NT4, the only real option for programmatically managing the directory was a package called adminmisc with perl. You might also piece together resource kit utilities, but this wasn't a comprehensive solution. In contrast, ADSI supports most languages, and you can use the other new controls that Microsoft offers like WMI and ADO (or ADO.NET) to control more than just the directory.

The AD LDAP controls are not well understood and therefore are underutilized by organizations that have implemented Active Directory, but these controls represent one of the key strengths of Active Directory compared to other vendors. For a description of the controls, including the three new ones, see Appendix E. In addition, you can find detailed information about programmatically using these controls at the Microsoft MSDN Web site: http://msdn.microsoft.com/library/en-us/netdir/ldap/extended_controls.asp.

The AD controls are extremely useful but not widely known

Directory-Enabled Services

With Active Directory, you can use the configuration partition to store information about directory-enabled services. Because the configuration partition is replicated across every domain controller, this service information is readily available to clients.

You can place service information in the configuration partition

An excellent example of integration of a service with Active Directory is Microsoft Exchange 2000, which is an e-mail, calendar, and messaging service. Exchange 2000's predecessor, Exchange 5.5, offered limited LDAP functionality in an application-specific directory. Exchange 5.5's directory held both service configuration information and user information. Exchange 2000 stores all this information in Active Directory. The service

What Impact Does Exchange Have on Active Directory?

In terms of AD usage, it depends on how many users are mailbox-enabled. There are a couple of Exchange processes that regularly interact with AD. Exchange servers query the GC concerning mail routing. The frequency of this traffic suggests that any Exchange server should have solid connectivity to a GC. In addition to this process, there is a service called RUS (Recipient Update Service) that interacts with AD. In contrast to the mail-routing process, there is one RUS for each domain that has Exchange users. Each of these RUS services interacts with a domain partition, ensuring that Exchange users have the proper Exchange attribute values. RUS runs from an Exchange server, but that server doesn't have to be in the domain for which it is responsible. RUS is an example of software that uses the Change Notification and Dirsync controls noted in Appendix E.

In addition to these system processes, there are a few user-driven processes that impact Active Directory. When addressing an e-mail, you can use several pre-configured queries (such as All Users or your Default Address List) to find lists of Exchange users. These lists result in LDAP queries, but the results of common queries are cached locally. Additionally, the scope of these predefined queries can be redefined—although Microsoft doesn't tell you this. The user-driven public folder functionality is based on entries in the domain partition. Therefore, changes to public folders can result in replication traffic. So in summary, the impact largely depends on how you implement, and how Exchange is used. I'd strongly recommend testing your configuration prior to deployment.

configuration information in stored in the configuration partition at DN `cn=Microsoft Exchange,cn=Services, cn=Configuration,dc=mydomain,dc=com`. User-specific information, such as the location of a user's mailbox, is now simply an attribute of the user entry in the domain partition. A variety of user-specific messaging information like the instant message (IM) connected status is stored in Active Directory.

Exchange 2000 extends the user object class by modifying the schema with auxiliary classes. Exchange 2000 goes overboard in terms of schema modifications. It doubles the total number of both classes and attributes in AD, and it recreates many existing user attributes with little reason. This practice goes against the X.500 directory standard recommendations. In addition to the user schema modifications, Exchange 2000 defines several object classes to support the service configuration information stored in the configuration partition.

Exchange 2000 extensively modifies the schema

Exchange 2000 offers many impressive features that are worth further examination, but such a discussion is beyond the scope of this book.

Schema

The schema employed by Active Directory has been discussed a little, in the previous section Schema Partition. AD employs a schema that is consistent forest-wide. Should a schema modification be needed in one domain partition, all the domain partitions must have this modification. The schema is fairly fragile in the existing AD implementation, because some portions of definitions are immutable: they cannot be modified. In some cases, if you define a class or attribute incorrectly, your only choice is to deactivate it. As a result, any error in schema definition input could be fatal. This shortfall in functionality is supposed to be remedied with the .NET Server 2003 release. With that product, you can deactivate a definition, modify it, and then reactivate it.

The AD schema has a strong set of default definitions, but a weak model for additional changes

The AD schema can be an area of integration problems because of a few nonstandard implementation decisions made by Microsoft. These decisions don't violate the LDAP standard, but they do violate some of the X.500 standards that most LDAP directories follow. For example, Microsoft has implemented the

Some nonstandard Microsoft decisions threaten directory integration

surname (sn) attribute in a nonstandard way. The X.500 definitions are clear that sn is a multivalued attribute, whereas AD implements sn as a single-valued attribute. This kind of issue can cause serious problems when multiple values are expected in interactions between the two directories.

The lack of flexibility to add syntax definitions is a failing of the AD schema

Another example of a lack in the AD schema is that syntaxes are hardcoded into AD, without the possibility of manual additional of a syntax definition beyond the default 18 syntaxes. .NET Server 2003 will add 9 new syntaxes for a total of 27 default syntaxes, but it doesn't promise to allow manual definition of your own syntaxes. This limitation is serious, because all attributes and matching rules are built on top of syntaxes, and a limitation to creating your own syntax translates into a limitation on designing your own attributes, which means a limit to the types of useful and customized data you can store in the directory. Should you want another LDAP directory to interoperate with AD, this might also be a limiting factor. In fairness, several other LDAP implementations do not allow new syntaxes to be defined; nonetheless, hardcoded syntaxes remain a limitation.

Classes

AD employs class inheritance and structural rules

AD uses a single class inheritance model in which only one class can be superior for any given object class. This inheritance model is common among directories despite the limitations it imposes. AD also makes use of structural schema rules. The attribute possSuperiors contains the names of the classes allowed to contain entries of a particular class. The attribute systemPossSuperiors serves the same purpose, except it cannot be modified. A series of attributes with the system prefix serve this same purpose of keeping some definitions constant so AD won't stop working as Microsoft designed. The allowedChildClasses attribute on an entry lists the names of all classes that an entry of this object class is allowed to contain.

An object class definition is stored in an entry of the `classSchema` object class. This entry has four attributes that define which attributes can be associated with an entry of that object class: `mustContain`, `mayContain`, `systemMustContain`, and `systemMayContain`. The values of these attributes are the mandatory and optional attributes for the object class, along with the required system attributes.

Microsoft chose to add operational attributes to the definition of the `top` class. So the AD `top` class has 69 optional attributes and 4 mandatory attributes. This nonstandard modification of the `top` class guarantees that every entry will have the operational attributes that AD requires for basic functionality, but the modification is not compliant with the X.500 standards. Microsoft also chose not to implement the abstract class `alias`. Alias entries represent an entry in one place but point to the real entry elsewhere in the directory. Microsoft downplays this lack of functionality, claiming it can be produced via other mechanisms; but I disagree, and lack of support severely limits interoperability with other vendors. Although you can add your own `alias` class, the LDAP-integrated client software from Microsoft is missing the `alias` support specified in the LDAP standard, thus violating the standard and creating a problematic situation.

Operational attributes are included in the `top` class definition

User entries are the most important entry in AD. Several attributes of the `user` object class have unique values and are valid as an RDN: `cn`, `userPrincipalName`, `canonicalName`, `sAMAccountName`, `objectGUID`, and `objectSID`. The `user-PrincipalName` attribute is the fully qualified Kerberos account name, for example brian@mycompany.com. This is the account brian, in the Kerberos realm mycompany.com. Although the format is similar to an e-mail address, it is not the e-mail address of the person associated with the user entry. The `objectGUID` and `objectSID` attributes both are used to assign a unique identifier to the entry. These identifiers are assigned by the domain controller with the RID Master FSMO role. The value of `objectSID` plays an important part in AD security, as it is

The user object class holds a lot of information and importance

placed in ACLs associated with entries. The DN of an entry is not placed in an ACL to denote to whom to give access, but rather the value of the `objectSID` of an entry. The `altSecurityIdentities` attribute links the user account with an external Kerberos principal or external public key certificate. The `userCertificate` attribute stores an entry's public key certificate, issued by a certificate authority (CA) trusted by Active Directory. There are many other user attributes that hold various settings, but these are too numerous to detail here.

The computer object class helps manage the client

Entries of the `computer` object class are also prominent in AD. Information about the computers that have joined a Windows domain is stored in the corresponding computer entry. The `computer` object class is a subclass of the `user` object class, and several of the security-related user attributes are used to support basic functionality. Additionally, the *fully qualified domain name (FQDN)* is kept in the `dNSHostName` attribute. Information about the operating system of the computer is kept in the `operatingSystem`, `operatingSystemHotfix`, and `operating-SystemVersion` attributes. The `servicePrincipalName` attribute serves a critically important purpose. It denotes the Kerberos authentication service names supported by the computer. These names are required for a specific service on that computer to support Kerberos authentication.

Attributes

Active Directory uses attributes in a standard way, with few surprises. By default, AD supports a lot of attribute definitions, which can be very useful.

Linked attributes provide an automated method for an attribute of one entry to be automatically connected to an attribute of another entry

One interesting feature AD implements is the idea of *linked attributes*. A linked attribute creates a connection between two entries in the directory. For example, my user entry in AD will have an attribute `manager` with a link to the RDN of my manager's user entry. My manager's user entry has a `directReports` attribute that links to the RDN of my user entry and possibly other entries. Adding a value to my manager's `manager` linked attribute automatically results in a modification to another entry's corresponding `directReports` linked attribute. AD makes use of linked attributes in several novel ways to ease administration of the directory. For example, user and group entries have a special link via the `member` and `memberOf` attributes respectively. If I add a user entry to the `member` attribute of a group entry, the group's entry is automatically added to the user's `memberOf` attribute. This functionality has obvious benefits in terms of managing the consistency of information. You can manually define your own linked attributes. For details on this functionality and guidelines for creating your own, see the relevant URL list in Appendix G.

Management

The directory management features of Active Directory are also substantial. As discussed earlier, AD uses a distributed directory design and offers a well-designed administrative application interface (MMC). In addition to these management features, AD provides multimaster replication, LDIF, control of what attributes are indexed by the directory, an amazing graphical administrative application called ADSI Edit, and outstanding security features. Microsoft also has an additional product called Microsoft Metadirectory Services (MMS) that offers automated management of directory integration.

ADSI Edit allows an administrator to browse the directory namespace. You can examine each entry in detail. Attributes are interactively listed by menu so you can view unfamiliar entries and easily make changes. ADSI Edit uses the ADSI components described earlier in the chapter, which in turn use the LDAP protocol.

ADSI Edit provides powerful directory browsing and editing in an easy format

Active Directory's LDIF functionality follows the standards presented in Chapter 5. Microsoft offers an application interface called LDIFDE to process LDIF input and output. In addition to

Active Directory supports LDIF and offers some extended capabilities

LDIF format, LDIFDE supports a variant format using comma-separated values (CSV). The CSV format is convenient for an administrator who is unfamiliar with LDIF, because Microsoft Excel can be used to quickly make bulk changes.

Replication

In the section Naming Contexts and Partitions, I discussed the three types of partitions that Active Directory allows. The schema and configuration partitions are replicated across every domain controller in the forest. The many domain partitions are replicated across each domain controller in a domain, as well as partially replicated to each of the global catalog servers in the forest. The section Sites discussed the details of how domain controllers in one site can pass replication traffic to domain controllers in another site. But I didn't cover how Active Directory accomplishes replication within the same site, nor the features that are used to accomplish the replication.

AD uses multimaster replication

Every domain controller can be written to, and it is considered an authoritative master for the partitions it holds. As a result, Active Directory must use a multimaster replication topology for these partitions. The multimaster model used employs a ring topology in which any domain controller is linked to two other domain controllers. Changes that are passed to one domain controller are also passed along to its partners. Redundant connections are automatically created for large rings so every domain controller is at most three hops from all the others. Figure 7-8 shows a possible replication topology of the entire AD forest namespace that was last pictured in Figure 7-3. In the figure, the squares represent domain controllers (DCs). The circles represent domain controllers that are also global catalog (GC) servers. Each domain controller is named by the first letter of the domain followed by a number. The root domain has two DCs. The Muppet domain also has two DCs. The Yourdomain domain has three DCs. The Sales domain has five DCs. The global catalog (GC) role is held by only two domain controllers:

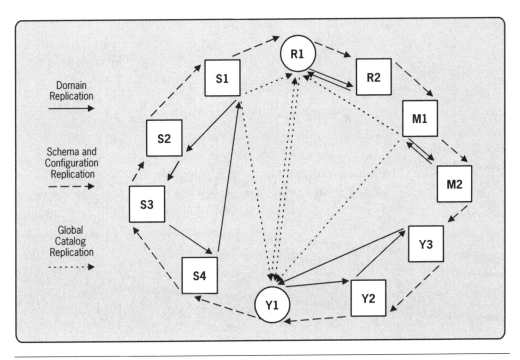

Figure 7-8   Active Directory replication topology

R1 and Y1. The number of DCs and GCs is arbitrarily chosen in this example; AD allows as many DCs per domain and GCs per forest as desired.

Only changes are ever replicated across the wire to minimize the network traffic between domain controllers. In addition, the mechanism used to replicate the changes ensures *propagation dampening*. Propagation dampening prevents a change from endlessly replicating around the ring, or to the same domain controller more than once. If the entry simply disappears, there isn't anything left for a replication partner to discover, which makes it difficult for deletions to replicate properly to all domain controllers. AD makes use of a *tombstone* to ensure that a deletion replicates properly. A tombstone is an entry that has been deleted. Users can no longer access it, but replication

AD replication traffic is efficient

partners can do so to ensure that they know that the entry is no longer accessible. After a period of 60 days, the tombstones disappear automatically. These Active Directory features ensure that replication is efficient.

Changes are passed between replication partners using a notification and request

Imagine a change is made to a partition on a domain controller, or it has been passed changes from another domain controller. After five minutes, that domain controller contacts its replication partners about this change (and any that have been made in that five-minute period). It sends a change notification that there is new information to be replicated, and this notification includes a special tracking number called an *update sequence number (USN)*. The USN is unique to each domain controller and tracks each change to that domain controller. The partners use this USN to track what changes they need to request. The partners then check their internal database of the changes they have already requested to make sure it isn't a USN that they have requested before. If it is new, the partner requests the change and updates its information. It is important to remember that replication takes time to propagate across all the domain controllers, so information in Active Directory should be considered loosely consistent at any one point in time.

Collisions can occur, but the effect is minimized

Because changes can be written to the same entry on more than one domain controller, a collision during replication is possible. One factor that limits collisions is that AD tracks changes on an attribute level. For example, imagine someone changes the cn attribute of Brian Arkills's entry on one domain controller, and at the same time someone else changes the member attribute of Brian Arkills's entry on another domain controller. Because the changes are tracked at the attribute level, they will not collide during replication, and both will be replicated without problem. AD also uses other factors to limit collisions. Every attribute in AD has a corresponding version number that uniquely tracks how many times that attribute has been changed during its lifetime. This version number eliminates most collisions at the attribute level. Timestamps and the unique identifier number of the originating domain controller help to decide which change wins collisions on the same attribute of an entry. When a change is made to the same attribute of an entry on two different domain controllers, the attribute version number, a timestamp, and the domain controller's unique ID number are stored as part of the USN in case alternative resolution methods are needed. The latest version number wins first; but if the change is made before the replication cycle is complete, the different changes may have the same version number. Then the modification with the later timestamp wins the collision. System time between domain controllers is synchronized by default. If the timestamp is identical on the colliding changes, the change that originates from the domain controller with a lower ID number wins. This is a purely arbitrary factor, but it ensures that there is a clear winner in every collision. This combination of factors works well to reduce any negative effects from collisions.

Indexing

Attributes that are frequently searched on, like `objectClass,` `cn`, or `sn`, are indexed by the directory. Indexing makes an attribute more readily available on the domain controller that hosts that domain partition. This design can decrease the overall time spent responding to queries. In addition to the default

Indexed attributes speed directory response

AD's Replication Model Surpasses That of Other Vendors

The flexibility of Active Directory's replication model enables it to host multiple master servers. The features employed to perform replication are impressive when compared to those used by other vendors' solutions. When other vendors allow multimaster replication, it is usually at the cost of some other functionality. This is an area of strength for the product, which is surprising given its time on the market relative to other products.

set, you can index other attributes by modifying their schema definitions. However, be aware that there are performance implications of selecting additional attributes for indexing. Indexing multivalued attributes or attributes with nonunique values can be costly in terms of storage space and time to write to disk and can also affect search operation performance. Perform a careful analysis to determine which attributes should be indexed to optimize search performance.

Data Architecture

MMS provides full-featured metadirectory functionality

Microsoft Metadirectory Services is a metadirectory product similar to those mentioned in Chapter 5. MMS has connectors for most major directories and database products. You use a connector to import data into the MMS database. Once data has been imported, data manipulation and business rules can be applied to the data from multiple sources. MMS offers some standard data manipulation functionality in addition to supporting more customized scripting. After the data has been assimilated into a consistent form via manipulation and rules, MMS can push the data back to the source systems. The processed data can overwrite the original data in the source system or alternatively create a parallel instance of the updated data.

Special Configuration Parameters

You can configure many Active Directory administrative parameters for the LDAP interface. All of the configurable parameters are stored in the Policies container in the configuration naming context, as noted in the earlier section Configuration Partition. You can modify all of these parameters with a variety of methods, although Microsoft usually prescribes a specific method that you can find in its knowledge base for each specific parameter.

What Tool Should I Use to Change Parameters?

In general, you can use any LDAP client (like ldp.exe or ADSIEdit) to modify these settings. In some cases, there is a special MMC snap-in. You should understand that no matter what method you use, LDAP is employed to change the directory information. Generally speaking, there is no special "voodoo" provided by one tool over another. Even Microsoft support personnel can lose sight of this. Personally, I find that ldp.exe gives me the most diversity in functionality. I'd rather have a single tool that works for all jobs than a plethora of MMC snap-ins for each job.

Here are the parameters you can configure:

- **MaxPageSize parameter**—Determines the largest page size allowed in a search using the paged control; default=1000

- **MaxActiveQueries parameter**—Determines the largest number of outstanding queries that the DSA will support; default=20

- **InitRecvTimeout parameter**—Determines how long the DSA will wait for an RPC request to another DSA; default=120 seconds

- **MaxConnections parameter**—Determines how many TCP connections the DSA will support at any one time (only clients that have successfully completed the bind operation count against the limit); default=5000

- **MaxConnIdleTime parameter**—Determines how long an LDAP client can remain idle before the DSA will drop the connection; default=900 seconds

- **MaxNotificationsPerConn parameter**—Determines how many searches using the notification control (as described in Appendix E) are allowed per connection; default=5

- **MaxQueryDuration parameter**—Determines how long the DSA will work on any particular requested client operation (paged searches are counted by each page, and when the limit is reached, the partial results are returned); default=120 seconds

- **MaxResultSetSize parameter**—Determines the largest amount of data in bytes the DSA will return for any search operation; default=262144 bytes

- **MaxTempTableSize parameter**—Determines the largest temporary table that can be created to calculate the result for a search using the sort control; default=10000 entries

- **MaxPoolThreads parameter**—Determines how many threads the DSA process will have available to process client requests; default=4

Security

AD security integration is impressive

Active Directory employs all three of the security concepts introduced in Chapter 5: authentication, authorization, and privacy via encryption. AD's security model is fairly robust and offers a level of integration that is rare when compared to other products. For example, the rigors of deploying a public key infrastructure (PKI) is made simpler by the built-in secure key distribution that AD supports. This will fuel future security developments in digitally signed code within an AD environment.

Authentication

AD authentication is primarily Kerberos via SASL support

AD employs SASL-based authentication and supports Kerberos v5 as well as the preexisting NTLM authentication. The account used to authenticate to AD can be stored internally or externally to AD. If the account is stored externally, a proxy shadow account must be created internal to AD, with a mapping to the external Kerberos account or PKI certificate. Generally speaking, users don't need to specify the full DN of their account entry to bind but can just specify the RDN, along with the domain partition. The RDN of account entries is unique across the domain partition. But a fully qualified account name (in other words, a DN) is also accepted.

Active Directory also supports the use of smart cards as an authentication method. Smart cards look like credit cards, but they have a limited processor and memory. They store a user's private key and can do the encryption and decryption calculations required to support PKI. The smart card together with a personal identification number (PIN) can be used instead of the traditional username and password.

Smart cards are supported by default

Doesn't Microsoft's Kerberos Violate the Standards?

There was quite a bit of hysteria when Microsoft first released Windows 2000. Microsoft passed some authorization data inside the Kerberos TGT, and some people felt this design violated the Kerberos standard. This customization meant that existing KDCs (key distribution centers) couldn't replace a Microsoft KDC. However, after further examination, the furor dissipated. Microsoft simply used a field that had been set aside for any data that a vendor might want to place in it. And a precedent from another vendor with this field had already been implemented. Although it's true you can't replace a Microsoft KDC, there are ways to reduce your dependence on a Microsoft KDC, should you need to deploy Active Directory.

Since then, MIT (the driving force behind Kerberos) and Microsoft have worked together more closely, resulting in greater interoperability and more reliability. Many organizations take advantage of the Kerberos interoperability features to eliminate the unnecessary proliferation of accounts. Some organizations rely on a preexisting MIT KDC and then configure shadow accounts in Active Directory to supply the authorization data.

Authorization

*AD authoriza-
tion uses ACLs
exclusively*

AD uses an ACL model for authorization. An ACL can be applied to a partition, container, entry, or attribute. The ability to specify an ACL at any level in the directory is useful. The attribute-level ACLs are particularly helpful when you want to give access to the entry, but not to private information in one or more attributes on that entry. The actual ACL definition is stored on the `ntSecurityDescriptor` attribute of the entry being secured. This attribute stores the access settings, owner information, and auditing configuration. The access settings are known as the *discretionary access control list (DACL)*. These include access control entries (ACEs) that specify the identity, the level of access being granted or denied, and possibly the affected attributes of the entry. The level of access can be defined by permission sets or via 13 incremental permissions (see Table 7-1).

Table 7-1   Permissions available in Active Directory

Incremental Permission	Read Access Set	Write Access Set	Full Control Set
All Validated Writes		X	X
All Extended Rights			X
Create All Child Objects			X
Delete			X
Delete All Child Objects			X
Delete Subtree			X
List Object			X
List Contents	X		X
Modify Owner			X
Modify Permissions			X
Read All Properties	X		X
Read Permissions	X		X
Write All Properties		X	X

In a similar fashion, if you are defining attribute-level access, you can use attribute sets (called extended rights) or individual attributes in ACLs. For more detail on incremental permissions and extended rights, see Kouti and Seitsonen's *Inside Active Directory*.

You can use only authentication identities, which loosely correspond to four groupings: users, computers, groups, and well-known security principals. The well-known security principal grouping corresponds to the dynamic entries discussed at the end of a prior section Configuration Partition. What exactly these entries represent is dynamically calculated at the time of access. Some of the more useful dynamic entries available are listed in Table 7-2. Several of these entries are useful in the context of ACL inheritance, which is described next.

Authentication identities correspond to four sets

A further ACL feature is support for inherited container permissions, so you can specify an ACL on a container to apply to all subordinate entries of that container. Inherited permissions are statically applied, not dynamically, which means that when a change is made, it is applied to the `ntSecurityDescriptor`

AD supports static inheritance of ACLs

Table 7-2   Well-known security principals

Name	Purpose
Authenticated Users	Any principal (process, computer, or user) that has been authenticated.
Creator Owner	The entry that creates another entry. This can be set on a container as a placeholder for new entries subordinate to the container.
Everyone	Anything, whether or not it has authenticated.
Interactive	Any principal that has authenticated to the same local computer as the resource.
Network	Any principal that has authenticated at a different computer than the resource.
Self	A placeholder for the entry itself. This can be set on a container to give each entry beneath access to itself.

attribute of each of the subordinate objects. Dynamic inheritance doesn't copy the ACL to the subordinate entries; instead, at the time of access, the ACL of the entry and all parent containers are checked. Perhaps Microsoft will change from static to dynamic inheritance in a future release.

AD's default ACLs can be modified

In addition, a directory administrator can define the default ACL for an object class so all entries of that class automatically inherit a certain default ACL. This approach can be useful when your entire environment is different from the assumptions Microsoft made. The combination of all of these ACL features is powerful.

Dynamic authorization and other factors would be nice additions to AD

However, AD uses only standard ACLs for authorization factors. Client IP addresses, client encryption (along with algorithm and key strength), and dynamic authorization are not supported as authorization factors. You cannot—but should be able to—prohibit access either via a specific authentication method like cleartext or to specific IP addresses. Several other vendors do support these features. Dynamic authorization, like that which the Directory Server product offers, allows access control to be based on the value of the attributes of the requesting user. This type of access control may seem esoteric, but it can prove to be incredibly useful. For example, if you wanted to give access to all users who are members of a particular organizational unit (OU), dynamic access would permit you to do so directly, without explicitly creating a security group for this purpose. Microsoft is aware of this product weakness and of its customers' desire for this functionality. Enhancements and features are in the pipeline for future upgrades to Active Directory.

Privacy

Certificate integration with Active Directory is without equal among directory vendors

An overview of Active Directory security wouldn't be complete without mention of the public key support. The public key certificate integration is nothing short of impressive. Microsoft supplies certificate authority server software as a standard service in Windows 2000. These certificate authority servers can be configured to publish certificates that contain the public key for a user directly to AD. This integration eliminates much of the grueling administrative work that other certificate solutions demand. CRLs are also automatically published in AD. Certificates can even be automatically allocated to users or computers via policies. Certificate policies are flexible and can reduce the amount of manual intervention needed. Because manual intervention is the leading drawback to certificate technology, this is a significant feature. Certificate integration provides the basis for many other security features, like SSL support for the directory itself, the Windows Encrypted File System (EFS), and other applications.

Why Active Directory?

Active Directory's comprehensive LDAP functionality and advanced features have compelled many organizations to choose it for their LDAP directory. The rate at which companies are adopting AD is impressive compared to that achieved by other vendors.

The adoption rate of Active Directory is high

Performance, scalability, and usability are critically important to the success of a directory. Independent tests indicate that AD performs very well with extremely large numbers of entries. Many companies have found that Active Directory can run their enterprise directory without issue. Perhaps more telling is how easy Active Directory is to use. General users are shielded from the messy syntax and details of LDAP, exactly as they should be.

Active Directory scales well

Also important is the ability to integrate with your organization. AD incorporates an above-average number of integration features, along with additional useful services that make it very attractive. However, Microsoft pushes its customers toward Microsoft solutions in none too subtle ways. As a result, true integration with other platforms and software solutions is usually poor, with an emphasis on encouraging migration onto a

Integration features are abundant, but there is rampant distrust of Microsoft

Microsoft-only solution. Microsoft's history has bred a level of distrust that is dangerous even with a clear dominance of the software market. Despite the number of excellent integration features, your organization may still distrust Active Directory's ability to integrate in your environment. However, Active Directory does integrate well with other products.

Active Directory is easy to manage

Microsoft designed AD with the goal of simplifying management. In addition to ADSI and the MMC interfaces, Microsoft continues to develop tools, applications, and scripts to make a directory administrator's job easier. Replication is easily managed and has few problems. The design supports distribution across physical locations very well, with a wealth of options. Installation and configuration are simple and well documented, and the delegation of authority is extensive. Manageability is a clear strength of AD.

Active Directory security is very good

The security employed by AD is lacking little. Support for strong authentication methods, strong and integrated encryption support, and an authorization model to protect resources are among the features that make AD a secure choice. I think Microsoft needs to go further with its authorization model and include support for more authorization factors. But Active Directory's existing security support is impressive compared to that of other directory solutions.

The bottom line is whether AD meets your NOS needs; the Windows client integration features are without equal

The major factor in evaluating whether AD will meet your LDAP directory needs is answering whether AD meets your network operating system needs. AD is built primarily to support and extend the functionality of the Windows network operating system. It is clear that the wealth of features AD offers is available only to Windows clients operating within the context of the Windows network operating system. If the strengths and functionality that Windows offers aren't relevant to your organization, AD definitely won't be the best solution for you. However, if the majority of your clients are Windows-based, you will be hard pressed to find another solution that is as well integrated or fully featured.

Microsoft is on record with a promise that some of the strict design specifications that are in place to support the Windows network operating system will be removed in a parallel Microsoft LDAP directory offering in the near future. You can read more about this by looking for information about AD/AM (Active Directory Application Mode) on the Microsoft Web site under .NET Server 2003. This new offering removes the domain namespace boundaries so you have complete freedom in designing the namespace, and it offers schema flexibility. You are, however, required to provide any advanced external security authentication and authorization. Though AD/AM still requires the Windows platform, this is an exciting development that will help Microsoft compete more directly with other products. Hopefully wider platform support will follow. When taken with the many other enhancements in the works, like dynamic authorization, Microsoft's late entry in the directory space doesn't seem to be holding the company back at all.

The future looks bright for Microsoft's directory products

8

Directory Server

Several key IT staff at the University of Michigan introduced LDAP to the world, and they led the process to standardize it. Later, several of these innovators left the University of Michigan to work at Netscape, helping to create an LDAP server product. For many years Netscape Directory Server was the only commercial LDAP server product and it continued to be the dominant product even after other products appeared. As a result, Netscape Directory Server has considerable name recognition.

There is a rich history behind this product

Many years after its emergence, Netscape Directory Server became iPlanet Directory Server when the Sun-Netscape Alliance was formed. After the dissolution of the Alliance, Netscape reverted to the original name for its product, while the Sun product became Sun ONE Directory Server. Although the company associated with the product has changed, the product name itself, Directory Server, has never changed. Currently, both company's products and documentation are remarkably similar, so this chapter is equally applicable to either product. Many people are still confused about which company owns Directory Server, especially now that there are two separate and nearly

The Directory Server product has changed hands many times

identical products. However, the companies themselves have added to the confusion by leaving references to Netscape and iPlanet within the software and documentation. For the purpose of limiting confusion, I'll refer to the products as simply Directory Server.

Performance and stability are strengths of Directory Server

The experience gained by Directory Server's long history is undeniable when you compare reliability and performance benchmarks to those of other vendors. Independent reviews of LDAP servers such as the one by Network World, http://www.nwfusion.com/reviews/2000/0515rev2.html, show that Directory Server clearly leads in performance comparisons. Comparison reviews also favor the stability of Directory Server over other LDAP servers. For large enterprises, performance comparisons and stability are critical factors in choosing a product.

Directory Server integrates with other products

Both Sun and Netscape offer several complementary products that integrate with Directory Server. These include server products for identity management, metadirectory management, enterprise calendar, e-mail, and certificate management among

Sun or Netscape: Confusion Reigns

The dissolution of iPlanet has created a great amount of confusion about the future of the product. This confusion has been compounded by a lack of clear explanation on the iPlanet Web site and by the difficulty in getting previously available documentation. Much change continues to occur. For example, I've changed all the URLs associated with this product more than once. These URLs may have changed again by the time you read this book.

As far as advice on which vendor to choose, I can't say that the dust has settled enough yet for me to offer an opinion. Your choice may be influenced by other complementary server products you select or the responsiveness of product support. I had a hard time starting any dialog with Sun over the course of two months, but perhaps my experience wasn't typical.

others. Some of these products are briefly touched on later in the chapter.

Directory Server is not tied to a network operating system. Although the majority of implementations are on the Solaris platform, a significant number are implemented on Windows. Sun Solaris, Linux, Microsoft Windows NT4, Microsoft Windows 2000, Hewlett-Packard HP-UX, and IBM AIX comprises the supported server platforms.

Directory Server supports multiple platforms

Starting with Solaris version 8, Directory Server is included with the operating system. Many system functions rely on the Directory Server. Sun customers may use the Directory Server for any purpose up to a certain number of user entries, after which a license must be purchased.

Directory Server is also integrated into the operating system

Flexibility

Directory Server supports the widest diversity of platforms of any LDAP product. This flexibility to choose the platform is important to many customers. One side note is that the directory path of critical components will vary between platforms, although this is documented reasonably well online.

Namespace

The namespace employed by Directory Server doesn't employ any unique technology or complexities, as we saw with Active Directory. The product documentation encourages modeling your namespace after DNS using RFC 2247; however, it also supports the use of X.500 style naming. LDAP service location for clients (for example, by using DNS SRV records) has not been specially addressed, as it has in other products. There is support for automatic configuration of Solaris-based LDAP clients.

Directory Server employs a standard LDAP namespace

Other software and services rely on the Directory Server namespace

Several other Sun and Netscape products use Directory Server as the source of their namespace. For example, the Sun ONE Identity Server stores its identity information in the Directory Server namespace. This information incorporates identities, roles, policies, application and service configuration, preferences, access controls, and administrative rights. Other products make similar use of Directory Server as a namespace. For a limited overview of these directory-enabled services, see the section, Directory-Enabled Applications.

The LDBM database underlies the Directory Server namespace

Directory Server makes use of LDBM database technology to support directory naming contexts. Many databases might be used to support a directory namespace, and multiple databases can even support a single naming context. For more on this support, see the section, Database Functionality.

Some default configuration information is stored in a special naming context

Some information related to the Directory Server configuration is created by default in the directory namespace. Directory Server uses this information to enable and disable operation. How Directory Server responds to any particular client request is affected by the values stored in this special naming context. To explore this default information further, see the following section, Naming Contexts.

Naming Contexts

Creating a Directory Server naming context requires three steps

With Directory Server, a naming context is one of the root suffixes of the directory namespace. Every naming context corresponds to a database. To create a naming context, you complete three steps:

1. Add a DN value to the `namingContexts` attribute of the root DSE.

2. Create a root entry for this naming context.

3. Create a database corresponding to the naming context and associate it with the naming context.

The installation process creates two default naming contexts that correspond to a special configuration naming context and a naming context intended for user data. You can create additional naming contexts during installation following the steps I just outlined. If you create a naming context after installation via the administrative console, Directory Server performs the first and third steps for you; you must then manually create the corresponding entry via LDIF or an add operation.

Two initial naming contexts are created by default; you must complete additional steps to create more naming contexts

The online documentation that refers to the configuration naming context is confusing, and it does a poor job of explaining the two configuration naming contexts. Every Directory Server has a `cn=config` naming context that holds the local configuration data for that server. In addition, there is another configuration naming context named `o=NetscapeRoot`, which exists on only a single Directory Server. The `o=NetscapeRoot` naming context stores configuration data for administration of one or more servers. This naming context stores the entire distributed directory's configuration information. In addition to being used by Directory Server, other products including Mail, Certificate, and Metadirectory use it to store their configuration information. By directing the Administrative Console toward the server with `o=NetscapeRoot`, you can view and manage all the servers in one spot.

The configuration naming context can be confusing

Good Documentation

Learning a new product is difficult without good documentation, and Directory Server has an excellent set. My experience with the online Directory Server documentation has been very positive. The examples are diverse, and there is a decent level of detail. Directory Server also offers supplementary material on how to design and implement. However, the default naming contexts are poorly documented.

The configuration naming context stores critical information

The configuration naming context includes special authentication identities, plug-in configuration (under `cn=plugins,cn=config`), the database configuration settings (under `cn=ldbm database,cn=plugins,cn=config`), indexing information (under `cn=index,cn=databaseName,cn=ldbm database,cn=plugins,cn=config`), and support for all actions that cannot be performed through existing LDAP operations, such as start or stop of the service. Figure 8-1 shows the layout of `cn=config`. To find details about the configuration parameters stored within this naming context, see the following sections: Database Functionality, Indexing, Chaining, Plug-ins, Replication, and Special Configuration Parameters.

The other initial naming context is configurable and waiting for use

The second naming context initially created during installation is intended for user data. By default, you choose the name of this naming context; however, if you select express installation, Directory Server uses a name that matches the LDAP `dc` component string of the DNS suffix of the server. So if I ran express

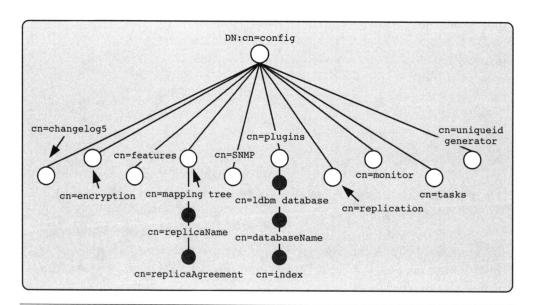

Figure 8-1   Configuration naming context

installation on dir1.mycompany.com, this naming context would be `dc=mycompany,dc=com`. This naming context is empty and only needs to be populated with Mycompany's directory data.

Database Functionality

Like OpenLDAP, LDBM database technology underlies Directory Server. The database is the unit of indexing, replication, and storage. All indexing, replication, and storage activities are performed on a database as a whole. Therefore, if you need a different configuration for any of these functionalities on different portions of the directory, you will need to configure multiple databases. By default there is a single database, but multiple databases are supported. In contrast to OpenLDAP, you can dynamically add databases without service outage.

A database underlies every naming context

Naming contexts are associated with a database that processes all operations. A special attribute, `nsslapd-state`, at the root entry of a naming context determines what the directory does with requests for entries in a given suffix. The value `backend` indicates the normal state where the database processes all operations. In contrast, the value `disabled` prevents any operations from succeeding. The value `referral` indicates that the directory should return the referral value stored in the `nsslapd-referral` attribute for all requests to this naming context. In contrast, the value `referral on update` indicates that only update-oriented requests return the referral, and all other requests are processed by the database.

You can configure where Directory Server sends a request

The attribute `nsslapd-backend` is used to specify the name of the database or database link associated with a naming context. This attribute is multivalued; but to make use of multiple values, you must employ special distribution functions to determine which value is used for any given request. Mycompany might specify two databases for a naming context if the number of entries in the naming context is significantly large. Special

You can associate multiple databases with a naming context, but there are drawbacks

assistance from Sun or Netscape is needed to obtain the plug-in necessary for proper distribution when you use multiple databases per naming context. There are also several restrictions on this type of naming context that result in your not being able to move an entry out of a database.

Indexing

Indexing options are flexible

You may configure separate indexing options on each database. Presence, equality, approximate, substring, international, and browsing (virtual list view) are all the possible indexes for attributes. Multiple types of indexing are allowed for each attribute, and a different collection of indexing types is allowed for each attribute.

Some of the index types are limited to usefulness in specific situations

The approximate match (or soundex) index implemented by Directory Server works only with the English language. The details of what types of matches work with the approximate index are in the online documentation. The international index is used to associate special language-specific matching rules with attributes so they can be sorted and searched for in accordance with the rules of the language. This approach enables a directory in one locale to have different language behavior from a server in another locale—even if the directory entries are identical on both servers. The browsing index speeds use of the virtual list view control—a control you may remember from previous chapters. The Directory Server management console uses this control.

The indexing configuration is represented in directory entries

The indexing configuration information is in entries within the configuration naming context in three different locations. Each entry that represents an index has five attributes that specify the indexing applied to that database. `nsSystemIndex` is a Boolean value that indicates whether the index is mandatory for basic directory operation. Mandatory indexes cannot be removed. `nsMatchingRule` denotes the OID of a collation order. This allows the index to order attributes as desired. `cn` specifies the attribute to be indexed. `Description` is used to provide a meaningful description of what the index does. `nsIndexType` denotes the type of indexing to perform, as well as which attribute values should be indexed. Valid values of this attribute include those listed in Table 8-1.

In general, when you want to create an index on a database, you create an entry under the container `cn=index,`
`cn=databaseName,cn=ldbm database,cn=plugins,cn=config`
where `databaseName` is the name of the database to which the index applies. There are a couple of exceptions. International indexing requires the use of matching rules together with the OID for the locale desired. The browsing or virtual list view indexing is configured via a different mechanism that is executed via the `vlvindex` command. There are two initial sets of indexes. The system indexes are required for Directory Server to work properly, and can't be deleted or modified. The system indexes are listed in Table F-1 in Appendix F. The default indexes, which apply to all databases, are listed in Table F-2 in Appendix F. You can modify the default indexes. To find the default indexes, look in the container `cn=default indexes,`
`cn=config,cn=ldbm database,cn=plugins,cn=config`.

Index entries are stored within the `cn=config` *naming context*

Table 8-1   Valid indexing types

Index Type	Kind of Index
	No value indicates all indexes should be created
none	Disables indexes for that attribute
pres	Presence index
eq	Equality index
approx	Approximate index
sub	Substring index

Referrals

An external referral is called a default referral within the product documentation. One default referral is allowed for the directory. In addition, you can set one default referral per naming context (per database). The documentation calls these latter instances *suffix referrals*. Suffix referrals are valid regardless of whether that naming context is disabled. All these default referrals are not entries in the directory; instead, they are a configuration option stored as an attribute of the naming context. Using this design, default referrals work even if the database associated with the naming context is disabled or unreachable.

The documentation calls all other referrals *smart referrals*. Smart referrals redirect clients from any directory entry that isn't a suffix. A smart referral simply uses the `ref` attribute as specified in the Internet-draft regarding LDAP referrals. Smart referrals have two options that let you specify whether the referral redirects on all requests for the entry or just on modify requests.

All Directory Server referrals use the LDAP URL syntax according to the standard.

Chaining

Chaining is supported by Directory Server, and the way it is implemented deserves more detail than the brief coverage in Chapter 5. You will recall that with chaining, the LDAP server chases the referral instead of the client. With Directory Server, chaining is enabled via a special object class that directs the server to channel requests to a chaining plug-in. The chaining plug-in is enabled by default. An entry of this object class can have no children, and it holds only a single attribute. This attribute is a database link to another directory server, not an LDAP URL as referrals normally are. Chaining is supported only to other instances of Directory Server, not to LDAP servers from other vendors.

Directory Server chaining can sidestep another issue that referrals don't. With referrals, the client must bind again to the server to which it is redirected. With chaining, this action is handled by the first server. Not only that, but with referrals you usually need a copy of the binding entry on each server. Chaining can eliminate this requirement.

Chaining eliminates some restrictions of referrals

Multiple levels of chaining are allowed. This is called *cascading chaining.* Loops in chaining are detected and prevented by a special LDAP control called Loop Detection. By default, you must enable this control on each database. To enable the control on the database specified by the entry, add the OID of the Loop Detection control, `1.3.6.1.4.1.1466.29539.12`, to the `nsTransmittedControls` attribute in the `cn=config, cn=chaining database,cn=plugins,cn=config` entry. The Loop Detection control then uses the `nsHopLimit` attribute described next to detect loops.

Chaining can traverse multiple levels, but loops and excessive chaining can be prevented

The `nsHopLimit` attribute limits the number of times a request can be passed to another server via chaining. This attribute is used to prevent looping or to limit operations that cause excessive chaining. There are several other attributes that affect the behavior of chaining; for more detail, turn to Appendix G for the URLs to the online documentation.

A hop limit restricts the number of chaining operations from a single request

Plug-ins and requests that use controls have implications when chaining is encountered. Additional configuration to allow plug-ins and controls to work is required by default. This default lack of functionality limits the security exposure and is therefore a good thing. Adding the OID of an LDAP control to the `nsTransmittedControls` attribute of the `cn=config, cn=chaining database,cn=plugins,cn=config` entry allows

By default, special operations may fail during chaining

Chaining Is a Great Idea

Chaining is a powerful feature that represents the maturity of this product. One of the key differences between LDAP and X.500 directories is that the LDAP client must chase referrals, whereas the X.500 client has chaining to do this extra work. By borrowing this key functionality, Directory Server has made up for one of LDAP's weaknesses and placed itself ahead of other products.

requests using that control to chain for the chaining database specified by the entry.

The chaining con-figuration details are stored in a variety of special attributes

The database links associated with a naming context that is chaining to a remote server are stored under the entry `cn=chaining database,cn=plugins,cn=config`. The `nss-lapd-referral` attribute is used to indicate the remote naming context that this database link will manage. The `nsMultiplexorBindDN` attribute stores the binding account, whereas `nsMultiplexorCredentials` stores the password. The remote server is indicated by specifying an LDAP URL to just the server's hostname via the `nsFarmServerURL` attribute.

Operations and Clients

Directory Server feature functionality can be extended, but the default functionality is quite handy

Directory Server is fully LDAP v3 compliant, and the product has actively implemented IETF drafts related to LDAP. Functionality special to Directory Server is typically implemented via a plug-in API that has been documented to allow further extension. For details on the plug-ins provided by default, see the following section titled Plug-ins. Directory Server offers a good selection of LDAP controls, featuring the most critical and useful IETF drafts that have been proposed. Client integration is adequate but can't be considered a strength of the product.

Clients

Directory Server relies primarily on command-line executables
for client functionality. The command-line executables
ldapsearch, ldapmodify, and ldapdelete are provided to enable
normal client operations. Full online documentation is available
at http://docs.sun.com/source/816-5608-10/utilities.htm#12904.
In addition to this user-oriented client software, the primary tool
for administering the server and the directory contents is the
Administrative Console, a graphical Java application that can
be run remotely.

The command-line applications are the primary client

However, there are also some graphical interface clients available for typical users. For example, the Netscape Communicator browser is designed to work well with Directory Server.
It provides support for

The Netscape browser also provides client support

- Searching for users, groups, phone numbers, and other
  attributes

- Sending an e-mail message to multiple recipients using
  LDAP lookups

- Configuring the list of LDAP servers to search

- Importing LDIF files

- LDAP URL support

There are also a few other Sun products that provide a graphical interface that may be appropriate for client users that have
special directory roles. iPlanet Delegated Administrator and
iPlanet Console are two such products (for more information,
see the following section, Management).

Directory-Enabled Applications

Sun and Netscape provide several useful LDAP-enabled applications and utilities that are designed for Directory Server in their
respective Directory Server Resource Kits. In addition, many
other server products from Sun and Netscape use Directory

A plethora of directory-enabled applications use Directory Server

Server. The Sun ONE Web Server, Netscape Enterprise Server, Sun ONE Calendar Server, Netscape Calendar Server, Sun ONE Messaging Server, Netscape Messaging Server, and Sun ONE Web Proxy Server all use Directory Server to authenticate users, and to provide some authorization information like group membership for access control. Sun ONE and Netscape Messaging Server also store distribution lists in Directory Server and use it to determine mail routing. Sun ONE and Netscape Certificate Server store user certificates and CRLs within Directory Server. Some of the other products that make use of Directory Server include Sun Directory Proxy Server, iPlanet BillerXpert, iPlanet ECXpert, iPlanet SellerXpert, iPlanet Market Maker, Sun Portal Server, and Netscape Certificate Management System.

Programming Support

Directory Server development support is rich

As you might expect with a product with such a long history, there are a wide range of resources available for developers. Sun and Netscape provide software development kits (SDKs) for the LDAP API in C and Java, and a perl version is available at http://mozilla.org. In addition to these development kits, there are code samples and other software kits. Vendor documentation is pretty good but tends to lag behind the product release. Appendix G lists several relevant URLs for this documentation. Sun and Netscape host answer forums that can be a source of information. In terms of additional help, I'd recommend these books:

- *LDAP Programming with Java* by Rob Weltman and Tony Dahbura

- *LDAP: Programming Directory-Enabled Applications with Lightweight Directory Access Protocol* by Tim Howes and Mark Smith

Of course, if you'd rather not do your own development, Sun or Netscape's Professional Services will do the work for you for a fee.

Controls

By default, Directory Server provides ten controls that extend the functionality of the server. Some of these controls provide support for functionality I have already mentioned, like chaining, while others support functionality I haven't discussed yet, like proxy authorization. What follows is a short description of each control. For greater detail, go to the online documentation at http://docs.sun.com/source/816-5616-10/controls.htm#999558, although note that not all the controls are well documented.

Directory Server supports many controls enabling further functionality

- **Manage DSA IT control** (2.16.840.1.113730.3.4.2)— Used to access entries that return referrals on client requests. This enables an LDAP client to manage the reference entry.

- **Persistent Search control** (2.16.840.1.113730.3.4.3)— Similar to the other persistent search controls discussed in Chapter 3, Appendix A, and E. You can specify tracking specific types of changes or all changes. The specific types break into the common modify-oriented LDAP operations: add, delete, modifyRDN, and modify. Results are returned with a special reference that can be used to obtain additional information about the type of change, the change number within that server's change log, and the old DN of the entry (if applicable). You use the reference with the Entry Change Notification control to query the server for the additional information. To end execution of the Persistent Search control, you can either send an abandon operation or unbind.

- **Entry Change Notification control** (2.16.840.1.113730.3.4.7)—Used to discover additional information about a specific change. It is returned to a client that has issued a search with the Persistent Search control.

- **Password Expired control** (2.16.840.1.113730.3.4.4)—
  Notifies a user to immediately change a password. This
  control is sent to the client if a password has been reset
  or if this is the client's first time logging in. If password
  policy has been enabled on the server, the user is allowed
  to send only an operation changing the password; all
  other operations are refused.

- **Password Expiration Warning control**
  (2.16.840.1.113730.3.4.5)—Used to indicate to the client
  that a password will expire soon. The number of seconds
  until expiration is included in the client message.

- **Virtual List View Request control**
  (2.16.840.1.113730.3.4.9)—Used with the search operation, this control allows the client to specify that the
  server return a subset of the search results in a special
  order and number and starting at a specific index. This
  capability is particularly useful for LDAP-enabled applications like e-mail clients, which allow users to scroll
  through a potentially huge number of user entries but
  display only a limited number of sorted entries beginning
  with a specific entry. This control is mentioned in
  Chapter 3 and Appendix E.

- **Virtual List Response control**
  (2.16.840.1.113730.3.4.10)—The matching pair to the
  Virtual List View Request control. This control is returned
  to a client that has issued a Virtual List View Request.

- **Server-Side Sort control** (1.2.840.113556.1.4.473)—
  Used with the search operation. It allows a client to retrieve results in sorted order as specified by the client.
  This control is described in Chapter 3 and Appendix E.
  Directory Server doesn't deploy the matching pair to this
  control, Sorted Search Response control
  (1.2.840.113556.1.4.474), a design that does not follow
  the draft standard specification.

- **Proxy Authorization control**
  (2.16.840.1.113730.3.4.12)—Used to assume the identity of another entry for the duration of a request. The
  control is intended primarily for use by servers that act
  on behalf of other users. This control can be used with
  any operation other than bind. A server process can have
  a single connection to the LDAP server but execute various client requests in the context of the user submitting
  the request. Within the operation, you also specify the
  proxy DN, the DN of the entry you are impersonating.
  Success requires that the proxied entry has granted your
  DN the appropriate proxy rights.

- **Chaining Loop Detection control**
  (1.3.6.1.4.1.1466.29539.12)—Used to detect and prevent an arbitrarily long sequence of chaining references
  that might be a loop. When a chain reference first occurs, the server sets this control with a maximum number
  of hops when it sends the request to the next server. This
  number is configurable using the `nsHopLimit` attribute,
  which by default is set to 10. Each subsequent server
  decrements the hop count. If a server receives a request
  with this control set and a hop count of 0, then the
  server returns an error message to the client.

Plug-ins

Directory Server allows the directory functionality to be extended via plug-ins. These plug-ins are special code components that can be installed and enabled to provide functionality
that is outside the default configuration. This description sounds
very similar to that of an LDAP control. But in general, plug-ins
are used to provide functionality that isn't directly related to a
client request or response. More specifically, plug-ins let you
extend and control the directory functionality without relying
on the client invoking a control. Many plug-ins are related to
checking the validity of client input for a specific syntax for

*Plug-ins extend direc-
tory functionality*

searching and sorting. For example, many of the language- and locale-specific syntax rules are implemented via syntax plug-ins. These plug-ins are called by the search system for ordering and matching.

Plug-ins give you greater control over built-in functionality

You can also write your own custom syntax-checking plug-in to enforce specific rules not known to the vendor-supplied plug-ins. For example, say that as the directory administrator you wanted every access control specifier to be checked for validity (further suppose that there is no schema-checking process). Because controls require that the client invoke them, if you deployed this validity check via a control, you would have no guarantee that every access control specifier was valid. Other LDAP servers incorporate this type of functionality in the schema-checking process without giving any choice on the configuration. As the directory administrator, you have no control over whether the access control specifier is checked for validity, aside from turning off the entire schema-checking process. But with Directory Server, you can control this smaller piece of functionality, electing to turn it off or on without affecting any other functionality. You might still turn off all schema checking, but you now have the luxury of picking and choosing which syntaxes to check. You can also write your own custom syntax-checking plug-in to enforce specific rules not known to the vendor-supplied plug-ins.

Plug-ins Are Also a Great Idea

The ability to write your own component that will augment an off-the-shelf product is a wonderful idea. In a way, this ability takes a bite out of part of the open source argument. If I can augment the product to do what I want, I'm less eager to see the core code. The company holds the responsibility for the core code, and I have the flexibility I desire. It's too bad that other LDAP vendors haven't given us this option. Kudos to Directory Server for wisdom.

The configuration for each Directory Server plug-in has a separate entry and set of attributes under `cn=plugins,cn=config`. Because many of the plug-ins supply syntax-checking, their configuration is limited to an on/off toggle. But some plug-ins are more complex and have extensive configuration. All plug-ins are instances of the `nsSlapdPlugin` object class, which inherits from the `extensibleObject` object class. As you'll recall, `extensibleObject` is the most flexible object class, with every defined attribute available to it.

Plug-ins are represented by entries in the directory

There are 31 plug-ins provided with Directory Server. Roles, class of service, multimaster replication, chaining, database operation, language-specific LDAP operation, password encryption, and ACL resolution are each supported directly or indirectly via plug-ins. As alluded to earlier, each of the 12 supported syntaxes is implemented via plug-ins. I don't discuss these plug-ins in detail here, but you can find a complete list with descriptions in Appendix F.

Many of the features that Directory Server offers are enabled via plug-ins

Schema

The core schema deployed by Directory Server includes all schema elements included in any Internet standard related to LDAP. There are some inconsistencies based on proprietary changes to classes, attributes, and syntaxes. In total, the core schema defines 12 syntaxes, 45 object classes, and 126 attributes. The schema can be extended from the default core that is supplied. Many supplemental schemas are available to support companion products that leverage Directory Server. Directory Server supports turning off the schema-checking process.

Directory Server employs all schema elements defined in Internet standards

Schema definitions are defined in LDIF format and are integrated at Directory Server startup. These files are stored in a special file directory on the server, which varies based on the underlying platform. Definitions are stored within the directory in an entry with a special DN: `cn=schema`. This entry doesn't

The schema comes from LDIF files and is placed in a special directory entry

have its own naming context (with a separate database) but is created from the schema file definitions at the service startup. Every object class and attribute supported are listed on this entry, under the `objectclasses` and `attributes` attributes. In addition to this file-based initialization, the schema are replicated between Directory Servers.

Schema inconsistencies can occur within the model employed by Directory Server

Schema replication is supported in both single-master and multimaster models. In either model, the schema must be consistent across all the servers. Otherwise, errors will ensue, and both schema and directory replication can fail. The schema can become inconsistent if a schema element is defined differently via the local LDIF schema files. When schema changes that overlap are made on the same master, they are resolved by the last change made. However, serious functional issues can occur in a multimaster model. If schema changes are made on two different masters, inconsistencies will result. Because of this functional limitation, it is strongly recommended that you always make schema modifications to the same master.

Groups

Directory Server provides both static and dynamic groups

Both static and dynamic groups are supported. Static groups are of object class `groupOfNames`, with a multivalued `member` attribute with the DN of each entry that is a member. The DN of another static or dynamic group can also be a value of `member`. This is called a *nested group*. Dynamic groups are of the object class `groupOfURLs`, with a multivalued `memberURL` attribute that contains a URL search filter. These search filters are evaluated at the time of access to generate the list of group membership. In contrast to static groups, the DN of another static or dynamic group is not a valid value of `memberURL`. However, you can create an entry with both the `groupOfNames` and the `groupOfURLs` object classes. This group entry would allow you to define both dynamic and static membership with nested groups. Because Directory Server uses dynamic membership and doesn't implement a back reference (called a linked attribute in Chapter 7) like Active Directory does, there is no simple way to enumerate all the groups to which a given entry belongs.

Roles

Roles are like groups, but they take the opposite approach. Instead of listing the DN of member entries on the role entry, the DN of the role entry is listed on each of the member entries. In other words, the user entry asserts its memberships, instead of the role asserting the membership. This is more conducive to being able to list every role assigned to a given entry, while being less conducive to listing every entry that belongs to a role.

Roles provide a different approach to grouping entries

To enable this functionality, every user entry has two special operational attributes called `nsRole` and `nsRoleDN`. `nsRoleDN` provides a mechanism to explicitly add the entry to a role. If I wanted to add myself to a role, I'd add the DN value of the desired role to my `nsRoleDN` attribute. `nsRole` is a read-only attribute maintained by the directory itself, and it lists every role to which the entry belongs. In actuality, the value of this attribute isn't statically maintained; it is dynamically calculated upon request. As a result, `nsRole` can't be used in any search filter. The value of `nsRole` is based on the value of `nsRoleDN`

Two special operational attributes enable this functionality

Group Functionality Is One of Only a Few Weaknesses

This lack of functionality of groups represents one of the few weaknesses of Directory Server—other products have superior functionality on this point. There are definitely ways to overcome this weakness, but it doesn't appear that this problem is being actively worked on. For nested memberships, I can imagine a control or plug-in that would do the recursive checks and limit looping within this recursion. For dynamic memberships, a back reference would suffice and eliminate the need for roles.

for that entry plus any of the dynamic and nested roles that may apply.

Although there are many object classes, only three are used in practice

There are several types of role entries, with many object classes representing them. Table 8-2 lists all these role object classes and gives a brief description of each. In practice, only three of the object classes are used to create entries: `nsNestedRoleDefinition`, `nsManagedRoleDefinition`, and `nsFilteredRoleDefinition`. *Managed roles* are the basic role entry. *Nested roles* provide a mechanism to have one role belong to another role. *Filtered roles* allow the membership of a role to be determined dynamically via a search filter.

Two limitations require careful planning to enable effective access control via roles

Roles are not compatible with chaining in all cases. Both an entry and its role entry must exist on the chained server or else the role mechanism (which automatically updates `nsRole`) will fail. If your servers are fully replicated, using roles will not be an issue; but otherwise, it will require careful planning. Of course, you probably wouldn't use chaining if you had a fully

Table 8-2   Role object classes

Object Class	Superior	Special Characteristics
`nsRoleDefinition`	`ldapSubEntry`	Just a `cn` and `description`
`nsSimpleRoleDefinition`	`nsRoleDefinition`	Just a `cn` and `description`
`nsManagedRoleDefinition`	`nsSimpleRoleDefinition`	Just a `cn` and `description`
`nsComplexRoleDefinition`	`nsRoleDefinition`	Just a `cn` and `description`
`nsNestedRoleDefinition`	`nsComplexRoleDefinition`	Equivalent to a nested group; a DN-based mandatory `nsRoleDN` attribute enables the nesting
`nsFilteredRoleDefinition`	`nsComplexRoleDefinition`	Equivalent to a dynamic group; a search filter in a mandatory `nsRoleFilter` attribute enables the dynamic membership

replicated environment. Roles are also dangerous with respect to user access control. Users are typically given full control of their entries, but this design lets them join any role they want, thus compromising access control based on roles. This limitation requires careful access control definition and awareness among directory administrators.

You can inactivate role entries, a step that inactivates all the entries that belong to that role. This might be an effective way to temporarily disable authentication to a set of entries. Reactivation of the role re-enables access to that set of entries. You can also delete role entries, though deletions can cause problems because of the way roles are implemented. Each entry that asserts membership in a deleted role is not automatically updated, unless the Referential Integrity plug-in is configured to search the `nsRoleDN` attribute for deleted role entries. For more information on plug-ins, see the earlier section Plug-ins, and for additional material on the Referential Integrity plug-in, see Appendix F.

You can inactivate or delete role entries

Class of Service (CoS)

The Class of Service (CoS) mechanism is used to associate a single attribute value on many entries. This is an important mechanism in simplifying management of recurring data. CoS values are calculated dynamically at the time of the request for the attribute. This results in a significantly smaller storage profile. However, the attribute that is dynamically asserted cannot be used in a search filter. The usefulness of CoS is limited to attributes that you wouldn't use to find entries. But regardless, CoS is somewhat useful, and it represents an important feature that deserves further development. In fact, this is the only mechanism of its kind on any LDAP server.

Class of Service (CoS) is used to assert an attribute value on many entries

An example of a situation in which CoS might be used demonstrates its usefulness. At Mycompany all of the person entries at Muppet HQ have the same address. If Muppet HQ moved, it

CoS's usefulness demonstrated

would be annoying to modify all the addresses manually, although LDIF could be used to speed this process. CoS simplifies this process even further by providing a way to make a single modification that affects all these entries at once.

Dynamic values can be dynamically asserted via CoS

You can use the Class of Service mechanism to dynamically assert a static attribute value or to assert a dynamically determined value. In the Muppet HQ example, a static value is asserted. However, the value could be asserted in a dynamic fashion. Consider another example: Luke Skywalker is the manager of a team of people within the Engineering organization at Mycompany. Each of their person entries reflects this relationship with an `o=Engineering` attribute pair. However, there is a big shakeup at Mycompany, and Luke's entire team is reorganized into the Marketing organization within Mycompany. CoS allows Luke's team members to have their o attributes dynamically linked to the value of Luke's o attribute. Each team member's o attribute is linked to the `manager` entry, which in this case indicates Luke's entry. CoS follows this path to Luke's entry and uses his o value for each team member's entry. Sounds pretty tricky, huh? Let's take a look at how this works.

There are three kinds of CoS definition entries and only one CoS template entry

Table 8-3 lists all the CoS object classes. Of these object classes, only four are commonly used: `cosTemplate`, `cosClassicDefinition`, `cosIndirectDefinition`, and `cosPointerDefinition`. `cosClassicDefinition`, `cosIndirectDefinition`, and `cosPointerDefinition` are used to specify the scope of affected entries and are called CoS definition entries. A *CoS definition entry* determines the scope of affected entries by its placement in the directory; all child entries below the parent of a CoS definition entry are affected. All the CoS definition entries have a mandatory `cosAttribute`. The `cosAttribute` specifies which attribute will have its value asserted. The `cosAttribute` can be multivalued; more than one attribute can be asserted. Each of the

Table 8-3   CoS object classes

Name	Mandatory	Allowed
cosDefinition		aci,cn,cosAttribute,cosSpecifier, cosTargetTree,cosTemplateDN,uid
cosSuperDefinition	cosAttribute	cn,description
cosClassicDefinition	cosAttribute	cn,description,cosSpecifier, cosTemplateDN
cosIndirectDefinition	cosAttribute	cn,description,cosIndirectSpecifier
cosPointerDefinition	cosAttribute	cn,description,cosTemplateDN
cosTemplate		cn,cosPriority

three types of CoS definition entries also has an attribute called a specifier. The *specifier* is used in determining the value of the attribute specified in `cosAttribute`. The specifier attribute is used differently for each object class, allowing fine-grained control of how attributes are evaluated based on the object classes of an entry. This diversity in how the attribute is used provides a richer mechanism.

Before looking at the details of each of the specifier attributes, we first need to take a look at the `cosTemplate` object class. A `cosTemplate` entry is called a *CoS template*. A CoS template is usually placed in the same directory container as the CoS definition entry, but this placement isn't required. You use a CoS template to assert one or many attribute values, and it can have an assigned priority in case more than one template matches a specifier (more on specifiers later). Higher numbers have higher priority, but zero is the highest priority. The key purpose of a CoS template is to statically define the value of the attribute being asserted. To achieve this purpose, all attributes need to be available to it. So in summary, I define a CoS template with the static value of the attribute I'm asserting via CoS.

The CoS template entry determines the attribute value indicated by `cosAttribute`

How Does cosTemplate Have All Attributes Available to It?

I don't know, and I couldn't get any answers about it. The documentation and configuration files indicate that `cosTemplate` inherits from the `top` class, but I suspect that the `extensibleObject` object class is also involved in an undocumented, behind-the-scenes hack. This would give entries of this object class the ability to add any defined attribute, which is clearly required for the functionality provided by this object class.

Isn't CoS Neat?

I really like CoS. I think the ability to quickly modify a bunch of disparate entries is a dandy of a feature. It might be a little complicated, but system administrators are paid to understand complexities. Directory Server needs to overcome the search filter weakness of CoS in future releases for CoS to be worthwhile. Otherwise, as a systems administrator, I'd rather just write a script that manually does all the modifications.

Pointer CoS

Pointer CoS determines resolution by directly pointing to a template entry with the value

The simplest type of CoS is pointer CoS. With pointer CoS (a `cosPointerDefinition` entry), the specifier attribute is `cosTemplateDN`. `cosTemplateDN` indicates a DN of a CoS template. A base-level search commences using this DN as the baseDN, and a presence search filter with the value of the `cosAttribute` (which is the name of an attribute). The value returned from the template is then asserted on all the affected entries. Consider Figure 8-2, which uses the Muppet HQ example (where the address was changed) to illustrate how pointer CoS works.

The CoS definition determines that the `postalAddress` value will be asserted for all entries below the Muppets OU. It speci-

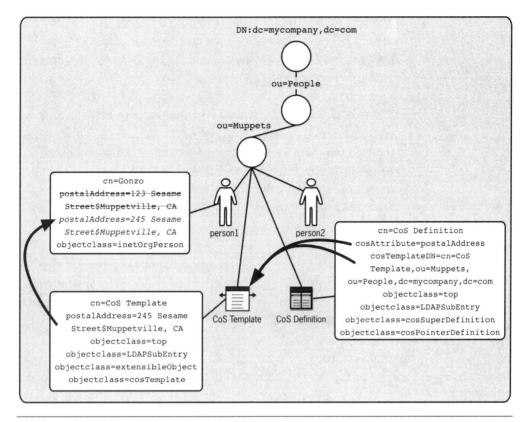

Figure 8-2   Pointer CoS example

fies the CoS template for resolution of the value. The CoS template specifies the `postalAddress` value, and this value overrides the static value on Gonzo's entry as well as all the other entries under `ou=Muppets`.

Classic CoS

The second type of CoS is called classic CoS. Classic CoS (a `cosClassicDefinition` entry) is similar to pointer CoS in that a CoS template provides the value of the attribute indicated by `cosAttribute`. However, the DN of the CoS template is not completely indicated by the specifier attribute `cosTemplateDN`.

Classic CoS determines resolution using a dynamic mechanism to point to a template entry with the value

The DN of the CoS template is formed by prepending "cn=" to the value in the classic CoS attribute `cosSpecifier` and appending the DN in `cosTemplateDN`. Figure 8-3 provides an example of classic CoS.

The CoS definition determines that the `postalAddress` value will be asserted for all entries below the People OU. It specifies the CoS template for resolution of the value is also under the `ou=People` container, and that the `cn` of the template should be determined by the value of the o attribute on the target entry. For Luke's entry, the value of o is Engineering, so the CoS template that applies is `cn=Engineering`. This CoS template specifies the `postalAddress` value, and this value overrides the static value on Luke's entry. In combination with many more CoS templates, this approach could be used to dynamically assign everyone's address based on the organization to which each person belongs.

Indirect CoS

Indirect CoS determines resolution by using a normal entry instead of a template entry

The third type of CoS is called indirect CoS. With indirect CoS (a `cosIndirectDefinition` entry), the specifier attribute is `cosIndirectSpecifier`. `cosIndirectSpecifier` indicates an attribute *on the target entry*. The target entry's attribute contains a DN value. This DN value is used as if it were a CoS template (but it doesn't need to be a CoS template). The attribute indicated by `cosAttribute` is queried on this DN, and the value returned is asserted by CoS. With indirect CoS, each target entry's attribute may have a different DN value and thus have a different value for the CoS attribute. Consider Figure 8-4, which uses the Luke Skywalker reorganization example (when the o was asserted via the manager's entry) to illustrate how indirect CoS works.

The CoS definition determines that the o value will be asserted for all entries below the Staff OU. It specifies the `manager` attribute will specify the DN used to resolve the value.

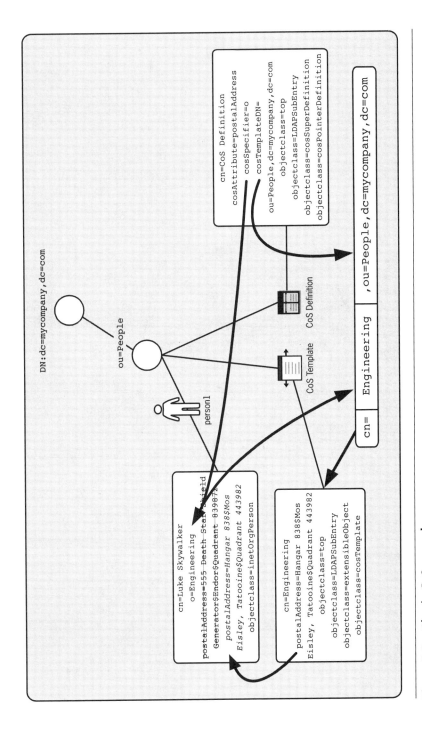

Figure 8-3   Classic CoS example

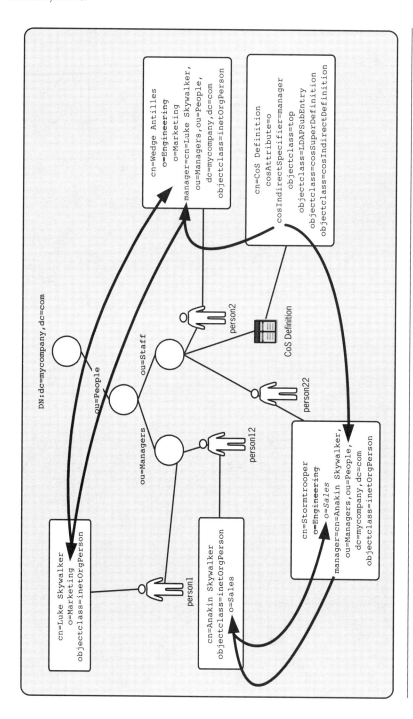

Figure 8-4   Indirect CoS example

On Wedge's entry, his `manager` attribute indicates Luke's entry. Luke's entry has an o attribute value of Marketing, so Wedge's entry gets the same value. However, on the Stormtrooper entry, the `manager` attribute indicates Anakin's entry. Anakin's entry has an o attribute value of Sales, which is applied to Stormtrooper's entry.

Management

Sun offers many products that provide additional management control. A short summary of the most interesting of these products follows, and you can find more information and management products under Sun's online documentation at http://docs.sun.com/.

Many Sun products provide additional directory management functionality

Sun Directory Proxy Server provides an LDAP proxy (or gateway) that, together with customer-defined rules, intelligently redirects LDAP client requests to an LDAP server and vice versa. Mycompany might deploy this proxy product to provide an extra layer of privacy to keep its directory information safe.

An LDAP proxy provides a layer of privacy control

iPlanet Console provides a GUI-based interface for administration of users and groups and for editing ACI statements. This is a useful tool for anyone who doesn't like the command line, and it reduces the level of detail you need to understand by walking you through many actions. It also includes a graphical Directory browser for operating directly on individual entries or subtrees.

A GUI-based console provides an alternative to the command line

iPlanet Delegated Administrator provides an HTML-based interface (via Java) for administration of user and group management, roles, Class of Service, and user certificates, among many other things. But even more important is how it predefines six levels of delegated directory administration via special roles. This layered delegation can help Mycompany give the most appropriate level of control to its staff.

An HTML-based interface is also provided

Sun's metadirectory provides a diversity of interoperability

iPlanet MetaDirectory's connectors speak primarily LDAP and SQL. In addition, custom connectors provide connectivity to specific products like Active Directory. Finally, a special customizable connector allows file-based input sources. This diversity maximizes the directories and data sources that can be integrated. Mycompany might use this metadirectory product to integrate an application-specific or NOS directory.

Useful management tools are provided

On a more mundane topic, Sun also provides a set of management tools and scripts for Directory Server. These tools support easy backups, LDIF operations, configuration activities, and service management. Online documentation is available at http://docs.sun.com/source/816-5606-10/index.html.

Replication

Three types of replication roles determine the replication model used by Directory Server

Directory Server defines three types of replicas. Labeling these types differently is largely for the purpose of understanding the replication functionality employed. A *master replica* allows both read- and write-oriented LDAP operations. A *consumer replica* is read-only and is a replicated copy of another master replica. The consumer server returns a referral to the master replica for all add, modify, modifyRDN, and delete operations. This referral reflects the fact that the consumer server is read-only, and that writes must be made to the master server. A *hub replica* is a consumer replica that distributes directory entries via replication to other consumer replicas. Directory Server replication follows a push model. In other words, the master replica (which might also be a hub) initiates replication. A consumer replica cannot request updates.

A replication agreement defines the configuration of replication

Replication agreements control which consumer replicas receive replication from a master replica. These agreements determine the target consumer, the database to replicate, scheduling for the replication, the authentication for the connection, and the encryption used for the traffic. The scheduling options include recurring periodic replication, a specific schedule, or immediate replication as changes happen. SSL encryption is fully supported via replication. Multiple-master replication is configured by setting up two replication agreements, one on each of the two master replicas. Each replication agreement uses a server thread as well as a file descriptor.

A change log tracks all changes to a master replica. This change log is used to determine what changes should be replicated to consumer replicas. Only the directory uses the change log; however, this data can be shared with clients through the Retro Change Log plug-in, which allows access to a parallel copy of the change log via LDAP. This separate and parallel change log can be enabled and disabled independently of the one used strictly by the replication process. Changes for multiple replicas on a master server are logged to a shared change log.

A change log is used to track the modifications that should be replicated

In a multiple-master architecture, collision resolution is determined by the last change made. Each change includes a timestamp that is used for determining collision resolution. If the server can't determine a resolution for a collision, manual resolution by a directory administrator is required. The replication process automatically flags the entry with a special operational attribute `nsds5ReplConflict`. Naming collisions result in the second entry having its DN appended with the `nsUniqueID` attribute, so the second entry has a globally unique value.

Replication collision resolution is handled automatically in most cases

There are some requirements when you use replication. A special entry called the Replication Manager entry is required to support replication. This entry exists on both the master and consumer replica servers. This entry has a special level of authorization on the consumer server and is not restricted by access controls set on the consumer server. Because of the sensitivity of this entry, it cannot be in the replication data. The Attribute Uniqueness plug-in cannot be used with multiple-master replication. The Referential Integrity plug-in can be run only on a single-master server in a multiple-master architecture.

Some configuration requirements are required in a replicated environment

The schema is replicated

The directory schema is replicated with the replica by default. In fact, the first steps performed in every replication transaction are verifying and replicating the schema as required. These steps help to ensure that the remainder of the replication can succeed. If part of the schema was missing and an entry included that schema element, the directory would have problems. After the schema has been replicated, the remainder of directory data replication proceeds.

Special Configuration Parameters

cn=config holds all the configuration parameters

The earlier section Naming Context highlights the importance of the information stored within `cn=config`. Most of the feature-specific configuration options available have been covered; however, there are many more options that can be configured.

Common configuration options are offered, only with greater functionality

These configuration options include the common ones that other products offer. However, Directory Server adds an additional layer of control. For example, the directory administrator can set resource limits on a per-user basis to restrict the basic LDAP functionality that a client is capable of performing. These limits include the maximum number of entries returned in an operation, a time limit, an idle timeout, and the maximum number of entries that will be examined to perform a single operation. Of course, these limits can be set at the server level as with other products, but Directory Server provides a greater degree of flexibility than its competitors.

Many options are configurable

Other options include turning off all access control checking, control over what operations are audited to a log file, control over what level of detail is written to the error log, control over the number of nested groups allowed, password lockout features, and SSL settings. Performance tuning options like maximum number of file handles available or threads per connection are also available.

The full details of the information stored in the configuration naming context are well documented online at http://docs.sun.com/source/816-5608-10/config.htm#12904.

See online documentation for more details

Security

Directory Server uses a variety of security features ranging from traditional access control to advanced features that are unique in the marketplace. Along with groups and roles, I introduced some of the basic functionality that enables the security features in the earlier section Schema. In addition, a full range of authentication and encryption methods is supported. However, the really exciting features are within the authorization support, where Directory Server exceeds all other LDAP server products in sophistication and sheer number of authorization factors available.

Directory Server offers a diversity of security features, with significant authorization features

The authorization features include the ability to proxy authorization to another account, dynamic group-based authorization, role-based authorization, and authorization based on the comparison of attribute values. Also available is the ability to restrict access based on the client's authentication method, IP address, DNS hostname, or the time of access. Directory Server also supports dynamic inheritance of authorization controls as well as access control macros for repetitive access controls. The number of authorization features and the complexity of functionality they provide are overwhelming.

The authorization features form an overwhelming list

Authentication

Among the authentication methods that Directory Server provides are anonymous authentication, simple authentication, simple authentication over TLS, authentication via certificate-based identity, and DIGEST-MD5 authentication with SASL. Like most LDAP servers, the basic unit of authentication is focused on the entry representing the client user. The password is

Directory Server supports common authentication methods

stored as an attribute of the user entry, and other authorization information is stored as part of this entry. For example, password history can be stored to keep a user from reusing old passwords. If nsAccountLock is set to TRUE, it will inactivate an entry's ability to bind. It can also be set on role entries to inactivate all the users associated with that role.

Certificate authentication is supported

In addition to password-based authentication, you can configure clients to use certificate-based authentication. You use the userCertificate attribute of the user's entry to store the certificate in binary format for the client. The DN indicated by the certificate must either match the DN of the user's entry or be mapped to this entry.

Pass-thru authentication simplifies the client experience

Directory Server supports pass-thru authentication. This means that one Directory Server passes credentials to another Directory Server so the client user doesn't have to bind to each server separately. It also means that the user's entry doesn't have to be replicated to every Directory Server to access data stored in that server. This functionality requires the Pass Thru Authentication (PTA) plug-in. This plug-in has a few useful configuration options. For example, you can specify that the two Directory Servers encrypt all pass-thru authentication communications. For more details, go to the online documentation, Chapter 16 of the *Administrator's Guide*, at http://docs.sun.com/source/816-5606-10/pasthru.htm#1068035.

Support for proxy authorization lets you access the directory with my rights

Although proxy authorization isn't an authentication method, it is used to impersonate another identity. As a user with access to specific directory resources, I can give the proxy right for my user entry to another user's entry. That user can then impersonate me, accessing directory resources as if a bind operation had been issued with my user entry. This other user does not need the password of my account to exercise the proxy right I've delegated. Instead, the other user employs proxy authorization at the time of each request to the directory by specifying the Proxy Authorization control. The control requires a single value known as the *ProxyDN*. Only users who have been specifically given proxy rights can impersonate my entry. To give the proxy right to another user, I must define a special statement called an access control instruction (ACI) that gives the other user account some specific subset of the directory access rights I hold.

Authorization

With Directory Server, an ACI is the essential unit used to define the directory access controls. A collection of access control instructions is called an access control list. An ACI is logically represented as an attribute of an entry, called the `aci` attribute. Each ACI can have multiple values that together form an access control list. There are four components to an ACI entry: a target, heading, permissions, and bind rules. By default, the access control specified in the `aci` attribute of an entry affects that entry and every child entry below that entry. This default behavior occurs only when the ACI target isn't specified. Application of the ACI to all child entries is accomplished via a feature unique to Directory Server called dynamic inheritance.

The ACI is the basic unit of access control

Inheritance occurs when a configuration setting, in this case an access control, propagates to children entries. With static inheritance, the access control is copied to each of the entries below it. Microsoft's Active Directory is an example of an LDAP server that uses static inheritance. With dynamic inheritance, the access control is never copied to subordinate objects. Instead, when a user tries to access an entry, the access control of that entry and every parent container must be checked. When more than one ACI applies, the union is effective. Denying access takes precedence over allowing access, so a deny all at the root of the directory would effectively restrict everyone from the entire directory.

Directory Server employs dynamic inheritance, and multiple ACIs may apply

There is a subtle difference between static inheritance and dynamic inheritance. This difference can affect performance dramatically, depending on how you make use of access controls

Inheritance has an implication on performance

in your directory. Static inheritance inflicts a load at the time of applying access controls, whereas dynamic inheritance increases the potential burden at the time of access. Minimizing this burden involves carefully crafting the ACIs. This task can almost be an art form, and it is best to test the configuration for performance impact.

The syntax of ACIs is complex; Appendix F covers ACIs in detail

In fact, the syntax and specific access control factors that ACIs provide are complex enough that they require extended coverage and study. For this reason, I've placed the extended overview of ACIs in Appendix F. Each of the components of an ACI is given specific attention, the access control factors offered are highlighted, and a number of examples are presented to illustrate the proper use of ACIs.

Macros can simplify complex or repetitive ACIs

Because ACIs can become complex and lengthy, Directory Server offers a feature to help simplify them. This feature is called *macros*. Macros can reduce the number of ACI statements needed when a repeating pattern of ACIs is required. They can also simplify a nonrepetitive ACI.

Macros allow variable substitution within an ACI

Macros are placeholders that are used to represent a DN, or a portion of a DN, in an ACI. In other words, a portion of the target DN can be saved as a variable to be plugged in later in the ACI statement. Macros are essentially dynamic DNs in ACIs. You might use a macro to save a DN in the target and later use this saved DN in the bind rule of the ACI. When used with wildcards, a single macro ACI can replace multiple ACI statements throughout the directory. Having many ACIs is bad for performance and also harder to administer. Macro ACIs, including examples, are also covered in detail in Appendix F.

Privacy

Directory Server supports both SSL and TLS

SSL v2, SSL v3, and TLS are available by default for session encryption. Several encryption algorithms are provided, including

RC2, RC4, DES, and Triple DES. Key lengths of 1024 bits are supported with TLS.

The `cn=encryption,cn=config` entry holds the server encryption settings. On this entry you can configure the SSL session timeout, whether encryption is allowed or required, and enable which of the available algorithms can be used by clients. These settings transcend the authorization controls specified in ACI statements. So if you require session encryption here, all client access must be encrypted whether or not the ACI access control requires it.

The encryption settings are highly configurable

Why Directory Server?

The strengths of Directory Server are numerous. Along with these features, it enjoys a great number of deployments and a historical advantage. Directory Server also benefits from broad multiplatform support, enabling server platforms of Solaris, Microsoft Windows NT or 2000, HP-UX, and IBM AIX. Sun has plans to support Linux this year. Sun also has plans to implement DSML support this year.

Multiplatform support and widespread deployment are good signs

Of course, the most critical performance number is how many client search operations can be performed per second. Directory Server ranks well ahead of all competitors, with only Active Directory coming close. An independent head-to-head comparison of LDAP servers two years ago gave Directory Server the highest marks in almost every performance test run. You can view those results at http://www.nwfusion.com/reviews/2000/0515rev2.html.

Directory Server has the best performance on the market

The product documentation is clearly the best of all the LDAP server products. The administrator's guide does an excellent job of documenting the features. All confusing topics are illustrated

The documentation is also the best

with several examples. An installation guide walks through the installation process. In addition, performance recommendations are given. Deployment and design documentation is extremely helpful, and this is provided in the form of an excellent deployment guide. This guide outlines the key steps Mycompany should take to deploy Directory Server. This is the only product that publishes this type of information, although much of the deployment guide could certainly be used for other products. Look in Appendix G for URLs for all this documentation.

Directory Server offers the most security features

Earlier I noted that Directory Server has the most access control factors of any product. Dynamic groups and values are very useful features to reduce management costs, and other products don't have them. The security features offered are clearly the most extensive, and ongoing development is under way. But several of the dynamic features have a major limitation that limits usefulness. For example, the attribute value that has been asserted via CoS can't be returned in a search filter. I'd also like to see the redundancy provided by groups and roles merged. I think an approach using linked attributes would be very beneficial.

The basic server functionality is significant

While supporting most of the functionality its competitors do, Directory Server also implements unique functionality. The plug-ins are a great idea, and other vendors should follow this direction, under a common standard. The CoS (Class of Service) is very cool and holds the promise to simplify directory management. Chaining support is nice, and the pass-thru authentication support makes this even nicer. The chaining support lets you increase server (and directory) capacity without any additional client configuration or headache.

Directory Server leads the pack

In summary, Directory Server is clearly still the leading LDAP server product. The product has set a high mark for other products to meet. Directory Server should satisfy any company's needs.

Appendixes

A

Client LDAP Operations Appendix

Draft Controls

PSEARCH

M. Smith, "A Simple LDAP Change Notification Mechanism," INTERNET-DRAFT <draft-ietf-ldapext-psearch-01.txt>, August 1998.

http://www.ietf.org/proceedings/98dec/I-D/draft-ietf-ldapext-psearch-01.txt

TSEARCH

M. Wahl, "LDAPv3 Triggered Search Control," INTERNET-DRAFT <draft-ietf-ldapext-trigger-01.txt>, August 1998.

http://www.uni.torun.pl/~mgw/internet-drafts/draft-ietf-ldapext-trigger-01.txt

DIRSYNC

M. Armijo, "Microsoft LDAP Control for Directory Synchronization," INTERNET-DRAFT <draft-armijo-ldap-dirsync-00.txt>, August 1999.

http://sunsite.ics.forth.gr/pub/systools/internet-drafts/draft-armijo-ldap-dirsync-00.txt

LCUP

M. Smith, "LDAP Client Update Protocol," INTERNET-DRAFT <draft-ietf-ldup-lcup-01.txt>, June 2001.

http://www.ietf.org/internet-drafts/draft-ietf-ldup-lcup-01.txt

Table A-1   LDAP persistent search control OIDs

Control	OID
PSEARCH	2.16.840.1.113730.3.4.3
TSEARCH	1.3.6.1.4.1.1466.29539.10
DIRSYNC	1.2.840.113556.1.4.841

Chaining

http://search.ietf.org/internet-drafts/draft-sermersheim-ldap-chaining-01.txt

Virtual List View

http://search.ietf.org/internet-drafts/draft-ietf-ldapext-ldapv3-vlv-04.txt

C language API

Table A-2 lists the functions in the C language API for LDAP.

Table A-2   LDAP API functions

Function	Description
ldap_open() ldap_bind() ldap_bind_s() ldap_simple_bind() ldap_simple_bind_s() ldap_kerberos_bind()	Opens a connection to the LDAP server. Returns a connection handle that is used by all other function calls based on this connection.
ldap_kerberos_bind_s()	Used to authenticate to the directory via the methods described by the function name.
ldap_unbind() ldap_search() ldap_search_s()	Unbinds and closes the connection.
ldap_search_s() ldap_modify()	Searches the directory. The _s version works synchronously, but has a time limit parameter.
ldap_modify_s() ldap_modrdn()	Modifies an entry.
ldap_modrdn_s() ldap_add()	Changes the RDN of an entry.
ldap_add_s() ldap_delete()	Adds an entry.
ldap_delete_s()	Deletes an entry.
ldap_abandon()	Abandons the operation in progress (in other words, the synchronous operation in progress).
ldap_result()	Reads LDAPMessage structure for an asynchronous operation.
ldap_msgfree()	Frees the memory space from the LDAPMessage structure from a previous ldap_result(), ldap_search_s(), or ldap_search_s().
ldap_result2error()	Converts the LDAPMessage structure into more usable error codes.
ldap_err2string()	Converts a numeric error code into a descriptive error string.
ldap_perror() ldap_first_entry() ldap_next_entry()	Prints the error message.
ldap_count_entries() ldap_first_attribute()	Retrieves entries from the LDAPMessage structure in an orderly fashion.

Continued

Table A-2   Continued

Function	Description
ldap_next_attribute() ldap_get_values()	Retrieves attributes in an orderly fashion from an entry in the LDAPMessage structure.
ldap_get_values_len() ldap_count_values()	Retrieves an attribute value. Non _len version used for nonbinary string data only.
ldap_count_values_len() ldap_value_free()	Counts the values returned by the two functions above.
ldap_value_free_len()	Frees memory space used by the attribute values returned by the functions above.
ldap_get_dn()	Gets the DN of an entry specified in the LDAPMessage structure.
ldap_explode_dn()	Separates the DN returned by the function above into an array of RDNs.
ldap_dn2ufn()	Converts the DN returned by the function above into a user-friendly format.

B

Schema Appendix

Schema Formats

The schema can be defined in several different formats, which can be confusing unless you know to expect slightly different formats. Different vendors use different formats. The LDAP RFCs generally use the *BNF format*, but vendors are not required to use this format in their documentation or implementation. The *ASN.1 format* is also used throughout the LDAP standard, and it is generally the choice of vendors. Vendors that developed from the first LDAP implementation at the University of Michigan use the *slapd.conf format*.

Each format has the syntax for an object class and attribute presented, followed by examples of each. Chapter 1 includes an example of the `person` object class definition in the ASN.1 format. To quickly illustrate the basic differences between formats, let's look at the same `person` definition and at the definition for the `cn` attribute. For your convenience, I've included the ASN.1 `person` definition again.

The schema must be defined in a pre-determined format

ASN.1 Object Class Syntax

Brackets indicate optional parameters, CAPS indicate required elements, lowercase indicates supplied variables. These notes are different from those for the slapd format!

```
objectclassname OBJECT-CLASS ::= {
    SUBCLASS OF { superclass }
    [KIND objectclasskind]
    [MUST CONTAIN { attribute1 | attribute2 ...}]
    [MAY CONTAIN { attribute3 | attribute4 ...}]
    ID oid}
```

Example
```
person OBJECT-CLASS ::= {
    SUBCLASS OF { top }
    KIND abstract
    MUST CONTAIN { sn, | cn}
    MAY CONTAIN { userPassword | telephoneNumber |
        seeAlso | description }
    ID 2.5.6.6}
```

ASN.1 Attribute Syntax

```
attributename ATTRIBUTE ::= {
[SUBTYPE OF supertype]
[WITH SYNTAX syntaxname {syntaxbounds}]
[EQUALITY MATCHING RULE equalmatchingrulename]
[ORDERING MATCHING RULE ordermatchingrulename]
[SUBSTRINGS MATCHING RULE submatchingrulename]
[SINGLEVALUED]
ID oid}
```

Example
```
commonName ATTRIBUTE ::= {
SUBTYPE OF name
WITH SYNTAX DirectoryString {ub-common-name}
ID id-at-commonName }
```

BNF Object Class Syntax

Brackets indicate optional elements, CAPS indicate required elements, lowercase indicates supplied variables. These notes are different from those for the slapd format!

```
(oid NAME 'objectclassname' SUP superclass
objectclasskind MUST (attribute1 $ attribute2) MAY
(attribute3 $ attribute4) )
```

Example
```
( 2.5.6.6 NAME 'person' SUP top STRUCTURAL MUST ( sn
$ cn ) MAY ( userPassword $ telephoneNumber $
seeAlso $ description ) )
```

BNF Attribute Syntax
```
(oid NAME 'attributename' [DESC 'description']
[OBSOLETE] [SUP supertype] [EQUALITY
equalmatchingrulename] [ORDERING
ordermatchingrulename] [SUBSTR submatchingrulename]
SYNTAX syntaxname {syntaxbounds} [SINGLE-VALUE]
[NO-USER-MODIFICATION] [USAGE attributeusage] )
```

Example
```
( 2.5.4.3 NAME 'cn' SUP name )
```

Slapd.conf Object Class Syntax
Brackets indicate optional parameters, CAPS indicate supplied variables, lowercase indicates required elements.

```
objectclass OBJECTCLASSNAME
[oid OID]
[superior SUPERIORCLASS]
[requires LISTOFATTRIBS]
[allows LISTOFATTRIBS]
```

Example
```
objectclass person
oid 2.5.6.6
superior top
requires
    sn
    cn
allows
    userPassword
telephoneNumber
seeAlso
description
```

Slapd.conf Attribute Syntax
```
attribute ATTRIBUTENAME [ALIAS] [OID] SYNTAX
[ATTRIBUTEOPTIONS]
```

`ATTRIBUTEOPTIONS` allows the nondefault values of "operational" or "single" to be specified. These show that the attribute is operational, not generally returned to clients, and single valued. I believe you can also define attribute options, such as language code support, here.

Example
```
attribute cn commonName 2.5.4.3 cis
```

Even with the simple examples I have chosen, there is more going on here than I can cover briefly. Some of the differences can be explained by lack of support for schema functionality like subtyping. Some of the differences result from definitions working together with other definitions like syntax and matching rule definitions, and some of the formats link the definitions in different places.

The formats are summarized here; you can find full details online

Knowing the formal syntax of these formats is worthwhile only if you want to extend the schema of a directory or understand the relationship between existing schema elements. The syntax of the formats can be complex; so if you aren't interested in modifying the schema, the knowledge isn't useful. You can find good resources for all the formats and common schema elements online. These resources explain the basics of the syntax, so you can decipher schema definitions for yourself. For the URLs of these online resources, see Appendix G. The BNF format is what is used by the LDAP standards documents to describe the recommended schema definitions, but any of the formats can be used. The LDAP standard does not require that the BNF format be used by an implementation.

Common Syntaxes

Table B-1 lists common syntaxes that are used in other schema definitions. These syntaxes will be of interest to you if you modify the schema of your directory or need to understand what values are allowed in specific attribute types.

Table B-1   **Common schema syntaxes**

Name	OID	Description
Binary	1.3.6.1.4.1.1466.115.121.1.5	0 or 1
Bit String	1.3.6.1.4.1.1466.115.121.1.6	Strings of binary
Boolean	1.3.6.1.4.1.1466.115.121.1.7	TRUE or FALSE
Certificate	1.3.6.1.4.1.14666.115.121.1.8	Binary encoding of X.509 certificate
Certificate Pair	1.3.6.1.4.1.14666.115.121.1.10	Sequence of two certificates
Country String	1.3.6.1.4.1.1466.115.121.1.11	Two-character code as defined in ISO 3166
DirectoryString	1.3.6.1.4.1.1466.115.121.1.15	UTF-8–based text string
DistinguishedName	1.3.6.1.4.1.1466.115.121.1.12	DN string
DIT Content Rule Description	1.3.6.1.4.1.1466.115.121.1.16	Used to define content rules for an object class
Facsimile Telephone Number	1.3.6.1.4.1.1466.115.121.1.22	Telephone number with fax parameters included
Fax	1.3.6.1.4.1.1466.115.121.1.23	Fax images in octet string syntax; oddly, octet string syntax isn't noted in the RFC
Generalized Time	1.3.6.1.4.1.1466.115.121.1.24	Time with time zone specified
IA5 String	1.3.6.1.4.1.1466.115.121.1.26	International Alphabet 5 String; contains ASCII and some nonprintable escape characters
INTEGER	1.3.6.1.4.1.1466.115.121.1.27	An integer
JPEG	1.3.6.1.4.1.1466.115.121.1.28	JPEG images encoded in JFIF
Matching Rule Description	1.3.6.1.4.1.1466.115.121.1.30	Used to define matching rules
Matching Rule Use Description	1.3.6.1.4.1.1466.115.121.1.31	Used to define matching rule use definitions
MHS OR Address	1.3.6.1.4.1.1466.115.121.1.33	
Name AND Optional UID	1.3.6.1.4.1.1466.115.121.1.34	A DN string with optional UID string
Name Form Description	1.3.6.1.4.1.1466.115.121.1.35	Used to define the name form of an object class, in other words, specify an RDN

Continued

Table B-1   Continued

Name	OID	Description
Numeric String	1.3.6.1.4.1.1466.115.121.1.36	A string of numbers
Object Class Description	1.3.6.1.4.1.1466.115.121.1.37	Used to define an object class
OID	1.3.6.1.4.1.1466.115.121.1.38	An OID string
Other Mailbox	1.3.6.1.4.1.1466.115.121.1.39	String used to denote mail system and mailbox location
PostalAddress	1.3.6.1.4.1.1466.115.121.1.41	Sequence of directory strings denoting a postal address
Presentation Address	1.3.6.1.4.1.1466.115.121.1.43	
PrintableString	1.3.6.1.4.1.1466.115.121.1.44	Text string with a restricted set of printable characters
Telephone Number	1.3.6.1.4.1.1466.115.121.1.50	Telephone number string in international phone format
UTC Time	1.3.6.1.4.1.1466.115.121.1.53	Printable string with time
LDAP Syntax Description	1.3.6.1.4.1.1466.115.121.1.54	Used to define a syntax
DIT Structure Rule Description	1.3.6.1.4.1.1466.115.121.1.17	Used to define a structural rule for an object class
OctetString	1.3.6.1.4.1.1466.115.121.1.40	Binary data in BER form

In several cases, the RFC 2252 authors deviated from established types and redefined the existing types for no clear reason. Some of the preexisting definitions are listed in Table B-2, because some LDAP vendors may choose to use the definitions with a differing OID.

Common Matching Rules

Tables B-3 through B-6 list common matching rules that are used in LDAP schema definitions. These rules will be of interest

Table B-2 Common syntaxes with OIDs that deviate from original

Name	OID
PrintableString	2.1.0.1.1
Boolean	2.5.5.8
PostalAddress	2.5.4.16

to you if you modify the schema of your directory or need to understand how values are compared in specific attribute types. All the common matching rules noted in RFC 2252 are included, as well as a few critical ones not noted in the RFC. The rules are listed in four separate tables by the type of matching rule: equality, ordering, substring, or subschema.

Table B-3 Equality matching rules

ASN.1 Matching Rule	OID	OID of Syntax	Description
`objectIdentifierMatch`	2.5.13.0	1.3.6.1.4.1.1466.115.121.1.38	Used to match OIDs and other numeric identifiers
`distinguishedMatch` also known as `distinguishedName Match`	2.5.13.1	1.3.6.1.4.1.1466.115.121.1.12	Follows the rules for DNs, with each RDN checked
`caseIgnoreMatch`	2.5.13.2	1.3.6.1.4.1.1466.115.121.1.15	Case ignored, and spaces ignored if at beginning or end, or used in repetition
`numericStringMatch`	2.5.13.8	1.3.6.1.4.1.1466.115.121.1.36	Matches numeric strings and ignores spaces
`caseIgnoreListMatch`	2.5.13.11	1.3.6.1.4.1.1466.115.121.1.41	Uses caseIgnoreMatch to compare lists of DirectoryStrings
`integerMatch`	2.5.13.14	1.3.6.1.4.1.1466.115.121.1.27	Matches values as integers

Continued

Table B-3   Continued

ASN.1 Matching Rule	OID	OID of Syntax	Description
bitStringMatch	2.5.13.16	1.3.6.1.4.1.1466.115.121.1.6	Compares bit strings to ensure that bits match
telephoneNumberMatch	2.5.13.20	1.3.6.1.4.1.1466.115.121.1.50	Case ignored, and all spaces and hyphens ignored
presentationAddress Match	2.5.13.22	1.3.6.1.4.1.1466.115.121.1.43	Compares PresentationAddress strings
uniqueMemberMatch	2.5.13.23	1.3.6.1.4.1.1466.115.121.1.34	Uses distinguishedMatch rule to compare DN strings, and uses bitStringMatch to compare uid RDNs
protocolInformation Match	2.5.13.24	1.3.6.1.4.1.1466.115.121.1.42	Uses octetStringMatch rule to compare ProtocolInformation strings
generalizedTimeMatch	2.5.13.27	1.3.6.1.4.1.1466.115.121.1.24	Matches strings of GeneralizedTime. Unspecified minutes or seconds are assumed to be zero
caseExactIA5Match	1.3.6.1.4.1. 1466.109. 114.1	1.3.6.1.4.1.1466.115.121.1.26	Matches an IA5 string, case does count
caseIgnoreIA5Match	1.3.6.1.4.1. 1466.109. 114.2	1.3.6.1.4.1.1466.115.121.1.26	Matches an IA5 string, case is ignored
caseExactMatch	2.5.13.5	1.3.6.1.4.1.1466.115.121.1.15	Matches strings; case is significant, but spaces are ignored if at beginning or end, or used in repetition
booleanMatch	2.5.13.13	1.3.6.1.4.1.1466.115.121.1.7	Matches a Boolean
octetStringMatch	2.5.13.17	1.3.6.1.4.1.1466.115.121.1.40	Matches a sequence of octet strings

Table B-4   Ordering matching rules

ASN.1 Matching Rule	OID	OID of Syntax	Description
`generalizedTimeOrdering Match`	2.5.13.28	1.3.6.1.4.1.1466. 115.121.1.24	Orders strings of GeneralizedTime
`caseIgnoreOrderingMatch`	2.5.13.3	1.3.6.1.4.1.1466. 115.121.1.15	Orders strings while ignoring case

Table B-5   Substring matching rules

ASN.1 Matching Rule	OID	OID of Syntax	Description
`caseIgnoreSubstringsMatch`	2.5.13.4	1.3.6.1.4.1.1466. 115.121.1.58	Matches a string with a wildcard in any position, while ignoring case
`telephoneNumberSubstrings Match`	2.5.13.21	1.3.6.1.4.1.1466. 115.121.1.58	Matches a PrintableString with a wildcard in any position; case does count, but spaces and hyphens are ignored
`numericStringSubstrings Match`	2.5.13.10	1.3.6.1.4.1.1466. 115.121.1.58	Matches a NumericString with a wildcard in any position, spaces are ignored

Table B-6   Subschema matching rules

ASN.1 Matching Rule	OID	OID of Syntax	Description
`IntegerFirstComponentMatch`	2.5.13.29	1.3.6.1.4.1.1466. 115.121.1.27	Matches the first integer in a sequence of integers
`objectIdentifierFirst ComponentMatch`	2.5.13.30	1.3.6.1.4.1.1466. 115.121.1.38	Matches the first OID component in an OID sequence

C

Stanford University Directory Architecture

Environment

The Stanford community consists of approximately 1,500 faculty, 8,000 staff, and 14,000 students. The extended community includes over 25,000 alumni. The university is organized in seven schools, several of which regularly receive top honors in national reviews. Many notable research projects are undertaken in over 100 locations, including the Stanford Linear Accelerator Center (SLAC) and the Stanford Hospital.

This environment demands sophisticated IT resources that can be easily accessed in a distributed computing model. Some IT support is provided centrally, but each school and research project has autonomy and may deploy computing resources. Central IT helps support resources that must have centralized management. The Stanford directory architecture is an example of such a resource.

Stanford employs a network-wide user identity system for authentication that is based on Kerberos. This system is known as the SUNet ID system, and it can be used to access many network services, including e-mail, the directory, Web sites, a Windows infrastructure, and other services.

The Stanford directory architecture has evolved over time to meet Stanford's diverse needs. Some of the elements of the architecture are vendor provided, while others are custom written. This composite nature of the directory architecture, along with the large, diverse environment, provide an interesting example of a data architecture that is worth a closer look.

Source Systems

Stanford has several systems of record. These systems hold authoritative data about Stanford's business. Each of these source systems is owned by offices that are responsible for the data, not the central IT organization. For example, one source system comes from the Registrar, is based on Peoplesoft, and contains authoritative information about students. Another source system comes from Human Resources and contains authoritative information about staff and faculty. Other sources include data from SLAC and the Stanford Hospital. An ID card system for all Stanford-affiliated people also is a source system. This system maps a person's name to a unique ID card number. Figure C-1 shows the relationship between the many source systems and the central repository that integrates each of these source systems. This central repository is called the Stanford Registry.

Stanford Registry

The Stanford Registry is neither an LDAP directory nor any other kind of directory, but rather a database. The rationale behind the Registry being a database centers on the purpose and functional-

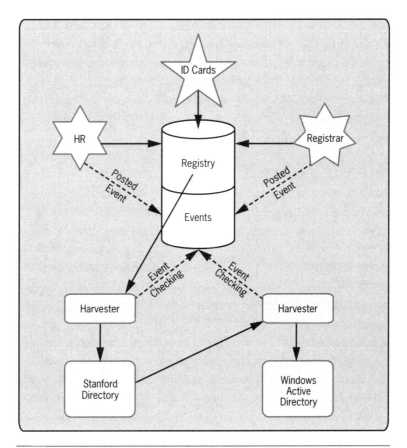

Figure C-1   Stanford source systems

ity it serves. A database meets several key requirements. Most notable among these requirements is the ability to make a large number of modifications and also to roll back data to a previously known state. The Stanford Registry provides a custom metadirectory functionality by amalgamating all the relevant data in one single repository. The Registry eliminates any potential duplication of information from the multiple sources, and it uses business logic specific to Stanford. For example, imagine a student who also works for the university as a staff member. At least two of the source systems hold authoritative information about this person. The Registry takes all the information and applies a rule that decides which information has more priority. In this example, some of the information from the student source is taken, and some from the staff source. The level of modification activity, reporting, and rollback-commit functionality required led to the decision to use a database for this metadirectory purpose.

The Registry gets information from the source systems via a periodic process involving XML formatted data. Because each of the source systems runs on a different platform, and each has a schema with slight variations from the others, the level of abstraction that XML provides is very useful. The Registry can then use the business rules it has defined to judge which source is ultimately more important or more current and whether values from multiple sources can coexist.

The Stanford Registry is a copy of the authoritative data, and not a referral that points back to the source database or directory. This means that any subsequent use of this data is read-only, or the authority of the source systems is put in jeopardy. So modification of data should be redirected to the authoritative source. However, for a subset of the data from the various source systems, specifically the person-related data set, the Registry is a co-owner of the authoritative data. Changes made to this subset of the data in the Registry propagate back to the source systems, just as all changes propagate to the Registry from the source systems. In other words, person data is replicated both ways.

In addition to information replicated from source systems, the Registry hosts a few other central information repositories. The Organization Registry holds an authoritative table of all the officially recognized departments, schools, and organizations associated with Stanford University. This organization data helps to provide unambiguous name resolution for applications that must differentiate between possibly ambiguous department names. For example, one application might call a department the `business school`, while another calls it the `Graduate School of Business`, while still another calls it the `GSB`. In addition to providing clear names, this data set also authoritatively establishes the hierarchical relationship between each department.

The Workgroup Registry provides a central place to define groups of people, such that the group definition can be reused for multiple services. This is similar to how groups are used in network operating systems like Windows, but it is platform independent so a group definition can be made once and be used by many services uniformly. Both departments and individual users can define groups for their own use.

The Authority Registry is something still in development, but its intent is to provide a central definition of who holds authority for specific responsibilities and administrative tasks. This will tie into the Organization Registry and will be used by network services to provide definition of roles and delegate administration. The Organization, Workgroup, and Authority Registries are incredibly important because the university employs a noncentralized computing administration model, and these repositories help to unify the distributed services that have been deployed by centrally defining groups and roles to make administration and interaction easier.

The Registry must provide privacy controls for information. As mandated by the federal law known as the Family Educational Rights and Privacy Act (FERPA), Stanford is liable for the privacy of student personal data. The university must honor a student's request to protect personal information. The Stanford Registry therefore has privacy settings for applicable data. Access controls are set on personal data attributes to protect the privacy of this data. All subsequent reuse of the data must also employ the same or a stricter level of privacy control.

Privacy Controls

The Registry provides the privacy control in an interesting fashion that is different from traditional access control list (ACL) methods. All users (student or otherwise) can specify three different privacy settings for each piece of information about their person. These settings are: `World`, `Stanford`, or `Self`. A `World` setting means that the information can be accessed by anyone. A `Stanford` setting means that the information can be accessed only by people who are members of the Stanford community. A `Self` setting means that the information is completely private, and only the person can access it. Of course, Stanford business processes and Stanford administrators must access data regardless of these settings to provide basic Stanford services. But these privacy settings ensure that general directory searches respect the rights of the person.

Each of the three privacy settings are placed in a special visibility attribute that is informally associated with the attribute it is intended to protect. For example, the `suVisibEmail` attribute holds the privacy settings that correspond to the mail attribute for each person entry. Almost every attribute that holds personal information has a corresponding visibility attribute. Even the person's name can be protected. Some attributes are grouped together in logical sets. For example, the `suVisibAffiliation` attribute protects the `affiliation`, `o`, and `ou` attributes. Another set covers all the personal attributes to simplify situations in which someone wants to treat all the information in the same manner.

These visibility attributes are then used as an authorization factor to determine whether any particular person has authority to access the informally linked attribute(s). Netscape Directory Server supports access control information (ACI) statements that provide this interesting authorization factor functionality. These statements can be associated with any container in the directory; but in Stanford's case, they are set at the root of the directory. The ACI statement allows a content-based access control to be implemented. In other words, the ACI statement specifies that the value of a special attribute of the requestor's binding entry must match a special attribute value of the targeted entry.

For example, imagine that I specify that my e-mail address has a privacy setting of `Stanford` (`suVisibEmail=Stanford`). Users who want to access the mail attribute of my entry must have a `suPrivilegeGroup` attribute on their entry with a value of `Stanford` to indicate that they are authorized to view my e-mail address. Otherwise, they will not get access. This functionality can be duplicated via traditional ACLs, but ACI statements allow for a much more dynamic application of access control than traditional ACLs do. Stanford's experience with the Netscape Directory Server product has been that the overhead involved with managing and processing attribute-level ACLs is greater than using ACI statements. For contrast, I will show how a comparable visibility is implemented in a traditional ACL model shortly when I turn to the Stanford Windows Infrastructure and Microsoft's Active Directory product.

Once all the data has been unified into the Registry, it is published in an LDAP directory, called the Stanford Directory, for subsequent use by services and applications. The method of moving the data from the Registry to the LDAP directory is a custom-designed process that is very interesting.

Directory Harvester

The directory harvester moves information from the Registry to the master directory server for the Stanford Directory. The directory harvester moves information in close to real time: as an update is made in the Registry, it is also reflected in the Directory. This functionality is enabled with the help of a special event database, which provides notification to the harvester of each change to the registry. The directory harvester is interested in only a subset of the information in the Registry. For example, it is not interested in the organization information, but it is interested in the people information. Stanford has more than one harvester, but the directory harvester is the most critical. It is unique among all the other harvesters: the directory harvester is the only one that retrieves information from the Registry for publication. All the other harvesters retrieve information from the Stanford Directory. These other harvesters tend to feed applications that require their own copy of the information, and can't look up the data via LDAP.

Event Database

The event database provides a way to track each change to an entry in a fairly simple manner. Each change results in an event posted to the Events database. The harvester keeps track of the last event ID it knows about and periodically checks the Events database for new events. So when a new event is posted, the harvester knows about it. The harvester queries the entry noted in the event and creates/deletes/modifies the corresponding directory entry. Events are triggered by each source system, but how each system accomplishes this event posting process differs between systems. For example, one source system parses an audit log of entry modifications every five minutes and creates events based on this information.

Stanford Directory

The Stanford Directory is currently run on the Netscape Directory Server product. A single-master replication model is employed, and this single master replicates the entire directory to two sets of directory servers. The first set of directory servers primarily provides mailbox resolution for the campus e-mail services. The second set of directory servers primarily provides a general white page service via a custom-designed Web interface. Each set provides a failover backup for the other set, but

helps to isolate service-intensive load to specific servers so
users from one service aren't arbitrarily impacted by other services. Incidentally in the short term, Stanford is actively migrat-
ing off Netscape Directory Server onto OpenLDAP. In the
longer term, Stanford will closely evaluate each of the products
to see which best meets its business requirements.

E-mail Service Integration

Stanford primarily runs a sendmail-based e-mail service in addition to other mail offerings. The sendmail service is integrated
to perform its lookup and routing of user SMTP information
against the LDAP directory. Usually this information is stored on
each individual sendmail server in the form of a database mapping or flat file; but when there are multiple sendmail servers
involved, the process of keeping these local mapping files synchronized while also up-to-date can be difficult. Information
about how you might integrate your sendmail service with an
LDAP directory can be found at http://www.iconimaging.net/
~jradford/sendmail/sendmail-ldap.html. Jason Christopher
Radford has provided these helpful online tips.

Web UI Integration

Currently at Stanford, directory searches are provided exclusively through a Web interface. In the future, LDAP protocol-
based clients may be allowed access. The Web interface, called
Stanford.Who, is quite friendly. A Web-based form is provided,
and the user can search based on name. You can also designate
a person's affiliation (student, staff, faculty) to help refine the
name search. Alternatively, you can search based on e-mail address, campus phone number, or Stanford's network ID called
the SUNet ID. Results include only the personal information
that is publicly accessible. A special Web authentication system
tied to the SUNet ID enforces the privacy access controls.

Updating Your Personal Information

In general, users can update their personal information via a Web interface called Stanford.You. This interface provides a portal for users to interface with the Registry (which co-owns their authoritative person data), without needing to know any specifics about the source system or Registry and the software it runs on. Users can view their personal information and modify it as needed. Additionally, users can choose privacy settings in this interface. This is a good example of the loose directory interconnection approach noted in Chapter 5.

Active Directory Harvester

The Active Directory of the Stanford Windows Infrastructure is a subscriber to the Stanford Directory via its own event harvester, as shown in Figure C-2. Stanford chose to harvest a minimum of person-related information to AD, so only name, the primary department affiliation, authorization group information (suPrivilegeGroup), and privacy settings were harvested. The primary department affiliation is used to determine where in the root domain of AD the user's account should reside. A hierarchy of organizational units that mimic the department hierarchy relationship at the university exists in the root domain for the accounts to be created within. A person's primary department affiliation determines the location of the account in this OU hierarchy. As a result, account administration can be easily delegated to the decentralized departmental Windows administrators across campus. The harvester is capable of moving accounts between departmental OUs when the primary departmental affiliation changes.

As shown in Figure C-2, the password information for a person's account is also written to AD. This is done via a separate process from the harvester, and tight security restrictions are placed on this data. The AD employs a Kerberos realm trust,

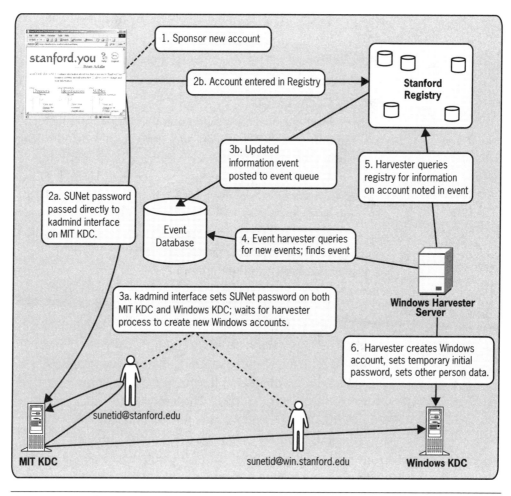

Figure C-2   Active Directory harvester

which along with using the `altSecurityIdentities` attribute, allows the existing MIT-style Kerberos 5 realm to authenticate all Kerberos ticket granting ticket (TGT) requests from Windows clients. The corresponding Windows account just functions as a shadow proxy account containing the proprietary Microsoft information. The passwords are written to AD to ensure that down-level clients that don't support Kerberos authentication can participate. At a later time when these down-level clients are no longer supported, this password synchronization will be discontinued.

Privacy Control in AD

Active Directory doesn't provide many authorization factors. For example, the ACI statement functionality discussed earlier isn't supported. Active Directory, however, does support inherited ACLs. When a person's entry is created by the AD harvester, it is placed somewhere beneath an Accounts OU. This OU has an inherited ACL that allows only the owner of that entry access to the entry. Inherited ACLs are statically applied in AD, so at the time of creation the setting is copied to the entry. This establishes the minimum level of access that all entries shares.

A special Windows-based service using LDAP code helps establish the more open access settings that people may have chosen. Active Directory supports the persistent search LDAP control, which enables this service to know whenever an entry has been modified. The service then checks the entry for two things, and takes action as needed. First, it creates membership in groups that match the values of the `suPrivilegeGroup` attribute of the entry. So a `World` and `Stanford` group are dynamically maintained by this service with memberships of all the appropriate entries. In actuality, there are far more groups dynamically created and maintained, and these groups correspond to the Workgroup Registry functionality described earlier. But for the purposes of privacy control, focus on just the two groups. Second, the service reads the privacy attributes set on the entry. The service compares the value of each of these attributes to the ACL it finds on the entry. If one of the informally linked attributes needs to have more access given (or access taken away), it has the authority to add an ACE to that entry's ACL. And of course, it uses the groups it is dynamically maintaining. This approach works quite well. If the special Windows service fails, no data is put at risk, because the default setting is more restrictive than the actual privacy desired.

Summary

As has been demonstrated already, a great number of applications and services participate in the overall directory architecture. I've purposely simplified the number of interactions that actually happen, so the general architectural concepts can be shown in a specific real-world environment. I cannot describe fully the schema definitions, data architecture, and directory functionality in the Stanford architecture. Hopefully this snapshot will be useful in illustrating how integration can be accomplished in a real-world setting. I appreciate the opportunity Stanford has allowed me to take in describing its environment.

D

OpenLDAP Access Control

<What> Element

You can form the `<what>` element in two ways. First, the asterisk * by itself indicates all the entries in the directory. Second, you can use a DN string. By default, the DN string is evaluated with regex pattern matching. For example, `dn=".*,ou=People, dc=Mycompany,dc=com"` would match all entries subordinate to the People OU in the Mycompany directory. Instead of using regex to evaluate the DN string, you can choose several other evaluation options (which OpenLDAP calls target styles) that closely correspond to the basic LDAP search scopes. These evaluation options include `base`, `one`, `subtree`, and `children`. Each of these options, except `children`, corresponds to a standard search scope and should be self-explanatory. For example, the `one` option indicates just the immediate child entries of the DN, not including the DN entry. The `children` option is similar to `subtree` in indicating all child entries of the DN, but it doesn't include the DN entry itself.

The <what> element uses a DN string or one of the common authorization groups

341

Attribute matching and search filters are also valid in `<what>` elements

Further flexibility on the `<what>` element is supported. You can replace or supplement the DN string option by either an LDAP search filter or an attribute list. The LDAP search filter is formed per the LDAP standard. The attribute list can be any valid attribute(s) of the entries indicated by the DN string or any valid attribute(s) in the entire directory, if the DN string is omitted. You would use the attribute list to control access to the attributes of an entry. In addition to the attributes noted above, two special attribute values are allowed: `entry` and `children`. `entry` denotes the DN of the entry specified by the DN string. `children` denotes the DN of entries that are subordinate to the DN string specified. The DN is not an attribute in the strict sense, but you must be able to indicate the DN of an entry so access to rename an entry can be controlled.

Several examples of valid `<what>` elements follow, and these illustrate the diversity of options.

```
access to dn=".*,ou=People,dc=Mycompany,dc=com"
    filter=(objectclass=user)
```

indicates all user entries subordinate to the People OU.

```
access to dn.base="ou=People,dc=Mycompany,dc=com"
    attr=entry
```

indicates the DN of just the People OU.

```
access to attr=cn
```

indicates the `cn` attribute of every entry.

`<Who>` Element

The `<who>` element uses a DN string or one of the common authorization groups

You can form the `<who>` element, sometimes called the authorization identity, in a multitude of ways. The two primary options are by a DN string or by inclusion in a special authorization group. The DN string option works as just described.

There are four possible values of the special authorization group: `anonymous`, `users`, `self`, and `*`. `anonymous` refers to any user who has authenticated anonymously or has not authenticated. `users` refers to any user who has successfully authenticated. `self` refers to an authorization identity that matches the DN of the entry specified in the `<what>` element.

In addition to these two primary elements, you can include these optional restrictions: inclusion in the membership of a group entry, a match of a DN-valued attribute indicated and the DN of the authorization identity, a match of the DNS domain of the client, a match of the IP address and port of the client, and a match of the server IP address and port that the client uses to connect.

IP address, DNS domain, attribute value matching, and group membership are also valid in <who> elements

You can use two other optional elements, but these are difficult to describe simply. One is called the set option, and it permits evaluation of complex combinatory logic of multiple expressions of DN strings, the special authorization designations, or DN-valued attributes. You can use the And & and Or | logical operators in these set expressions. The other optional element is called an ACI expression, and I covered it cursorily in Chapter 6.

Two advanced elements, ACI and logical sets, are also possible in <who>

Note: The <who> Options Aren't Fully Covered Here

For the sake of brevity, the full details of the less common options aren't included. To delve into these details, look at the *OpenLDAP Administration Guide* (http://www.openldap.org/doc/admin/) and the OpenLDAP FAQ-O-Matic (http://www.openldap.org/faq), search the OpenLDAP mailing list archives (http://www.openldap.org/lists/#archives), and, as a last resort, mail a query to the mailing lists.

I've included several examples here of valid <who> elements, and these should illustrate the diversity of options.

```
by dn=".*,ou=People,dc=Mycompany,dc=com"
```

matches any entry within the People OU.

```
by self
```

indicates the authorization identity mapped to the entry associated with the <what>.

```
by dnattr=manager
```

indicates the entry specified by the DN values of the `manager` attribute of the entry(s) specified in <what>.

```
by domain=.*\.mycompany\.com
```

indicates a client with any DNS hostname in the mycompany.com DNS zone.

```
by peername.exact=IP=10.123.123.123:1679
```

indicates a client with the IP address indicated, using port 1679.

```
by group=cn=mygroup,ou=Groups,dc=Mycompany,dc=com
```

indicates the entries specified by the DN values of the `member` attribute of the `mygroup` entry. Both the `member` attribute and the `groupOfNames` object class are assumed by default, but others can be specified.

<Access> Element

The <access> element sets common access settings or discrete privileges

The <access> element specifies the level of access that should be granted. You can use the set of six common access settings, or you can specify the underlying five discrete privileges incre-

Table D-1   Common access settings

Setting	Privilege	Explanation
none		No access allowed
auth	x	Allows authentication
compare	cx	Allows the compare operation
search	scx	Allows entry to be enumerated on a search operation
read	rscx	Allows entry to be returned on a search operation
write	wrscx	Allows any type of modify operation

mentally. The six common settings are none, auth, compare, search, read, and write. Table D-1 describes these settings. As listed, the settings are in increasing order of access.

Instead of using the common settings, you can employ the discrete privileges in custom combinations. The underlying five privileges are w (write), r (read), s (search), c (compare), and x (authenticate). You can set them, or add and subtract them from existing privileges, in whatever combination you desire. Later examples demonstrate adding and subtracting from existing privileges and how the order of resolution affect this option.

Discrete privileges can be set in uncommon combinations or incrementally

Evaluation of Access

Evaluation of access control follows a specific order. First, the <what> element is matched, then the <who> element is matched within that <what> directive. The first <what> element to be matched is the only directive that is applied, and any other matching <what> elements that come later are ignored. By default, the first <who> match determines the only <access> applied. Directives can be set at two levels, at the database level (the naming context level) and at the global level. Each of these

There is a specific order to the evaluation of access control directives. By default, the first match is the only control applied

levels can have multiple directives, and the order in which they appear determines the order of evaluation. Also recall that each `<what>` directive can have multiple `<who>` `<access>` pairs, and again the order in which they appear determines the order of evaluation.

You can set multiple access controls if you use the optional `<control>` element

However, the default behavior of the `<who>` element matching is configurable. Earlier when I stated there were only three primary elements in an access directive, I didn't mention that there is a fourth optional element. This optional element is the `<control>` element, which tells the access evaluation what to do once a `<who>` match has been met. The valid values are `stop`, `continue`, and `break`. The `stop` value is the default value when the `<control>` element isn't specified. `stop` means that once the `<who>` is matched, no further `<who>` elements are evaluated. The `continue` value means that additional `<who>` elements will be evaluated, and the next `<who>` element to match will also be applied. Note that the next directive might stop further evaluation by setting a different `<control>` value.

Comprehensive Example

The following example slapd configuration file demonstrates the multiple access control levels at the database level and at the global level and the flexibility of access control factors. It also shows what a basic configuration file looks like. I've added line numbers to make the commentary easier, but there are no line numbers in a real file.

```
1 include /usr/local/etc/schema/myschema.schema
2 referral ldap://root.openldap.org
3 access to * by * read
```

Line 1 defines the schema by including a file. Line 2 configures the default referral. Line 3 is a global access directive and gives read access to anyone, if a directive at the database level isn't matched. This can be dangerous from a security perspective, so think over this approach.

```
4  database ldbm
5  suffix "dc=mycompany,dc=com"
6  directory /usr/local/var/openldap
7  rootdn="cn=Admin,dc=mycompany,dc=com"
8  rootpw=n0lc@ncU
9  index uid,cn,pres,eq,approx,sub
10 index objectclass eq
```

Line 4 initiates a database, and all that follows applies to this database, until another database is initiated. Line 5 defines the suffix that is in the database, and line 6 is where the database file resides. Lines 7 and 8 set up the all-powerful administrative account. Lines 9 and 10 create indexes for the database. The uid and cn attributes have presence, equality, approximate, and substring operator indexes, and the objectclass attribute has an equality index. Note that all the subsequent access directives apply to this database.

```
11  access to attr=userPassword
12  by self write
13  by anonymous auth
14  by group=cn=admingroup,ou=Groups,dc=Mycompany,
    dc=com +w
```

Lines 11 through 14 are the first access directive for the database. This directive matches any access of the userPassword attribute throughout the database. Line 12 allows a user to write (and read) a personal password; but if the entry that is being accessed isn't your own entry, this line won't be matched. Line 13 allows an anonymous user to authenticate, which is important, because prior to authenticating you are anonymous. Note that authenticated users won't match this line. Line 14 allows the entries indicated by the DN values of the member attribute of the groupOfNames admingroup entry to overwrite (but not read) the password of any entry. Note that the order of the <who>

directives doesn't really matter in this example, because there isn't an overlap.

```
15   access to dn.exact="cn=Brian
     Arkills,ou=People,dc=mycompany,dc=com"
16   by dn="cn=Brian
     Arkills,ou=People,dc=mycompany,dc=com" write
17   by peername.exact=IP=10.123.123.123:1679 write
```

Lines 15 through 17 are the second access directive. Line 15 establishes that this directive applies to accesses to Brian Arkills's entry. Note that accesses of Brian Arkills's password would have been caught by the previous access directive. Line 16 allows Brian Arkills to write to his own entry. The DN string could just as easily have been replaced by `self`. Line 17 allows clients from the specified IP address and port to write to the entry. This IP address might be Brian's computer, so he has a backdoor in case he forgets his own password but is too embarrassed to have another administrator change it.

```
18   access to dn=".*,ou=People,dc=Mycompany,dc=com"
     filter=(objectclass=inetOrgPerson)
19   by dnattr=manager write
20   by self write
21   by dn=".*,ou=People,dc=Mycompany,dc=com" read
22   by domain=.*\.mycompany\.com search
```

Lines 18 through 22 are the third access directive. Line 18 matches an access to any `inetOrgPerson` entry that is immediately subordinate to the People OU. Note that both the previous access directives have a possible overlap with this directive, and they might apply prior to this directive, rendering this directive null. Line 19 allows managers to write to their staff's `inetOrgPerson` entries. Line 20 gives everyone write access to their own entry. Line 21 allows entries in the People OU to read each other's entry. This might not fit with Mycompany's privacy policy as it might be too permissive. Line 22 gives computers in the mycompany.com zone the ability to search the

People OU for `inetOrgPerson` entries. This would only apply if
the binding DN was outside of the People OU or anonymous.

```
23   access to dn.subtree="ou=Documents,dc=Mycompany,
     dc=com"
24   by dnattr=documentAuthor write
25   by users read
```

Lines 23 through 25 are the fourth access directive. Line 23
determines that this directive applies to entries beneath the
Documents OU. Line 24 gives the author of a document write
access. Line 25 gives the special `users` group, which stands for
all authenticated users, the ability to read entries in this OU.

E

Active Directory Controls
Appendix

The controls are presented in the order listed in the `rootDSE` entry.

- **Paged Search control**—Used with the search operation. This control allows a client to retrieve a result in small pieces. The OID 1.2.840.113556.1.4.319 specifies this control. This control is described in Chapter 3.

- **Get Security Descriptor control**—Used with the search operation. This control allows a client to retrieve the `nTSecurityDescriptor` attribute. The `nTSecurityDescriptor` attribute is not returned normally, even if explicitly requested. There are four flags used with this control to retrieve the different portions of the attribute. 0x01 is used to get the owner information, 0x02 is used to get the group information, 0x04 is used to get the DACL information (list of ACEs), and 0x08 is used to get the SACL information (audit settings). The OID 1.2.840.113556.1.4.801 specifies this control.

- **Sorted Search Request control**—Used with the search operation. This control allows a client to retrieve results in sorted order as specified by the client. The OID 1.2.840.113556.1.4.473 specifies this control. This control is described in Chapter 3.

- **Change Notification (PSEARCH) control**—Used with the search operation. This control allows a client to receive results from the server as long as the client-server session is kept alive. The operation never completes. It runs and returns results as new entries meet the search criteria. The OID 1.2.840.113556.1.4.528 specifies this control. This control is introduced in Chapter 3.

- **Show Deleted Objects control**—Used with the search operation. This control allows a client to find entries that have been deleted but not yet purged from the underlying directory database. Deleted entries are not normally returned by search operations, but this control includes them. The OID 1.2.840.113556.1.4.417 specifies this control.

- **Lazy Commit control**—Used with any of the operations that modify or add entries. This control allows a client to tell AD to postpone writing the results of the operations to disk, and to just store them in cache. This control allows a client to make a large number of changes without any loss of performance due to disk writes and therefore optimizes large changes. However, if the directory server crashes before the cache is written, the changes are lost. The OID 1.2.840.113556.1.4.619 specifies this control.

- **Directory Synchronization (DIRSYNC) control**—Used with a search operation. This control allows a client to find all changes to a directory partition since a point in time. The client presents information indicating a replication USN. The server returns all changed entries that are after this USN and before the current replication USN of the directory partition, and that match the search filter.

The OID 1.2.840.113556.1.4.841 specifies this control.
This control is introduced in Chapter 3.

- **Return Extended DN control**—Used with a search operation. This control allows a client to get a special DN for
  an entry that is guaranteed to remain accurate regardless
  of subsequent rename or move operations. The control
  returns a DN with the *globally unique identifier (GUID)*
  as a component. The GUID for an entry in AD never
  changes. This special DN could then be stored for an extended period of time, and still be used at a later time to
  reference the entry. The OID 1.2.840.113556.1.4.529
  specifies this control.

- **Tree Delete control**—Used with a delete operation. This
  control allows a client to delete a container and all children of the container. The operation is subject to access
  controls and will not cross directory partitions. The OID
  1.2.840.113556.1.4.805 specifies this control.

- **Cross Domain Move control**—Used with the modifyRDN
  operation. This control allows a client to move an entry
  from one domain partition to another. There are implications to moving any entry between domains that are used
  in conjunction with access control security, and you
  should read more about this control before using it. The
  OID 1.2.840.113556.1.4.521 specifies this control.

- **Statistics control**—Has little to no documentation. This
  control is installed on the Windows 2000 AD and apparently will return statistics on directory queries. There is
  some documentation of the control at http://msdn.microsoft.
  com/library/en-us/dnactdir/html/efficientadapps.asp.
  Microsoft has indicated it will be fully documented for
  the .NET Server release. Apparently it hasn't been documented to discourage use because the initial implementation of the control isn't robust. One wonders how this
  feature made it past the beta screening. The OID
  1.2.840.113556.1.4.970 specifies this control.

- **Verify Server Name control**—Used with the search operation. This control allows a client to specify which global catalog server to use when performing the search. This can be useful when replication may not have created the entry in all partitions. The OID 1.2.840.113556.1.4.1338 specifies this control.

- **Sorted Search Response control**—The response paired with the request detailed above. The OID 1.2.840.113556.1.4.474 specifies this control.

- **Search with Local Scope control,** also known as **Do Not Generate Referrals control**—Used with the search operation. This control allows the client to disable the generation of referrals by the server. Note that this is different from the client option not to chase referrals. Telling the server not to generate the referrals can reduce the client's processing time because entries with referrals aren't returned at all to the client. The OID 1.2.840.113556.1.4.1339 specifies this control.

- **Server Search Operations control**—Used with the search operation. This control allows a client to specify several options to control how the request is handled. Only two options are documented, one that does the same thing as the Search with Local Scope control, and another that enables the directory to honor search requests with a base DN outside the partition's base DN. By default, AD will give an error instead of returning a default referral for requests with a base DN outside the partition's base DN, but this flag changes that behavior. The OID 1.2.840.113556.1.4.1340 specifies this control.

- **Permissive Modify control**—Used with the modify operation. This control allows a client to perform operations that are usually illegal. Usually adding an optional single-valued attribute that already exists or deleting an optional attribute that doesn't exist on an entry returns an error. This control changes that behavior so the operation returns a success message. The OID 1.2.840.113556.1.4. 1413 specifies this control.

- **ASQ control**—Used with the search operation. This control allows the client to perform an extended match filter (described in Chapter 3), which lets you search the directory for values in an entry's DN. This control requires that you specify a single naming attribute to perform the extended match filter against. This control will be supported in the .NET Server release. The OID 1.2.840.113556.1.4.1504 specifies this control.

- **Virtual List View Request control**—Used with the search operation. This control allows the client to specify that the server return search results in a special order and number. This is particularly useful for LDAP-enabled applications like e-mail clients, which want to display a limited number of sorted entries beginning with a specific entry. This control was mentioned briefly in Chapter 3 and will be supported in the .NET Server release. The OID 2.16.840.1.113730.3.4.9 specifies this control.

- **Virtual List View Response control**—The response paired with the request detailed above. The OID 2.16.840.1.113730.3.4.10 specifies this control.

F

Directory Server Appendix

Default Indexes

The default indexes initially available are listed in Tables F-1 and F-2.

Table F-1   System indexes

Attribute	Indexes
dnComp	eq
objectClass	eq
entryDN	eq
parentID	eq
nsUniqueID	eq
aci	pres
numSubordinates	pres

Table F-2   Default indexes

Attribute	Indexes
cn	pres, eq, sub
givenName	pres, eq, sub
mail	pres, eq, sub
sn	pres, eq, sub
telephoneNumber	pres, eq, sub
mailHost	eq
member	eq
owner	eq
seeAlso	eq
uid	eq
uniqueMember	eq

Access Control Instructions (ACIs)

As noted in Chapter 8, ACIs are a topic worthy of extended study. This appendix gives an overview that illustrates their use and provides a handy reference.

ACI Targets

The ACI target indicates which entries or attributes are affected by the access control

The target of an ACI specifies a set of entries and attributes that are affected by this access control. The target can specify a single attribute of a single entry, every entry, or something in between. Specifying the target component is optional; no target means that the ACI applies to this entry and every child entry. You can use several different methods to designate the target entries. These methods let you target a set of entries in a particular subtree, a set of entries that match a LDAP search filter, a set of attributes, or a type of operation.

You can indicate a set of entries by specifying the DN of the target entries using a slightly modified LDAP URL format. The customizations to this format involve substituting a forward slash (/) for the hostname and port, allowing use of an asterisk as a wildcard for attribute values, and disallowing search filters, options, or controls. For example, both the following targets are valid examples of this method:

You can specify a set of entries using a DN-based method

```
(target = "ldap:///cn=Brian Arkills,ou=People,dc=my
    company,dc=com")
(target = "ldap:///cn=*,ou=*,dc=mycompany,dc=com")
```

The first target matches only my entry, whereas the second matches any entry with a cn attribute directly under any OU entry, under the mycompany.com namespace.

You can indicate a set of entries by specifying an LDAP search filter. Both the following targets are valid examples of this method:

You can also use an LDAP search filter to specify a set of entries

```
(targetfilter = "(|(objectclass=person)(uid=b*))")
(targetfilter = "(&(sn=Skywalker)(telephoneNumber=*))")
```

The first target matches all person entries or entries with a uid beginning with the letter "b." The second target matches entries with both a surname of Skywalker and a valid telephone number.

You can indicate a set of attributes using a special format. Both the following targets are valid examples of this method:

You can target a set of attributes

```
(targetattr = "cn || sn || telephoneNumber")
(targetattr = "uid")
```

The first target matches all the attribute types noted, so every cn, sn, and telephoneNumber attribute would be targeted. The second target matches only the uid attribute.

*You can target
LDAP operations*

Finally, you can target specific LDAP operations in combination
with a valid LDAP search filter. The following targets are valid
examples of this method:

```
(targattrfilters="add=objectClass:
    (objectClass=person)")
(targattrfilters="del=department:(department=Sales)")
```

The first target matches the add operation of the `objectclass`
attribute with a value of `person`, in other words, whenever a
person entry is created. The second target matches the delete
operation of the `department` attribute with a value of `Sales`, or
in other words whenever an entry leaves the Sales department.

ACI Heading

*The ACI heading
contains mandatory
operational infor-
mation and names
the ACI*

The ACI heading is essentially the version plus the name of the
ACI. The version is a required string that identifies the ACI version. "Version 3.0" is the most recent version. The name is also
required and can be any string that identifies the ACI. Use the
name to help you remember what the ACI does. An example
that shows all the components of an ACI follows the ACI component sections.

ACI Permissions

*The ACI permis-
sions denote what
operations are al-
lowed to target
entries*

The ACI permissions specify what rights apply to the target entries. In addition, the ACI permissions specify whether these
rights are allowed or denied. Recall that several ACI statements might apply to a specific target entry and a specific
user. Table F-3 identifies all the valid permissions and what
rights they give.

ACI Bind Rules

*ACI bind rules
specify who is af-
fected by the ACI*

The credentials and bind parameters that a user must provide
to match the ACI are defined by the ACI bind rules; the bind
rule designates the authorization identity. The methods to designate the user affected are varied, like the ACI target compo-

Table F-3 Valid ACI permissions

Permission	Rights Given
Read	Allows or denies whether directory data can be read
Write	Allows or denies whether directory data can be modified or created; attributes can be deleted, but not entries
Search	Allows or denies whether directory data can be searched; if the search permission isn't given on an entry, that entry will never be returned even in the event of a match
Compare	Allows or denies whether directory data can be compared; with the compare operation, the value of the attribute is not returned, just a Boolean
Selfwrite	Allows or denies whether the entry can add or delete itself from a group
Add	Allows or denies whether a child entry can be created
Delete	Allows or denies whether an entry can be deleted
Proxy	Allows or denies another entry to impersonate the targeted entry or entries using proxy authorization
All	Allows or denies all permissions

nent. These methods employ the greatest diversity of access control factors of any LDAP server on the market. They include specifying entries via a variety of means, including client computer identity, day or time, the client authentication method, and a dynamic access control factor that matches the value of attributes.

You can indicate a set of entries by specifying the DN of the target entries using a slightly modified LDAP URL format. This parallels the target method, except the prefix is different. For example,

You can specify entries directly

```
(userdn = "ldap:///cn=Brian Arkills,ou=People,dc=my
    company,dc=com")
```

designates my entry as the authorization identity. Wildcards are allowed, just as they were in the parallel target method. In addition to what I described in the earlier section ACI Targets, several special values are supported by this bind rule method. Table F-4 lists these special values.

You can dynami-
cally specify entries

In addition to directly specifying an entry, you can dynamically target entries via an LDAP URL subtree search filter. Only subtree search filters are allowed via this method. This method lets you specify entries based on whether they match a search filter at the time of access. Who is given access will change over time based on the search filter employed. A valid example of this method is

```
userdn = "ldap:///dc=mycompany,dc=com??sub?
    (|(sn=Skywalker)(sn=Solo))"
```

This example gives access to any entry under the mycompany.com namespace with an sn value of Skywalker or Solo. Wildcards are not allowed in the search filter, but you can use them in the base DN.

You can specify en-
tries via groups or
roles

You can also indicate a set of entries by specifying the DN of the target group or role in an LDAP URL format. Wildcards are not allowed via this method, nor are any LDAP URL options or search filters. However, you can specify multiple groups by delimiting the group DNs with || characters. The

Table F-4   Special values for bind rule by entry method

Special Value	Specifies Which Entries
ldap:///all	All defined directory entries have access
ldap:///anyone	All entries including anonymous users have access
ldap:///self	The entry being targeted
ldap:///parent	The parent entry of the entry being targeted

following example illustrates a valid use of this method of targeting groups:

```
Groupdn="ldap:///cn=Rebel Sympathizers,ou=Groups,
    ou=People,dc=mycompany,dc=com || cn=Imperial
    Stormtroopers,ou=Groups,ou=People,dc=mycompany,
    dc=com"
```

This example specifies all the entries that are members of the `Rebel Sympathizers` group as well as all the entries that are members of the `Imperial Stormtroopers` group. The following example illustrates a valid use of this method of targeting roles:

```
roledn="ldap:///cn=Sith,ou=Roles,ou=People,
    dc=mycompany,dc=com || cn=Jedi,ou=Roles,
    ou=People,dc=mycompany,dc=com"
```

This example specifies all the entries that are members of the `Sith` role as well as all the entries that are members of the `Jedi` role.

The client computer's IP address or DNS hostname can control access. Although this isn't a very effective means of restricting access control by itself, you can use it in conjunction with other bind rule methods to provide greater access control. Wildcards are allowed via these methods. This is a good thing, because adding every IP address on a single basis would make this method unusable otherwise. Valid examples of these methods are

You can specify client computers by IP or DNS name

```
ip="10.87.42.*"
dns="*.mycompany.com"
```

The first example allows all client computers on the 10.87.42.0/24 network. The second example allows all client computers with a DNS hostname suffix of "mycompany.com."

You can control the time of access

You can use the time of day and day of the week to control access. These methods are useful in combination with other methods, for example to allow only members of the temporary employee group access during business hours. This method is also useful to temporarily disable access during a directory maintenance window. Examples of usage are

```
dayofweek="tue"
timeofday="2359"
```

The first example allows access on Tuesday. Valid values are the first three characters of the name of the day. The second example allows access at 11:59 PM. Valid values are between 0 and 2359, where zero means midnight.

The method of authentication can restrict access

The authentication method negotiated by the client can help to control access. Again, this method is best applied in combination with another method. This method is especially useful in controlling access to entries with highly sensitive data. Requiring SSL is an effective means to protect the privacy of an entry. Most other LDAP servers support SSL but don't give you this level of authorization control. A valid example of this method is

```
authmethod="sasl DIGEST-MD5"
```

This example requires SASL DIGEST-MD5 authentication. Valid values include none, simple, ssl, and sasl (along with the specific sasl method).

You can use attribute values to dynamically restrict access

You can use a comparison of an attribute value of the target entry and the binding entry as a bind rule method. To pass this bind rule method, the value of the attribute specified on your binding entry must match the value of the corresponding attribute on the target entry. This is the most complex of the methods, but it offers functionality that isn't possible otherwise. For example, say you want to easily give a manager access to all the person entries of the people she manages. Without using this method, you would need several ACI statements—one for each entry. But using this method, you can specify the `manager` attribute and the value matching the DN of the manager's entry.

This method has two variations, which I describe separately. Typically, you specify the attribute type and value. A valid example of normal usage is

This method has two variations; typically, just the attribute pair is required

```
userattr = "favoriteDrink#Bantha Milk"
```

This allows entries with `favoriteDrink=Bantha Milk` to access each other. A more practical example is:

```
userattr = "relationshipToMycompany#employee"
```

The attribute `relationshipToMycompany` is a custom attribute on person entries, which Mycompany uses to specify the relationship each person has to Mycompany. This example allows all employees of Mycompany access to each other's entries. This might fulfill Mycompany's privacy policy without the use of groups with a large number of members. This specific approach is behind the privacy controls used by Stanford University described in Appendix C.

If the attribute specified has a value with a DN string, the value of the attribute isn't specified. Instead, you must specify one of four options: USERDN, GROUPDN, ROLEDN, or LDAPURL. These options indicate which DN of the user should be compared to the target entry attribute value. USERDN indicates the DN of the user's entry. GROUPDN indicates the DN of one of the groups the user's entry belongs to, including dynamic groups. If dynamic groups are used, this option requires extra processing and can become highly resource intensive. ROLEDN indicates the DN of one of the roles to which the user's entry belongs. If filtered roles are being used, this option can also be highly resource intensive. LDAPURL indicates that the DN of the user's entry

Attributes with a DN string syntax are treated specially

should be compared to the value of the attribute. However, the value of the attribute must be an LDAP search filter. The DN of the user's entry then must match the resolution of the LDAP search filter.

A valid example of the DN string option of this method is

```
userattr = "manager#USERDN"
```

This example grants a manager's entry access to her employees' entries.

Putting an ACI Together

Multiple components are allowed, and comprehensive examples follow

Now that I have explained all the components of an ACI, let's see what a complete ACI looks like and explore a comprehensive example. An ACI follows this format:

```
aci: (target1)...(targetX)(version 3.0;acl
    "name1";permission1 bind_rules1; ... permissionX
    bind_ruleX;) ... (version 3.0;acl "nameX";
    permission bind_rules;)
```

Note that many components allow multiples. Multiple targets, permissions, and bind rules can be specified. When multiple targets are designated, the resulting target is the union of the targets. Each of the following header/permission/bind rule pairs apply to this union.

A simple example that gives access to just my entry

Some examples will help illustrate how ACIs translate into practical access controls.

```
aci: (target="ldap:///uid=barkills,ou=Accounts,
    dc=Mycompany,dc=com")(targetattr=*)
(version 3.0; acl "Self access"; allow (read,
    search, compare) userdn="ldap:///self";)
```

This example targets my user account and all attributes of my entry. The header designates the version and names the ACI for reference. The permissions allow read, search, and compare access. The bind rules specify that the authorization identity must match the target entry. So I'd be able to write to my own entry with this ACI. This `aci` attribute would need to be set on my entry or on a parent entry anywhere above my entry.

Where an ACI is applied is important and can simplify the target. For example, if I want to give all account entries write access to themselves, the following ACI on `ou=Accounts, dc=Mycompany,dc=com` would do the trick:

Where the ACI is applied is critical

```
aci: (targetattr=*)(version 3.0; acl "Self access";
    allow (write) userdn="ldap:///self";)
```

The following example gives members of the `Sales-HR-admins` group access to all the members of the Sales HR admins department:

This example gives a group access to entries that match a search filter

```
aci: (targetfilter="(businessCategory=Sales)")
    (version 3.0; acl "Sales-HR-admins-write"; allow
    (write) groupdn ="ldap:///cn=Sales HR
    admins,ou=Groups,ou=People,dc=Mycompany,dc=com";)
```

The following example is an ACI on `ou=People,dc=Mycompany, dc=com`. It gives users the right to add any role, except the Admin role, to their own entry. This ACI additionally restricts the use of this right with an exhausting list of conditions. The add operation must be made using SSL encryption, from a client computer with a DNS host suffix of Mycompany.com, on a weekday during normal business hours, and from a specific class C IP address range.

This example demonstrates multiple bind rules and also the use of an inequality operator

```
aci: (targetattr="*") (targattrfilters=
    "add=nsRoleDN:(nsRoleDN != "cn=Admin,dc=Mycompany,
    dc=com")") (version 3.0; acl "Add Roles"; allow
    (write) userdn= "ldap:///self" and
    dns="*.Mycompany.com" and (authmethod="ssl") and
    (dayofweek="Mon,Tues,Wed,Thu,Fri") and (timeofday
    >= "0800" and timeofday <= "1700") and
    (ip="10.87.42.*");)
```

*This example
shows the use of
the complex at-
tribute value
method*

The following example ACI is applied to `ou=Documents,`
`dc=Mycompany,dc=com`. It gives all authors full control over
all their document entries:

```
aci: (targetattr="*") (version 3.0; acl
    "Doc author"; allow (all)
    userattr="documentAuthor#USERDN";)
```

You can find more information about ACIs online in the administrator's guide, Chapter 6, at http://docs.sun.com/source/816-
5606-10/acl.htm#997355.

Macro ACIs

As noted in Chapter 8, you use macros to simplify ACI statements by saving a portion of the target's information for later
substitution in the bind rule. This section briefly introduces the
syntax and specific functionality that macros enable.

*Three macro vari-
ables are available*

You can use three macro variables. Two of these variables match
the target's DN, and the other matches an attribute of the target
entry. (`$dn`) is an exact DN match. It saves the DN of the resource targeted in a request for later use. [`$dn`] is a sub-RDN
match. It saves the DN of the target for later use. When substituted in the bind rule, the DN of the targeted resource is examined multiple times, each time dropping the left-most RDN
component until a match is found. (`$attr.attrName`) is an attribute value match. It evaluates to the value of the attribute
named by `attrName` in the target. This can be used in combination with the complex attribute value matching bind rule
method. Table F-5 lists each of the variables and the methods
that are compatible with each.

Table F-5   Which methods support each macro variable

Macro	Used In:
($dn)	target, targetFilter, userDN, roleDN, groupDN, userAttr
[$dn]	targetfilter, userDN, roleDN, groupDN, userAttr
($attr.attrName)	userDN, roleDN, groupDN, userAttr

The following example grants search access to the members of any `cn=Admins` group in any subtree to the `ou=Groups` subtree under the same DN:

```
aci: (target="ldap:///ou=Groups,($dn),
    dc=Mycompany,dc=com") (targetattr="*") (version
    3.0; acl "Domain access"; allow (read,search)
    groupdn="ldap:///cn=Admins,ou=Groups,[$dn],
    dc=Mycompany,dc=com";)
```

Plug-ins

As noted in Chapter 8, plug-ins are an integral part of enabling the features of Directory Server. Table F-6 lists all the available plug-ins and gives a description of their purpose.

The plug-ins are documented in the online *Configuration, Command and File Reference Guide*, Chapter 3, at http://docs.sun.com/source/816-5608-10/plugconfig.htm#11284.

Table F-6   Plug-ins

Plug-in	Description
ACL	Enables ACL access checking
ACL Preoperation	Insufficient documentation is available
Chaining Database	Enables the use of DN syntax during a chaining operation
Class of Service	Allows sharing of attribute data
Internationalization	Processes collation orders and locales
Ldbm	Implements the local databases used by naming contexts
Legacy replication	Allows a Directory Server 5.1 to be a consumer of a Directory Server 4.1 master
Multimaster Replication	Allows two or more servers to be masters
Clear Password Storage Scheme	Enables the password encryption used by the CLEAR password storage scheme

Continued

Table F-6   Continued

Plug-in	Description
Crypt Password Storage Scheme	Enables the password encryption used by the Crypt password storage scheme
NS-MTA-MD5 Password Storage Scheme	Enables the password encryption used by the NS-MTA-MD5 password storage scheme; new passwords cannot be encrypted with this plug-in, but old passwords can be decrypted for authentication
SHA Password Storage Scheme	Enables the password encryption used by the SHA password storage scheme
SSHA Password Storage Scheme	Enables the password encryption used by the SSHA password storage scheme
PTA (Pass-Thru Authentication)	Enables one server to accept credentials from another server
Referential Integrity Postoperation	Checks dynamic attributes (`member`, `seeAlso`, `uniqueMember`, and `owner`) after a delete or rename operation; other attributes can be added to the search configuration, like `nsRoleDN`
Retro Changelog	Used to enable replication with older Directory Servers
Roles	Enables the use of roles
UID Uniqueness	Ensures that every `uid` value is unique
7-Bit Check	Checks that specified attributes in a specific suffix are 7-bit clean
Binary Syntax	Checks for binary data
Boolean Syntax	Checks for Boolean data
Case Exact String Syntax	Checks for case-sensitive strings
Case Ignore String Syntax	Checks for case-insensitive strings
Country String Syntax	Checks for a country string
Distinguished Name Syntax	Checks for a DN string
Generalized Time Syntax Zone	Checks for a date and time qualified with a time
Integer Syntax	Checks for integer data

Continued

Table F-6   Continued

Plug-in	Description
Octet String Syntax	Checks for octet strings
Postal Address String Syntax	Checks for a postal address string
Telephone Syntax	Checks for a telephone number
URI Syntax	Checks for Unique Resource Identifiers, including URLs

G

Online Reference Material

Chapter 1 Topics

Articles
An Introduction to LDAP, http://ldapman.org/articles/intro_to_ldap.html

What is LDAP, http://www.gracion.com/server/whatldap.html

LDAP Introduction, http://www.pinds.com/software/ldap-in-general

Directories and the Internet, http://www.networkmagazine.com/article/NMG20000508S0030

Directories and LDAP—Universal Access To Directory Information, http://developer.netscape.com/viewsource/rose_ldap.html

Intro to Directories and LDAP, http://www.stanford.edu/
%7Ehodges/talks/mactivity.ldap.97/index2.html

Special Report on Directories,
http://www.networkmagazine.com/article/NMG20000510S0002

ComputerBooksOnline: *Understanding and Deploying LDAP Directory Services Sample,* **Ch. 1**
http://www.computerbooksonline.com/chapters/ldapchap.htm

Database 101,
http://www.jobsecurity.com/jobsecurity/ courses/db101.htm

Why Do I Need a Directory When I Could Use a Relational Database? http://www.stanford.edu/~hodges/talks/EMA98-DirectoryServicesRollout/Steve_Kille/index.htm

Understanding X.500—Contents, http://www.isi.salford.ac.uk/
staff/dwc/Version.Web/Contents.htm

LDAP Supersites
An LDAP Roadmap & FAQ
http://www.kingsmountain.com/ldapRoadmap.shtml

LDAP World
http://www.critical-angle.com/ldapworld/ldapv3.html

LDAP World—LDAP v3 Core Specifications
http://www.innosoft.com/ldapworld/v3core.html

University of Michigan LDAP v2 Resources
http://www.umich.edu/~dirsvcs/ldap/doc/

Implementing Directory Services Resources Site
http://www.directoryservice.com/defaultmain.htm

The Burton Group—Directory Resources Center
http://www.tbg.com/directoryrc/

LDAPguru. Are You Ready for the LDAP Revolution?
http://www.ldapguru.com/

Directory Service Guides
http://compnetworking.about.com/cs/directoryservices1/

iPlanet—Home Page
http://www.iplanet.com/index.html

iPlanet Directory FAQ
http://www.iplanet.com/products/iplanet_directory/
directory_faq.pdf

**iPlanet Directory Server Administrator's Guide Chapter 5
Advanced Entry Management**
http://docs.iplanet.com/docs/manuals/directory/50/html/ag/
roles.htm#1115331

LDAP and NDS
http://www.nwconnection.com/nov.99/ldapn9/

Chapter 2 Topics

DNS
DNS Overview and General References
http://www.dns.net/dnsrd/docs/whatis.html

Allegiance Internet: An Explanation of DNS Records
http://support.digex.net/cst/dns/dns2.html

Referrals
Planning Referrals
http://developer.netscape.com/docs/manuals/directory/
deploy30/referral.htm

Escaping Special Characters
Re Escaping the special meaning of + in attribute value
http://www.openldap.org/lists/openldap-software/199911/
msg00215.html

Chapter 3 Topics

Programming Resources
ldap@umich.edu list by thread
http://www.umich.edu/~dirsvcs/ldap/archive/index.html#605

Netscape Directory SDK_ Source Code Release
http://www.mozilla.org/directory/

**Lighting Up LDAP: A Programmer's Guide to Directory
Development, Part 2**
http://sunsite.uakom.sk/sunworldonline/swol-09-1999/swol-09-
ldap2.html

PHP Manual—Function Reference—LDAP Functions
http://www.zend.com/manual/ref.ldap.php

IBM Redbook: Understanding LDAP
http://www.redbooks.ibm.com/pubs/pdfs/redbooks/sg244986.pdf

Encoding Resources
Sample Base 64 Encoding and Decoding (Q191239)
http://support.microsoft.com/support/kb/articles/Q191/2/39.ASP

Base64 Encode and Decode Base64 Files

http://www.fourmilab.ch/webtools/base64/

Directory Integration
Sendmail+LDAP HOWTO

http://www.iconimaging.net/~jradford/sendmail/
sendmail-ldap.html

eMailman(sm)—Public LDAP Servers

http://www.emailman.com/ldap/public.html

Desire Services Directory Services

http://www.desire.org/html/services/directoryservices/

PC-Pages Integrated LDAP Client

http://www.dante.net/np/ldap/

Chapter 4 Topics

X.500
Overview of X.500

http://www.stanford.edu/group/networking/directory/doc/ldap/2.
x500.html

X.500 Resources

http://www.nexor.com/x500frame.htm

"Understanding X.500—The Directory" online book by David Chadwick

http://www.isi.salford.ac.uk/staff/dwc/Version.Web/Contents.htm

ASN.1
Layman's Guide to ASN.1

ftp://ftp.rsa.com/pub/pkcs/ascii/layman.asc

ASN.1: Wherefore Art Thou?
http://www.isi.edu/gost/brian/security/asn1.html

ASN.1
http://www.netice.com/advice/Reference/Networking/Encoding/
ASN.1/

Schema Resources
LDAP Schema Viewer / Proposer
http://ldap.hklc.com/objectclass.html

Directory Schema Element References
http://www.cenorm.be/isss/Workshop/dir/Details/schemref.htm

Automated Schema Documentation Program
http://www.microsoft.com/windows2000/techinfo/
administration/activedirectory/schema.asp

Windows 2000 Schema
http://msdn.microsoft.com/library/default.asp?url=/library/
en-us/netdir/adschema/w2k.asp

iPlanet Internationalization
http://docs.iplanet.com/docs/manuals/directory/50/html/ag/i18n.
htm#2836267

ISSS-WS-DIR Directory Schema Definitions
http://www.cenorm.be/isss/Workshop/dir/Details/f_
schema.htm#objcl

Netscape Schema Reference
http://home.netscape.com/eng/server/directory/schema/
ocindex.htm

iPlanet Schema Reference
http://docs.iplanet.com/docs/manuals/directory/schema/
contents.htm

Chapter 5 Topics

Metadirectories
The Meta-Directory FAQ
http://www.directoryservice.com/WP/TBG/The%20Meta-Directory%20FAQ.htm

Enterprise Directory Infrastructure: Meta-Directory Concepts and Functions
http://www.directoryservice.com/WP/TBG/edimd.pdf

Meta Directory: The Technology Differences
http://www.directoryservice.com/WP/ISOCOR/MDTTD.htm

Microsoft Metadirectory Services Concepts and Architecture
http://www.microsoft.com/windows2000/techinfo/howitworks/activedirectory/MMSintro.asp

Active Directory Interoperability and Metadirectory Overview
http://www.microsoft.com/windows2000/techinfo/howitworks/activedirectory/identity.asp

Microsoft and Novell Take Fight to Metadirectory Front
http://www.nwfusion.com/archive/2000/88590_02-28-2000.html

iPlanet for Developers—Netscape Metadirectory Services
http://developer.iplanet.com/docs/articles/directory/metadirectory.htm

Sync or Swim? Will Your Merged Mail System Float Together or Drift into Chaos?
http://www.networkcomputing.com/901/901f22.html

Meta Directory
http://www.calendra.com/en/home/meta_directory.htm

Meta-Directories Cutting Through the Hype White Paper
http://www.esys.ca/publications/IC-6087.html

Directory Integration and the Metadirectory

http://www.win2000mag.com/Articles/Index.cfm?ArticleID=5584

Critical Path Ships Rearchitected Metadirectory

http://www.techinformer.com/english/crd_injoin_472707.html

MetaDirectory FAQ

http://www.netapps.org/Events/HTMLDocs/
workshopmetadirectoryfaq.htm

Strategies & Issues Unifying Diverse Directories

http://www.networkmagazine.com/article/NMG20010126S0001/1

DSML

DSML Helps Directories Work Together

http://www.nwfusion.com/news/tech/1122tech.html

Strategies & Issues Unifying Diverse Directories

http://www.networkmagazine.com/article/NMG20010126S0001

Directory Services Markup Language (DSML)

http://www.oasis-open.org/cover/dsml.html

Security

Transport Layer Security (tls) Charter

http://www.ietf.org/html.charters/tls-charter.html

Keep Your Data Secure from Prying Eyes: An Encryption Primer—SunWorld—March 1997

http://sunsite.uniandes.edu.co/sunworldonline/swol-03-
1997/swol-03-encrypt.html

Data Encryption Techniques

http://catalog.com/sft/encrypt.html

Stanford University
Stanford Directory Data Architecture Overview
http://www.stanford.edu/group/itss-ccs/project/registry/info_
infra_overview.html

Registries Project, Person Registry
http://www.stanford.edu/group/itss-ccs/project/registry/person_
registry/

Project Space Dog—Registry Extensions
http://www.stanford.edu/group/itss-ccs/project/spacedog/

Project Horton Main Index
http://www.stanford.edu/group/itss-ccs/project/horton/

Stanford Windows Infrastructure Documentation
http://windows.stanford.edu/doc.shtml

Chapter 6 Topics

U of Mich. Introduction to slapd and slurpd
http://www.umich.edu/~dirsvcs/ldap/doc/guides/slapd/
1.html#RTFToC1

OpenLDAP 2.0 Administrator's Guide
http://www.openldap.org/doc/admin/

OpenLDAP 2.1 Administrator's Guide (unreleased at time of print)
http://www.openldap.org/devel/admin/

OpenLDAP Faq-O-Matic Software FAQ
http://www.openldap.org/faq/data/cache/2.html

OpenLDAP Access Control FAQ
http://www.openldap.org/faq/data/cache/447.html

OpenLDAP Mailing List Archives
http://www.openldap.org/lists/#archives

OpenLDAP, OpenSSL, SASL, and KerberosV HOWTO
http://www.bayour.com/LDAPv3-HOWTO.html

OpenLDAP Release Roadmap
http://www.openldap.org/software/roadmap.html

OpenLDAP Manual pages
http://www.openldap.org/software/man.cgi

Building OpenLDAP
OpenLDAP Quick-Start Guide
http://www.openldap.org/doc/admin/quickstart.html

Configuring Solaris8 with OpenLDAP
http://www.ypass.net/solaris8/openldap/

How to Port OpenLDAP to Windows
http://www.fivesight.com/downloads/openldap.asp

OpenSSL
http://www.openssl.org/

MIT Kerberos
http://web.mit.edu/kerberos/www/

Heimdal Kerberos
http://www.pdc.kth.se/heimdal/

Cyrus's SASL Library
http://asg.web.cmu.edu/sasl/sasl-library.html

Chapter 7 Topics

Proposed SAMBA AD schema

http://www.unav.es/cti/ldap-smb/ldap-smb-AD-schemas.html#AD_
schemas

Active Directory Replication

http://www.microsoft.com/windows2000/techinfo/reskit/
samplechapters/dsbh/dsbh_rep_jfbg.asp

Microsoft TechNet

http://www.microsoft.com/technet/tcevents/itevents/spring00/
tnq40004.asp

MS Directory Services

http://www.microsoft.com/windows2000/technologies/
ldirectory/default.asp

Schema in Active Directory

http://www.unav.edu/cti/ldap-smb/AD-gluser.html

Linked Attributes in Active Directory

http://msdn.microsoft.com/library/default.asp?url=/library/
en-us/netdir/ad/linked_attributes.asp

Microsoft Windows 2000 Server Documentation

http://www.microsoft.com/windows2000/en/server/help/

LDAP Reference

http://msdn.microsoft.com/library/default.asp?url=/library/
en-us/netdir/ldap/ldap_reference.asp

Tracking Updates

http://www.microsoft.com/WINDOWS2000/techinfo/reskit/en/D
istrib/dsbh_rep_zcil.htm

Tracking Changes
http://msdn.microsoft.com/library/en-us/netdir/ad/polling_for_
changes_using_usnchanged.asp

Active Directory Schema Documentation Program
http://www.microsoft.com/windows2000/techinfo/administration/
activedirectory/schema.asp

The Inside Active Directory Book
http://www.kouti.com/

Chapter 8 Topics

Server Documentation
SUN Directory Servers
http://wwws.sun.com/software/products/directory_srvr/home_
directory.html

SUN Directory Server Documentation
http://docs.sun.com/db/prod/s1dirsrv

SUN Directory Server Documentation—Installation Guide
http://docs.sun.com/source/816-5610-10/index.html

SUN Directory Server Documentation—Deployment Guide
http://docs.sun.com/source/816-5609-10/index.html

SUN Directory Server Documentation—Administrator's Guide
http://docs.sun.com/source/816-5606-10/index.html

SUN Directory Server Documentation—Reference
http://docs.sun.com/source/816-5608-10/index.html

SUN Directory Server Documentation—Schema
http://docs.sun.com/source/816-5613-10/index.html

SUN Blueprints: Naming and Directory Services

http://www.sun.com/solutions/blueprints/browsesubject.html#nds

Programming Resources

Directory Server Plug-ins Programmer's Guide

http://docs.sun.com/source/816-6683-10/index.html

LDAP SDK for C

http://docs.sun.com/source/816-5616-10/index.html

Directory Server SDK 4.0 for Java Programmer's Guide

http://docs.sun.com/source/816-6388-10/index.html

Directory Server Resource Kit 5.1

http://wwws.sun.com/software/download/developer/5175.html

Index

Note: Italicized locators indicate figures/tables.

inform IT

YOUR GUIDE TO IT REFERENCE

Articles

Keep your edge with thousands of free articles, in-depth features, interviews, and IT reference recommendations – all written by experts you know and trust.

Online Books

Answers in an instant from **InformIT Online Book's** 600+ fully searchable on line books. For a limited time, you can get your first 14 days **free**.

Catalog

Review online sample chapters, author biographies and customer rankings and choose exactly the right book from a selection of over 5,000 titles.